South Asian Folklore

South Asian Folklore

A Handbook

Frank J. Korom

Greenwood Folklore Handbooks

GREENWOOD PRESS
Westport, Connecticut • London

Library of Congress Cataloging-in-Publication Data

Korom, Frank J.
    South Asian folklore : a handbook / Frank J. Korom.
        p. cm.—(Greenwood folklore handbooks, ISSN 1549–733X)
    Includes bibliographical references and index.
    ISBN 0–313–33193–6 (alk.paper)
1.   Folklore—Southeast Asia—Handbooks, manuals, etc.   2.   Southeast Asia—Social life
and customs—Handbooks, manuals, etc.   I.   Title.   II.   Series.
    GR308.K67   2006
    398.0959—dc22   2006000449

British Library Cataloguing in Publication Data is available.

Library of Congress Catalog Card Number: 2006000449
ISBN: 0–313–33193–6
ISSN: 1549–733X

First published in 2006

Greenwood Press, 88 Post Road West, Westport, CT 06881
An imprint of Greenwood Publishing Group, Inc.
www.greenwood.com

Printed in the United States of America

The paper used in this book complies with the
Permanent Paper Standard issued by the National
Information Standards Organization (Z39.48–1984).

10   9   8   7   6   5   4   3   2   1

Contents

Preface

This book is a modest attempt to introduce students to the vastly complex world of South Asian folklore. I call it modest, for even to list the genres and subgenres found in the region would require a volume larger than this one. I therefore decided to take a more open-ended approach that would allow me to selectively choose examples that illustrate theoretical and methodological points that are explored throughout the book. Although intended to engage and stimulate those who have no prior background in the study of the region's traditions, I hope that specialists will also find something of value in what follows. I have attempted to present previous and current debates in scholarship that reflect controversies specific to South Asia, but also general issues in the field of folklore studies that may not have received quite as much attention among regional specialists. I believe that nonspecialist folklorists can learn much from the South Asian materials and South Asia specialists can learn equally as much from the general literature on folklore scholarship.

The present work follows a structural format set in earlier volumes published in Greenwood's series of *Folklore Handbooks*. Because I have followed the earlier precedents, some redundancies appear in the text, which actually allows for each chapter to be read independently of the others. However, those with no background in the region's literature and culture may wish to read the introduction and final chapter first before diving into the numerous examples and their interpretations included in the third chapter. I have intentionally kept endnotes to a minimum, but the extensive—but by no means exhaustive—bibliography will serve to stimulate further exploration. I have also included a glossary of some of the more prominent foreign and technical terms used in the book to allow for quick reference while reading.

An annotated listing of Internet sites is included as well for those who wish to pursue the topic online.

Chapter one is introductory in nature, providing a minimum of general background for the uninitiated reader. It also explores what I hope this book will achieve. Chapter two dives into the concept of folklore and the history of how the discipline of folklore study developed in colonial India, before moving on to consider the limitations of cross-cultural analysis and exploring the prospects of indigenous categories as a starting point for contemporary studies. Chapter three provides extensive full-text examples of South Asian folklore culled from classical, printed sources and contemporary accounts, as well as my own experiences in the region over the course of a few decades. Chapter four provides overviews of prominent people and theories in the region first and then moves on to chart out some future directions for research. Lastly, chapter five includes overviews of important folkloric texts in the classical literature and then moves on to a closing discussion of folklore in contemporary literature and culture.

Some of the material included in this volume in reworked and updated form appeared in a few of my earlier essays. A portion of chapter one appeared in an essay titled "Why Folklore?" (1988), which was the inauguration lecture for the Regional Resources Centre for the Folk Performing Arts in Udupi, India. I thank H. Krishna Bhat, the director of RRC, and S. A. Krishnaiah, chief researcher there, for permission to reprint it. A part of chapter two appeared in 1989 as "Inventing Traditions: Folklore and Nationalism as Historical Process in Bengal." Thanks to the Institute of Ethnology and Folklore Research in Zagreb, Croatia, and its director, Ivan Lozica, for permission to reprint sections of that essay. The last section of chapter four recently appeared as "Uncharted Waters of Folklore Theory" in 2004. Malini Bhattacharyya, editor of the journal *Lokoshruti,* and Dibyajyoti Majumdar, editor of publications at the Folk and Tribal Cultural Centre in Kolkata, both deserve thanks for permission to reprint sections of it here. I have included the complete references to these earlier versions in the general bibliography. If I have shown a bias to Bengali materials, it is only because it is the area of the subcontinent that I know best.

I would also like to thank Margaret Mills of Ohio State University for first encouraging me to undertake this project and George Butler, my editor at Greenwood Press, who patiently awaited delivery of the manuscript. I am also grateful to Elizabeth Kincaid of Greenwood Press for her graphic design. Her valuable input has undoubtedly made the book more attractive. Thanks are due to Rosan A. Jordan and Frank de Caro as well for permission to reprint Robin Adair's bear narrative in chapter three. Lastly, I have used transliteration of terms from South Asian languages sparingly. Names, places, and text titles are not transliterated normally unless they appear so in quotations. This book is dedicated to all my teachers, past and present, and all the people in South Asia who have shared their lives with me over the past thirty years. Without them, this current endeavor would not have been possible. *Dhanyavād!*

One

Introduction

SOUTH ASIA AS A CULTURAL AND LINGUISTIC REGION

South Asia, as defined here, consists of the countries located on the Indian subcontinent, including Afghanistan, Pakistan, India, Nepal, Bhutan, Bangladesh, and Sri Lanka. The region is enormously variegated with regard to language and ethnicity, and hundreds of languages and thousands of dialects are spoken. It is the region of the world that gave us the great Indus Valley civilization, one of the oldest in prehistory. It is also the birthplace of four great religions: Hinduism, Jainism, Buddhism, and Sikhism. It has served as the crossroads of numerous conquerors, from Alexander the Great to Timur, culminating with the advent of the British raj, who colonized much of the region and opened it up to large-scale European influence. By the time of the establishment of the East India Company, India was already home to all the so-called major world religions.

Western interest in the region flourished during the British colonial period, and a score of researchers entered the subcontinent to study virtually every aspect of South Asian culture and society. Their motivation to study the region was at first a romantic one, but later positivists, here defined as those seeking empirical knowledge, also embarked on research. As we shall see, some of these early researchers understood ancient India to be the wellspring of religion and lore. Curiously, however, interest in the region waned somewhat during the period of decolonization after World War II. This fact notwithstanding, a resurgence of interest started in the 1960s and 1970s that has waxed and waned ever since. Today, South Asia still remains an important area of the world in geopolitical terms, as current global events after

The isolated city of Jharkot in Nepal. © Eye Ubiquitous / Corbis.

September 11, 2001, attest. Before we embark on our journey into the world of South Asian expressive forms, a brief introductory survey of language and regional culture areas will be useful.

Linguistic Overview

The Dravidologist Murray Emeneau was the first to define the Indian subcontinent as a linguistic region or area. He defines linguistic area as follows:

> The term "linguistic area" may be defined as meaning an area which includes languages belonging to more than one family but showing traits in common which are found not to belong to the other members of [at least] one of the families. (1964, 650)

Following Emeneau's lead, we will begin our inquiry by breaking down the linguistic area into a typology. There are four major language families in South Asia: Indo-Aryan (spoken by 73.3% of the population), Dravidian (24.5%), Austro-Asiatic (1.5%), and Tibeto-Burman (0.7%). Indo-Aryan is

Working elephants bathing in a river, Sri Lanka. © H. Sitton / Zefa / Corbis.

a subbranch of Indo-European; thus the vernacular languages derived from Sanskrit (spoken primarily in north India) are simultaneously Indo-Aryan and Indo-European, being closer to Latin and Greek than they are to other language families in South Asia. Sanskrit develops in the following manner: Vedic Sanskrit (1500 B.C.E.)→classical Sanskrit (1000 B.C.E.)→Prakrits (600 B.C.E.)→Apabhramshas (300 B.C.E.)→modern Indo-Aryan languages (900 C.E.). Tajik, Pashto, Urdu, Sindhi, Baluchi, Punjabi, Hindi, Gujarati, Bengali, Marathi, Oriya, Assamese, Nepali, and Sinhalese are all examples of contemporary Indo-Aryan languages.

The origins of Dravidian are less certain than those of Indo-Aryan, but many linguists feel that there is a strong possibility that it might be connected to the Ural-Altaic languages of Central Asia. Although so far there is no conclusive data, many linguists and archaeologists also believe that the indigenous language of the Indus Valley civilization was Dravidian. The Dravidian language family is divided into three branches: Proto-South Dravidian (i.e., Kannada, Badaga, Toda, Kota, Kodagu, Malayalam, and Tamil), Proto-Central Dravidian (i.e., Telugu, Kui, Kuvi, Pengo, Manda, Konda, Gondi, Tulu, Kolami, Naiki, Ollari, and Parji), and Proto-North Dravidian (i.e., Kurukh, Malto, Koraga, and Brahui). Tamil, Malayalam, Telugu, and Kannada are the four predominant Dravidian languages spoken today. Whereas Indo-Aryan languages dominate the northern geographic regions, Dravidian is spoken by the majority in peninsular India.

Austro-Asiatic languages are spoken mostly among tribal populations inhabiting central and eastern India. This family is divided into a western and an eastern branch. The western branch, which is called Munda, is further broken down into southern and northern branches. South Munda includes Sora, Gorum, Gutob, Remo, Gata, Kharia, and Juang, and North Munda includes Korku, Santali, Mundari, and Ho.

Tibeto-Burman, by far the smallest linguistic family in South Asia, has stronger linguistic and cultural affinities with Tibet and Burma than with India. It is divided into a Tibetan and a Burmese branch. The Tibetan branch consists of Tibetan, Rgyarung, Gurung, and the Himalayan branches, while Burmese is divided into Lolo and Kuki branches. Lolo is not important on the Indian subcontinent, but the Kuki branch consists of the tribal languages

The Hunza Valley in Pakistan. © Jonathan Blair / Corbis.

of Assam and the tribal territories of northeastern India that border China, Bangladesh, and Burma.[1]

Culture Zones

Anthropologists generally distinguish between four major cultural zones in South Asia, which are broken down into directional units. The two largest are the northern and southern. The southern zone corresponds roughly with peninsular India, where the Dravidian languages dominate. The northern zone (consisting of Orissa, Madhya Pradesh, southern Bihar, southeastern

Families at Marina Beach in India, 2003. © Chris Lisle / Corbis.

Cevbal Asia

Macs culture languas

Bengal, and Maharashtra) is known as the central transitional, where we see a heavier convergence of cultural and linguistic forms that mix elements of Dravidian and Indo-Aryan. This culturally rich region is a hybrid mixture of northern and southern patterns. The third zone is the northern Indo-Aryan, which includes a major portion of Afghanistan, Pakistan, and Bangladesh. A borderlands region rings the northern pattern in a grand arc from the Arabian Sea in the west, moving across the Himalayas (northern Pakistan, Ladakh, highland Nepal, and Bhutan) and finally culminating in the Bay of Bengal.[2]

Map Is Not Territory

The brief survey of languages and regional cultures presented above should give an indication of the incredible amount of diversity in the South Asian region. Yet there are also remarkable similarities that bridge Afghanistan in the extreme west with Bangladesh in the extreme east, and everything in between within the subcontinent. Not surprisingly, the folklore traditions of South Asia are as complex and variegated as the linguistic scenario. It will therefore not be possible for me to provide an exhaustive survey of folklore genres in this book, for this would require a multivolume endeavor (cf. George 1984, 55–146). Instead, I wish to provide a kind of road map to the folkloric terrain by describing and analyzing what has been done to date, what might be done in the future, and what still needs to be done as we move ahead with the serious study of the region's folklore. As we move further into the new millennium there is still much to be studied in South Asian folklore, for we have barely scratched the surface. On this gaping lacuna in our knowledge of the region's verbal art, A. K. Ramanujan has this to say:

> Linguists have classified and subsumed these speech varieties, or dialects, under 105 or so languages which belong to four language families. Of these 105 languages 90 are spoken by less than 5 percent of the entire population; 65 belong to small tribes. Including Sanskrit, 15 of the languages are written, read, and spoken by about 95 percent of the people. We, in universities outside India, have just begun to study a few of these languages. (1990, 3)

What Ramanujan has to say about India is equally true of the other countries of South Asia as well.

The study of South Asian folklore is still relatively young compared to European and American folklore studies, and it is still trying to free itself from its colonial legacy, which will be the subject of the next chapter's opening section. But why study folklore in the first place? Why is it important to understanding a group's ethos and worldview? The relevance of studying folklore generally and South Asian folklore specifically is discussed in the next section.

WHY FOLKLORE?

I hope that this book will mark the beginning of a new type of involvement between Euro-American and South Asian folklorists, because the need for genuine collaboration is dire. A newfound interest in collaborative work should not be driven simply by the need for further research, collection, and documentation, but by a serious desire to establish a mutual dialogue among indigenous scholars and students and their foreign counterparts. The need for intercultural (cf. Bharucha 2000) and, by extension, interdisciplinary dialogue should be an essential concern of all who share a passion for the expressive traditions of a region as complex as South Asia. After all, learning from each other is the only way to establish a truly international approach to the study of South Asian folklore.

The present moment in history is a prime time for such a dialogue to grow, because a new awareness of the importance of South Asian folklore is awakening after a relatively long slumber as a result of the movement of South Asian diaspora populations across the globe. The slumber to which I refer produced a host of misconceptions about the region's folkloric traditions, as well as the very concept of folklore itself. Throughout the following pages, I wish to attempt to clarify some of the misconceptions by drawing on a wide range of literature that exists disparately in dusty corners of university libraries. At the same time, I will provide samples of expressive traditions in chapter three to illustrate the underlying theoretical points that I seek to present elsewhere in the book. No such survey, however, can be exhaustive, as mentioned above. I therefore seek to be selective, not comprehensive.

The new awareness of the importance of South Asian folklore to which I am referring is primarily guided by performance studies of specific folk traditions in their natural contexts, be they urban legends swapped on a bus in New Delhi or ballads sung by an itinerant scroll painter in West Bengal. This approach seeks to study how texts are artistically presented by individuals or groups of performers to an audience that shares not only the immediate physical and ecological environment but also—and much more significantly—a sociolinguistic and cultural one that includes certain implicit shared assumptions about the universe (cf. Claus and Korom 1991, 5–45). But such shared assumptions are also contested, negated, or negotiated to create multiple meanings for members of an interpretive community.

Passengers squeezed together on a local bus in India often pass the time by swapping stories. © David Cumming; Eye Ubiquitous / Corbis.

From this perspective, the audience is a fundamental and integral part of the performance, for it shares the burden of responsibility of interpreting the validity and/or authenticity of what is being performed. A performance is thus emergent, constantly in the process of becoming, as the audience shares in and shapes the outcome in often very subtle ways that require the close attention of the folklorist or ethnographer. The range of expressive forms is thus infinitely expandable.

A performance approach to folkloristics, as the discipline of folklore studies is currently termed, begins with the assumption that the stuff comprising the materials folklorists study is first of all shared stuff and second of all a medium of aesthetic communication. A minimal definition of the discipline could therefore be the study of artistic communication in small groups, a concept posited by Dan Ben-Amos (1972). His broad definition is more suitable for the study of South Asia than a genre-based investigation (i.e., a list of kinds of folklore). It allows us to free ourselves from preconceived notions of what an epic, ballad, proverb, riddle, or tale is and to see how a particular community defines and labels its own performance traditions. Only then might we venture to make cross-cultural comparisons. I discuss this issue further at the end of the next chapter.

The job of the responsible and reflexive folklorist is thus to interpret the many possibilities that present themselves in the material he or she chooses to study. We must remember that folklore as an empirical bit of reality does not exist apart from our academic creation of it. There is nothing in the realm of human experience that is intrinsically folkloric.[3] Yet, having defined folklore in very broad and processual terms, the folklorist must be willing to accept the methodological challenge that confronts him or her. Folklore, as it is currently defined, is multidimensional and emergent. It speaks to us in a "polyphony of voices," as the Russian literary critic Mikhail Bakhtin (1981) would have it. Elsewhere, Bakhtin writes about the emergent quality of folklore production and consumption as follows:

> Behind each text stands a language system. Everything in the text that is repeated and reproduced, everything repeatable and reproducible, everything that can be given outside a text (the given) conforms to this language system. But at the same time each text (as an utterance) is individual, unique, and unrepeatable, and herein lies its entire significance (its plan, the purpose for which it was created). . . . With respect to this aspect, everything repeatable and reproducible proves to be material, a means to an end. (1986, 105)

For Bakhtin, as for many folklorists, each text is composed in the context of performance and thus must be studied not solely as the production of variants of a master narrative. Precisely because folklore is multivocalic and emergent, the well-trained folklorist must be competent in a number of disciplines that are sensitive to the context of performance in which a particular text is created. In other words, the serious study of folklore must include methodology and theory culled from anthropology, sociology, linguistics, history of religions, literary criticism, and so forth, to meet the future challenges of this interdisciplinary field of inquiry.

The goals of this book are many. My first intention is to stimulate an ongoing dialogue among Euro-American scholars, whose work is often dominated by comparative and international issues and theories, and South Asian scholars, who are often more concerned with the regional process of collection and documentation. Both types of research are, of course, necessary, for the advancement of scholarship depends on sound academic source material. Doing good research in folklore requires access to well-equipped libraries, coupled with participant observation or fieldwork over extensive periods of time. Combining book work with ethnographic description allows us to analyze both the text and the context of performance, as well as the many ways a particular item of tradition influences people's lives, expresses public consensus and opinion, and transforms or reinforces the participants' perception of the world. After all, any successful folk event is simultaneously *in*formative and *per*formative. Performances also have to be persuasive to be accepted by an audience as legitimate.

Why are both information and performance necessary? The folklorist would answer by saying that the goal of research in folklore is twofold. First, it is to preserve or revitalize the past of a culture that is perceived to be dying or in a state of decay. Second, it is to analyze historical change in traditions and recapture strands of their roots in an effort to describe and interpret the dynamics of the processes of folkloric production, commodification, and consumption. In colonial Bengal, for example, the early development of the discipline of folklore studies was inspired and guided by romantic nationalistic sentiment or, alternatively, by colonial forces that stressed misconceived notions of racial and cultural evolution.[4] Urban literary figures such as Rabindranath Tagore appropriated the verbal art of the so-called folk in an effort to awaken Bengali consciousness and arouse a pan-Bengali ethos among all the members of that society. It was an effort to reunite city and village, a dichotomy that resulted from the vagaries of urbanization.[5] I do not wish to suggest that the bolstering of nationalism and patriotism is a completely inappropriate approach to folklore studies. It is often necessary at a certain point in time to stimulate people to act, as it did in Bengal. History teaches us that nationalistic motivation lies at the core of the establishment of folklore studies throughout the world (cf. Blackburn 2003). But it can also be dangerous, and even deadly, when it becomes ideologically charged and motivated.[6] The point is, rather, that the study of folklore is much more than this. It is a complex approach to a variety of phenomena that require our attention in many ways.

Questions that one should ask when studying folklore generally include, what is the intellectual basis of the concept, what does folklore do, how does it achieve its effect, and how do we express ourselves through its many media? These are the questions upon which all folkloric inquiry should be based. Ideally, the study of South Asian folklore should be grounded in international scholarship in order to avoid parochialism. It should also be comparative and cross-cultural, yet this does not mean that we have to sacrifice the specifics of the local context. Folklore scholarship should begin from within and work outward, paying close attention to regional changes and variation. On the other hand, one cannot become totally absorbed in microscopic studies, because swimming adrift in ethnographic minutiae ultimately hinders international dialogue by limiting one's specialized and often esoteric knowledge to a small group of local experts. The comparative study of folklore works on the assumption that specialists will share their finely tuned data with others unfamiliar with that specific tradition.

The key to opening up an area of research to others is, of course, the publication of material in a concise manner that makes it coherent and accessible to the nonspecialist. The obvious trick in the latter is finding a writing style that can draw on specific local and regional issues to inform broader general theoretical issues and problems that are pertinent and of interest to a community of folklore researchers outside the specialized area of research. But we must remember that the texts of our research also become part of the process of folklore production. We create folklore in the most unsuspected places, without necessarily being cognizant of the fact that we ourselves are users and producers of folklore, and the scholar is no exception to this rule. Folklore is to humankind as water is to fish: we are engulfed by it but are not aware that we are immersed in it. Folklore permeates every aspect of life, and accepting unorthodox genres of both verbal and nonverbal art enables us to expand our understanding of the pervasive influence that it has on the human psyche.

There was a time in the United States and elsewhere when the study of folklore was not taken very seriously as an academic discipline, and in many academic institutions it still is not strongly represented. Scholars in other fields believed that folklore research was superfluous. As Alan Dundes once wrote, folklore for many was defined as false and was therefore equated with rumor and lies. So if folklore were false, then the study of folklore would be the height of folly. Dundes writes that the folklorist is thus "implicitly relegated to the role of a full-time student of error" (1990, 3). Fortunately, this phase has for the most part passed, although echoes of an anti-folklore bias continue to reverberate throughout academe. Even though departments of folklore studies in North America are few and far between, the scholarly study of folklore continues to flourish in other departments throughout the world. Folklorists have found homes in anthropology departments, language programs, and a variety of other social science and humanities fields. Due to the dearth of academic opportunities, an increasing number of folklorists also continue to enter the public sector to do what we might call applied folklore, which is putting folklore to work for the folk themselves (e.g., Baron and Spitzer 1992). Much interest has also been paid to the commodification of folklore for mass consumption in recent years, a phenomenon we might call folklorization.

South Asia has much to offer the international development of folklore scholarship. Its traditions are rich and diverse, but they have not been studied as extensively as many other regional traditions in other parts of the world. India is especially rife for international contribution due to its many academic folklore departments and research institutions, which have sprung up over the past few decades. As world awareness of India's folk traditions continues to grow, India will become both an object of further inquiry and a locus for the theoretical development of the field by indigenous scholars. Pakistan and Bangladesh also have their own national centers for folklore research, but much less is offered in those nations by way of academic training in folklore studies at the university level. However, as more and more information is disseminated from South Asia in general, it is likely that a greater number of foreign students will become more interested in South Asian expressive traditions, which should lead to more opportunities for collaborative research.

The development of folklore scholarship in South Asia should steer away from regionalism in favor of a concerted pan-South Asian effort. To be certain, national borders in South Asia do not correspond to the demarcation of regional traditions, and there is much shared lore in Afghanistan, for example, that can also be found at the eastern periphery of the Indian subcontinent in Bangladesh. Research in South Asia could ultimately contribute to international folklore studies by bringing to light specific aspects of the region's culture that may radically affect the future trends of comparative folklore scholarship. South Asian traditions suggest both similarities with and differences from other national and regional traditions, and scholars, both indigenous and foreign, should pursue the identification of the differences *and* similarities in order to advance our overall knowledge of folkloric traditions around the world.

So why should we study folklore in the first place? The study of folklore has the capability to answer questions about culture and society that other disciplines are less equipped to answer. It is not that folklore's raw materials are in any way more significant than those of other disciplines, but simply that the questions folklorists ask are framed in such a way as to shed new light on old problems. Furthermore, because so many other fields are more rigidly defined, they run the risk of dismissing certain interesting phenomena as being outside their domain of inquiry. This point is a useful one but should not be overemphasized, because many disciplines in the social sciences and humanities are coming to terms with multidisciplinarity. Academic disciplines are becoming more self-conscious, reflexively evaluating the very nature of the term "discipline." Academic discourses in postmodern society are no longer strictly demarcated into airtight compartments, and "sector leakage" from one field to another causes us to confront our conversational partners in many areas of research. In fact, much of the most interesting theorizing is being done under the general rubric of cultural studies.

If we use Clifford Geertz's (1983) analogy of an academic discipline as a literary genre, then it is possible to say that we are presently confronted with a case of what he calls "blurred genres," the spilling over of one field of study into another, and vice versa. Such an academic environment can be productive if it is not done in a random and eclectic manner. Each field of inquiry has much to offer the others, and because folklorists have drawn freely on the methodologies of other disciplines in the past, folklore studies is the exemplary interdisciplinary field. The result has been the development of a highly sophisticated theoretical base for the understanding of cultural performances and aesthetic traditions. The time has come for other disciplines to utilize the insights into cultural matters that folklore scholarship has to offer, by borrowing back ideas and concepts that have been tested and refined by folklorists, so as to contribute to the larger universe of academic discourse.

THE RELEVANCE OF FOLKLORE TO SOUTH ASIAN STUDIES

For much of its history, Indology has privileged written, especially classical, texts, even though, as we have already seen, the subcontinent abounds with orality and vernacular languages and dialects. This privileging of textual study recalls the infamous dichotomy drawn by anthropologist Robert Redfield (1960) between "great" and "little" traditions, in which he characterized the former as elitist, literary, classical, textual, and perpetuated by a reflective minority, and the latter as populist, nonliterary, folk, contextual, and perpetuated by an unreflective majority (cf. also Obeyesekere 1963; Sinha 1958). Such dichotomies privilege the great tradition at the expense of the so-called little traditions. Although Redfield's fieldwork concerned Mexico, he argued that the dichotomy was true of all civilizations. However, his student Milton Singer (1972) was particularly interested in India and called for a more contextualized study of these levels of tradition through what he called "cultural performances" that generated texts (cf. also Singer 1961). Singer's 1972 study is more subtly nuanced than his mentor's, yet it continued to draw a distinction between the great and little traditions, as the title of his book, *When a Great Tradition Modernizes,* attests (cf. Claus 1998, 214–21).

The problem with such tidy divisions is that they fail to see or acknowledge the dialogic interactions of what philosophers like Wittgenstein (1976) call "family resemblances" or what Collingwood (1933) terms "scales of form." In actuality, the boundary between oral and literate, folk and classical, little and great is highly porous, allowing materials to move back and forth freely. Only by recognizing this fact can we expand and advance our knowledge of South Asian culture. While it is true that Indian tradition makes a distinction between *mārga* (highway) and *deśī* (byway), by 1937, Ananda Coomaraswamy had already complicated the distinction between the two in a seminal article published that year. Discussing a variety of evidence and expressive forms in India that could be labeled as folk, popular, or classical, he convincingly concludes with the following statement:

> The point that we want to bring out is that the folk material, regardless of our actual qualifications in relation to it, is actually of an essentially *mārga* and not a *desī* character, and actually intelligible at levels of reference that are far above and by no means inferior to those of our ordinary contemporary "learning." (1937, 82)

Coomaraswamy's well-taken point is that what may be taken in one context as classical may be understood in another context as folk, or vice versa. We need to break down such divisive categories to truly get at the complex dynamics underlying South Asian expressive culture.

Ramanujan has assisted us greatly in regard to smashing questionable dichotomies. As he writes, "Past and present, what's 'pan-Indian' and what's local, what's shared and what's unique in regional communities, and individuals, the written and the oral—all are engaged in a dialogic reworking and redefining of relevant others. Texts then are contexts and pretexts for other texts" (1990, 5). Ramanujan thus calls for a more "interactive" model of South Asian expressive systems that recognizes the constant back-and-forth traffic between academic categories that have little relevance to everyday lived reality. His advocacy of an interactive model enables us to get beyond ethno-semiotic and class-oriented biases that have guided folklore studies for much of its developmental history, which is no less true of Europe than it is of South Asia. The folk and their lore are not just the "other" and its property in relation to us, but they are also, in fact, us and our property. From this perspective, the urban, learned Brahman priest communicates and expresses himself through folklore just as much as does the rural, uneducated peasant.

Another reason why folklore in South Asia matters is because it often provides alternative takes on long-held normative opinions about the region. Such concepts as *karma* (the law of cause and effect), categories as mythology, and behaviors as saint worship often take radically new meanings on the local level that are often at odds with our preexisting suppositions based on so-called classical textual material. In Hindu oral mythology, for example, the movement of divinity is often upward from earth to the heavens, whereas it is downward in Sanskritic mythological texts (e.g., Blackburn 1985). The oral tradition, in other words, while interacting with the literary tradition, also contests it and reinterprets it to provide alternative understandings, interpretations, and explanations of humankind's existential predicament.[7]

In this introductory chapter, I have written more generally about the pitfalls, problems, and prospects of studying South Asian folklore. The following chapter is more specific in nature; in it I attempt to situate the academic study of folklore in a historical and regional context that takes into account the political dimension of folklore and its study. In so doing, I point out the limitations of past studies and the prospects and possibilities of contemporary and future studies. Since the future always builds upon the present, and the present on the past, however, the following detailed analysis is mandatory for further refinement in our chosen area of inquiry, and to understand where we have been and where we are going. After all, learning from our past errors makes us better scholars in the future.

NOTES

1. Good overviews of the languages of the region can be found in George (1984, 3–52) and Zograph (1982).

2. For a succinct overview of the region's languages and culture zones, see Tyler (1973, 178–204). See also Maloney (1974) for a good general introduction to South Asia.

3. Folklore studies in this regard is similar to the academic study of religion. Jonathan Z. Smith, for example, makes the following point in the introduction to *Imagining Religion* (1982): "If we have understood the archaeological and textual record correctly, man has had his entire history in which to imagine deities and modes of interaction with them. But man, more precisely western man, has had only the last few centuries in which to imagine religion. It is this act of second order, reflective imagination which must be the central occupation of any student of religion. That is to say, while there is a staggering amount of data, of phenomena, of human experiences and expressions that might be characterized in one culture or another, by one criterion or another, as religious—*there is no data for religion*. Religion is solely the creation of the scholar's study. It is created for the scholar's analytic purposes by his imaginative acts of comparison and generalization. Religion has no independent existence apart from the academy. For this reason, the student of religion, and most particularly the historian of religion, must be relentlessly self-conscious. Indeed, this self-consciousness constitutes his primary expertise, his foremost object of study" (1982, xi). Similarly, scholars of folklore self-consciously create the object of their study by the careful selection of their data.

4. Abrahams (1993) traces the development of folklore studies generally, identifying its emergence in the romantic nationalist period in eighteenth- and nineteenth-century Europe.

5. Blackburn (2003) makes the same point about folklore studies in south India, specifically in Tamil country, where there was a romantic urban quest for what he calls the "vanishing village."

6. See, for example, Anzulovic (1999) on the uses and violent abuses of folklore in the historical context of Serbian nationalism.

7. For examples of such alternative understandings, see again Ramanujan (1990, 12–20).

Two
Definitions and Classifications

PREFATORY REMARKS

My task in the first section of this chapter is to trace the development of folklore studies in South Asia, which has culminated in a debate over the definition of folklore. By exploring the broader cultural contexts within which the study of South Asian folklore studies grew as one strand of a complex historical process interwoven with a number of currents ranging from religion and philosophy to politics and economics, I hope to provide a suitable context for the rest of this volume, especially for the contents of chapter three. The remainder of this chapter then considers the complicated issues surrounding classificatory schemes for the study of folkloric genres. I focus here specifically on Bengal, since one can viably argue that it is in colonial Bengal that the academic study of South Asian folklore was first developed. But in order to make my point, a few paragraphs concerning some ethnic stereotypes of Bengal will help to clarify the ethnohistorical sections and theoretical discussions that follow.

Bengal has been perceived as an anomalous area of the Indian subcontinent at various points in time. Manisha Roy points out that even the first Aryan migrants in India kept their distance from Bengal as they moved eastward into the Gangetic plain from the northwest. As she notes, Vedic Brahmans saw Bengal as peripheral and impure (1972, 2). This is partially due to the region's marginal geographic location but is also due to stereotypical images of Bengalis and their unique culture. To be sure, Bengalis themselves perpetuated this degree of difference with their somewhat xenophobic attitudes toward the outside world and their linguocentric ideas concerning their own tongue. This is not to say, however, that Bengalis could not adapt to new waves of influence and change. History bears out the fact that Bengalis not only adjusted to life under various foreign rulers but creatively enriched their own cultural traditions as a result of these encounters. The distinct sense of being a functional segment of the "other" while maintaining a comfortable distance from it adds to both the internal and external ambiguities concerning Bengali society.

Attitudes concerning Bengal are especially significant during the middle portion of the eighteenth century, when British colonialists first began to establish a firm foothold in the subcontinent. Unlike other foreigners who came overland from Central Asia and entered South Asia through the Khyber Pass, the British East India Company came by sea and entered India from the east. They thus encountered Bengalis prior to other Indians. This is an important factor, for the British initially simply assumed that Bengalis were representative of India's total population. In other words, when the British "thought they were seeing India, they were in fact seeing Bengal," as Ainslee Embree (1976, 131) suggests. This vision of India is obviously limited in scope and equally biased in interpretation. The British conception of Bengal was generally negative. They perceived Bengalis as being inveterate liars who had no moral scruples.[1] These unfavorable perceptions provided an ideology and justification for British imperial rule. According to Embree, it was a kind of rule that "demanded social distance" (1976, 133). The initial British attitude toward India was thus simultaneously characterized by a confident sense of familiarity and a conscious alienation and estrangement from those natives closest to them (i.e., the Bengalis).

The initial encounter between India and the British was, in a sense, buffered by Bengal, and the colonialists' myopic vision of India was mediated by a smoked lens that conditioned the norms of interaction between the rulers and the ruled. It is most important to keep in mind, however, that Bengalis were also imagining the British at the same time that they themselves were being imagined. This mutual process created an incongruous dialogue between Bengal's inhabitants and the British that remained enigmatic well into the twentieth century.[2]

Other sorts of paradoxes resulted from this encounter as well. For example, the British set up their headquarters in Calcutta and ruled both Bengal and the rest of their subcontinental holdings from that primary locus. What we have is an image of a peripheral center, since Calcutta, originally the British Indian capital city, was located on the geographic periphery of the Indian subcontinent.

It might be natural to assume that because of its central role, Bengal and its culture would have become a target object of inquiry by the domineering

Engraving depicting the English East India Company at Bombay in 1767. © The Granger Collection, New York.

new rulers of India. Curiously enough, this was not the case. There are factors that can be isolated as possible causes for this situation. One outstanding factor in this regard is a result of British expansionism. By the second half of the nineteenth century, they had met and subjugated a number of diverse peoples who were culturally dissimilar to Bengalis. The British were forced to reconceptualize India and change their initial view, since the new image often conflicted with the old one constructed around Bengal (cf. Embree 1976, 138). The new images were no less stereotypical than the old ones, but the British had to accommodate newly encountered peoples who were clearly distinct from Bengalis. It is important to remember that certain regions of India were more rebellious than others and, as such, drew more attention than the ones that had already accepted the new colonial system. Calcutta and its environs were one such area. It was the predominantly calm and relatively safe spot in the midst of an area, according to the British rulers, in constant strife.

The Bengalis, and especially the Hindus among them, became the first indigenous clerical workers for the British government, because they became involved with the new administration quite early on. It is generally true that Bengalis chose to deal with the new system first by learning its ways and then, once they understood its mechanisms, using that knowledge for subtler means of subversion. The British, however, were not at first aware of this silent yet powerful force, for they saw only those robust peoples such as the Pathans and Punjabis—those who were willing to raise arms against them—as a challenge to their hegemony. The seemingly acquiescent manner of the Bengalis with regard to the administration prevented them from being seen as an imminent political threat.

This passiveness, as perceived by the rulers, led to new stereotypes of the Bengalis by their British employers. They were seen as effeminate (cf. Sinha 1995). Bengalis were, according to British officials of the time, weak, non-resistant, easy to control, and endowed with an uncanny lack of volition compared to other races. This image was juxtaposed against that of the "masculine" violently resistant and openly subversive tribes that continued to be a constant thorn in the side of the British government (Rudolph and Rudolph 1976, 6–13).

The British were little concerned about the apparently passive, weak, and cowardly Bengalis, for they could not stand up to the aggressiveness of the new imperialists. Rather, they focused on the threatening forces typified by those untamed and less understood "others" who stood against the ruling party. A combined fear and fantasy of these empirical others stimulated a great interest among British professionals and nonprofessionals alike. Guided by an imperialist theory that mandated a philosophy of divide and rule, British civil servants went to the field to learn everything they could about these people, so that they might better control them. Thus, while the Indian countryside was being mapped and documented by curious government investigators in search of new oddities and antiquities, Bengal remained relatively unnoticed. Of course some seminal ethnographies written about India describe Bengal specifically, but these are few in number compared to the voluminous tomes compiled on other areas of South Asia. Put another way, it seems to be the case that the familiar was less worthy of documentation. Although the academic journals and monographs edited and written by British scholars reached only a limited indigenous audience, Bengalis had the slight advantage of having access to these printed materials in English. The reason for this is not only their strategic position in Calcutta, but also their Anglophile tendencies regarding education, an important issue I address below.

Another unique feature of the region is that Bengali intellectuals were among the earliest pioneers of ethnology and folklore in the subcontinent. It is not certain, however, if Bengali scholars felt the need to go to the field because they were aware that their British colleagues relegated their region to an inferior cultural position. While this attitude may have been a contributing factor, it was only tangential to the primary focus of native

Bengali anthropologists and folklorists. Their efforts were clearly a product *[Literary]* of a nationalist and somewhat romantic milieu. As the movement for inde- *[Scholars]* pendence gathered momentum, Bengali scholars and writers were at the *[led the]* forefront, reawakening their compatriots to the wonders of Bengali life and *[revolution]* custom. It was in this nationalist context that the study of folklore emerged as a discipline in Bengal. The bulk of this chapter is an attempt to delineate some of the factors that shaped the emergence of folklore studies and to suggest how this configuration lent meaning to the changing identity of colonial Bengal.

While I attempt to suggest the emergence of two separate strands of *[Real Sd]* folklore study—one influenced by the positivism of Auguste Comte, which stressed objectivity and empiricism, and the other a product of romantic nationalism—I also wish to suggest their interrelated nature. Neither meth- *[Romanticism]* odology developed in isolation from the other, for they both came out of the same urban intellectual milieu. The boundaries between positivism and romanticism-cum-nationalism were often obscured and permeable, allowing a constant exchange of ideas between the two. Positivism was imbued with romantic tendencies, and vice versa, since cultural encounters are never a one-way street. As David Kopf has pointed out, they are always a two-way process, a "merging of interests and identities" (1969, 5).

FROM THE BEGINNING

On June 23, 1757, Lord Clive of the British East India Company defeated Sirajudaula, the *navāb* of Bengal at the Battle of Plassey, and thus the Company Bahadur (the brave company) became the undisputed ruler of the region. By 1764 the East India Company had a firm foothold on the subcontinent. That year they began paying tribute to the titular Mughal emperor at Delhi. In return the British received extra land holdings, which amounted to what are now the provinces of Bihar and Orissa, both of which border Bengal (cf. Spear 1958, 465–480). As the British web of influence spread, the region's administration started becoming less efficient. The company's policy was obviously dominated by commercial interest rather than concern for fair rule. The scenario during those early years was largely one of pillage. Themes of British exploitation come up over and over in Bengali oral tradition, and the tyranny and oppression of the company in India were not unknown to the British public either.

The situation had deteriorated immensely by the time that Clive was ousted and replaced by Warren Hastings (1732–1818) in 1772. Hastings, being a scholar himself and a connoisseur of Indian painting, encouraged study and

Baron Robert Clive, founder of the empire of British India.
© The Granger Collection, New York.

research in Bengal. During his service, a number of eminent scholars were
brought to Bengal, including William Jones (1746–94), Charles Wilkins
(1750–1836), and Nathaniel Brassey Halhed (1750–1830). Hastings, who
had a deep interest in the classics himself, encouraged these and other scholars
to study Sanskrit so that they would be able to translate the classical literature
of India. After several years in India, Jones founded the Royal Asiatic Society of Bengal in Calcutta. Jones's presidential address on January 15, 1784,
stressed the need to study the Orient. This study was to be undertaken solely
by elite Europeans, however.[3] There were no Indians in his audience that
evening, and the first indigenous scholars to join the Asiatic Society did not
appear on the scene until 45 years later, in 1849 (Poddar 1970, 220). The

Illustration of Robert Clive fighting the Prince of Bengal. © Bettmann / Corbis.

Society's efforts were generally classical in orientation. Most of the British Orientalists in the Society consciously attempted to revitalize Hindu classical traditions, yet there were attempts made to steer the methodology of the Orientalists toward the "unlettered" aspects of Indian culture.[4] Rev. William Carey (1761–1834), for example, was the first faculty member of Fort William College, the center of learning and the locus of intellectual activity in Calcutta at the beginning of the nineteenth century, to be more concerned with rural Bengali ways of life rather than high culture. For this reason, Kopf labels him as the first cultural anthropologist of India.[5] Indeed, as Eugene Nida has stated, "good missionaries have always been good anthropologists" (1960, 253).[6] While we may not wish to agree absolutely with Nida, his observation is relevant to the Indian context, for in order to propagate the Christian faith, missionaries made it their goal to become well versed in all areas of knowledge concerning traditional India.

Carey was the greatest and least typical of the missionary anthropologists. He became professor of Sanskrit and Bengali at Fort William College in 1800 and occupied the post until 1831. Until Carey published his Bengali dictionary in 1818, it was a neglected language. This is ironic for a culture that places so much emphasis on the distinctness of its language. By promoting

British officers attend a dancing display presented by an Indian raja, 1813.
© Mary Evans Picture Library.

the study of Bengali, Carey raised the consciousness of Bengal's urban intellectual elite by forcing them to think more deeply about their own language
and traditions.[7] Some sympathetic admirers of Carey even claimed that he
single-handedly initiated what would later be called the Bengal Renaissance.

Carey's approach was an emic, or insider, one, describing and emphasizing
local culture through language to portray accurately the ways and customs
of the Bengali folk. His romantic vision of a pristine form of Bengali society,
undisturbed by the exigencies of urban life, was more of a fictional portrayal
than a factual one. Nevertheless, his advocacy was important to the Bengali
intellectual elite's vision of their own culture, because it acted as a foil against
their own urban points of view. Kopf states the following on this point:

> In essence, Carey sought to recapture a Bengali folk tradition that existed prior
> to or apart from the influence of Calcutta. It is significant that during the next
> five decades, whenever Bengalis themselves depicted life in a socially realistic
> manner, they turned their backs on Carey's area of perception, rural Bengal,
> and described the new social classes living in a new cultural milieu in urbanized
> Calcutta. (1969, 94)

The classical-versus-vernacular debate at Fort William fluctuated in intensity from year to year until finally reaching its peak in 1812. Carey, the only

English Orientalist and missionary William Carey baptiz-
ing the first Hindu convert, a carpenter named Kristno,
in the Hooghly River, India. © The Granger Collection,
New York. *Bengali's learned from colonialists not the other way around*

European faculty member supporting the vernacularist position, lost the battle. As a result of his defeat, the activities of the college remained primarily
classical until its closing in 1835, a consequence of the ultimate triumph of
Macaulayist educational reforms based on the premise that the "natives" had
more to learn from the colonialists than the other way around (cf. Macaulay *Bengali*
1835). Carey's influence at Fort William had introduced many native stu- *study their own lore*
dents to the study of Bengali oral lore. It was primarily those students who
created and stimulated a movement to revive interest in traditional Bengali
life among the upper classes, largely in reaction to the missionary attempts

to convert them to Christianity. Even liberal middle- and upper-class urban Bengalis reevaluated their own culture and religion in an attempt to become more conservative.

These were the days of Rammohan Roy, a leading intellectual figure of the time who founded the Brahma Sabha in 1828 in order to revive what he conceived of as the pure, traditional core of Hindu belief (cf. Halbfass 1988, 222–43). More need not be said about Roy here, but his activities marked the surge of new nationalist movements in Bengal. Roy died in 1833, and soon thereafter a proliferation of new journals emphasizing Hindu philosophy, literature, ethnology, and folklore began to appear in Calcutta. Again, these works were not always of scholarly quality, according to British normative standards, but they nonetheless served as instruments of the approaching Bengal reawakening.

The period of Hastings's rule coincided with the so-called golden age of British Orientalism. The classical interest of the Orientalists searching for India's lost golden age, coupled with the many popular journals printed by the missionaries at Serampore, led to what social historians have termed the Bengal Renaissance. The Bengal Renaissance was a climactic period in Indian history during which the rapport between foreign researchers and Bengali urban intellectual elites became so intimate and fine tuned that it led to the emergence of a new and transformed strand of thought that dominated urban attitudes concerning virtually all aspects of life.[8] The city came to play such an important role in Bengali intellectual life that metropolitan elites quickly lost sight of Bengal beyond the urban fringe. Attempts were even made to lure country folk to the city.[9] Rapid urbanization had the unexpected side effect of human alienation, which partially stimulated the identity crisis that urban intellectuals increasingly began to feel in the mid-nineteenth century. By the time that Fort William closed in 1835, the awakening of the Bengali intellectual elite was well under way. The awakening, however, was largely confined to the Hindu portion of Calcutta's population.

Hastings had been successful in motivating a scholarly interest in India, but his other reforms did not work out as well. The continued overbearing attitude of the British led to a reactive Islamic revival in the Muslim population. Hindus also attained a greater awareness of being oppressed. A series of strikes and minor agitations led to a temporary feeling of solidarity among various communities of Indians, a feeling that occasionally crossed barriers of religion. The movement culminated in the Sepoy Rebellion of 1857, an event referred to as a mutiny by the British. The rebellion is a significant event in the history of Indian folklore because it offers a major clue in helping us to understand why the British would suddenly want to radically reorient themselves and move beyond the urban environment in their academic endeavors. After the suppression of this insurrection, the British established a firmer rule and consolidated their power to an even further extent. By then they controlled much of the Indian subcontinent. But stiffer rule did not control dissidence, for the final dissolution of Fort William three years earlier in 1854 and the increasing political suppression imposed by the British led to another phase of revivalism. The heightened sense of interest in South Asian culture in all its aspects led to the opening of Calcutta University during the year of the rebellion.

[handwritten margin note: Suppression led to revivalism]

The Sepoy Rebellion deeply disturbed the British administration. Back in England, the Parliament debated how such an event could have occurred. No doubt the so-called mutiny was an embarrassment to the British Empire, and it led to a reevaluation of colonial methods and tactics. A movement to study the ruled folk filtered through the administration, and a lenient position toward the civil service examination was taken: the year 1859 saw the first Indians sitting for the exam, the group being predictably dominated by Bengalis. The reform, however, was purely cosmetic, since fewer than ten candidates received the opportunity each year. As late as 1915, only 5 percent of civil servants were of Indian origin.[10]

The Sepoy Rebellion of 1857–58.© The Granger Collection, New York.

Reach out
from Brief
Rive

The movement to study "the people" described above nonetheless caught on. As Mazharul Islam has written, "English officials were strictly directed to come closer to the people, to learn their language, and to honor their cultural heritage" (1970, 16). Although certain Englishmen, such as Halhed, did learn the language, no major bridges between the two cultures were built. The underlying assumption in the new policy was that better rule made exploitation more efficient.

Richard Dorson has stated that the above motivation, along with "a desire to test in a living laboratory the new anthropological hypotheses of E. B. Tylor (1832–1917) concerning primitive man" (1968, 333) were the two powerful impulses that inspired the overseas folklorists, as they were called.[11] A correlation of chronologies reveals that the history of folklore study in India closely parallels that in England. It is no wonder then that the sanctioning of an ethnographic and linguistic survey of India in 1901 followed the presidential address of Edwin Sidney Hartland (1848–1927) to London's Folk-Lore Society in 1900.[12] In his address, Hartland presented his empire theory of applied folklore. Dorson writes that "in that address he stressed the practical advantages for the governors, district officers, and judges of an enlightened mother-country in learning through folklore about the cultures of the native peoples under their dominion. Accordingly, the council for the Society had presented a memorial to the colonial secretary calling for a 'methodical survey' of the native tribes" (1968, 332). As a result of this *The Linguistic Survey of India* was inaugurated in 1903 by Lord Curzon and put under the direction of a brilliant linguist by the name of George Abraham Grierson (1851–1941). This was the first systematic survey of the subcontinent, including a richly detailed volume on Bengal that consisted of regional and dialectal examples of rhymes, proverbs, and tales.

As nationalism flourished, the British researchers continued their politically oriented scholastics. The great names of Indian folklore were usually to be found in association with areas of India outside Bengal. The name of William Crooke (1848–1923) came up in relation to studies pertaining to north India and what is now Pakistan, and Richard Carnac Temple (1850–1931) was mentioned in reference to the Punjab. These names stood out in the Folk-Lore Society. Grierson's name came up less often, although he was mentioned on occasion. However, his role as head of the *Linguistic Survey* put him in a position to promote the study of all aspects of folklore. His relentless attention to language led him to publish materials on 179 languages and 554 dialects spoken in India. Yet even though his publications were extensive, covering all regions of India's topography, he devoted much of his time to Bengal. Between 1873 and 1877, Grierson collected a massive amount of rhymes, songs, and tales from the Rangpur district of what is now Bangladesh. Of particular importance are Grierson's song collections. Before his time there were only a few sporadic reports of songs in daily newspapers. But Grierson gave attention to notational features of tunes and thereby stimulated indigenous interest in ethnomusicology. His material, though filled with hasty value judgments that taint his scholarship, deserves merit for the sheer volume of the work alone.

Until the establishment of the Folk-Lore Society in London (1878), amateurs and missionaries did most of the folklore collecting in India. The amateur work is dilettantish but could be useful as a valuable historical record of missionary research. Even though these accounts are biased, they contain a wealth of facts that are still relevant as background reading for ethnographic research today. Along with these accounts, bits of pertinent information were occasionally included in census reports, imperial gazetteers, and district manuals issued by the government of India. The period up to 1878 has been labeled the "formative phase" of folklore studies by Ashraf Siddique (1966, 52), during which the groundwork for the beginnings of positivistic scholarship were constructed. As the formative phase ended, there was a great flourishing of intellectual and cultural activity in urban Bengal. It was not limited to the academy but involved a large portion of the Bengali intelligentsia, even if only tangentially in some cases. By the end of this period, a fine ethnography of Bengal was available, which was being used by both scholars and native amateurs who wished to acquire descriptive background on Bengali society.[13] The time was now right for the growth of studies on Bengal.

Due to the formation of the Folk-Lore Society in London, a renewed interest was taken in India generally. India was already the center of a heated solar mythology debate between Max Müller and Andrew Lang (cf. Dorson 1955). The publicity caused by it was one factor in a general trend that created a certain romantic fondness for the exoticness of India in the minds of Europeans. As already mentioned, the subcontinent became a testing ground for field-workers who were trying to prove Tylor's evolutionary theories of culture. Researchers such as Sir Herbert Risley (1851–1911) poured into India to demonstrate that India was a prime target for such investigations. Along with the British scholars came the evolutionary ideas of Darwin, Frazer, Gomme, Hartland, and others. Risley's *Tribes and Castes of Bengal* (1891), for example, is the epitome of this trend. It is primarily a descriptive work, but Risley's interpretation of his material fits clearly into the anthropological research paradigm of the period. We notice in it glimpses of a survivalist who envisions a culture made up of remnants of the past arranged in a hierarchical fashion.

The web of scholarly influence extended beyond those Europeans studying in India to include a new generation of prominent indigenous researchers. Along with the development of nationalist movements, there was also a cadre of young Bengali scholars attempting to produce scientific work along the lines of the British ethnologists and folklorists. With the British Parliament's official sanction of ethnology in India (1901), these native scholars began to work diligently under the encouraging patronage of Bengali elites.

A predominant figure among these was Sarat Chandra Mitra (1863–1938). He was a prolific writer who contributed no fewer than 115 articles in various journals printed in Calcutta and Bombay.[14] There was not a single aspect of Bengali aesthetic culture left unprobed by Mitra. Mitra was influenced by Gomme's *Handbook of Folklore,* especially Charlotte Burne's 1914 revision, which laid out the imperialistic outlook of English folklorists of the time. It is not certain to what degree Mitra accepted the latent ideology of the discipline, but he did incorporate her typology of Indo-European folktales by using her categories as a basis for comparison and arrangement. Although Mitra's work seems archaic today, it is an important record of the positivistic strand in indigenous Bengali folklore scholarship. Mitra was by no means a field-worker. He was an armchair theorist who obtained most of his material from a Bengali journal called *Sahitya Parishad Patrika,* which was founded by Rabindranath Tagore in 1894. In part, Mitra's aim was to take the humanistic and nationalist accounts from this journal and test them by using the common ethnoscientific methodology of the period. There was certainly a strong sense of competition between the nationalists/humanists and the social scientists. Yet the positivists were a small minority and had to rely to a certain degree on nationalist patrons. In the final analysis a significant number of Bengali intellectuals tended to side with their nationalist comrades rather than with their senior British colleagues. Indigenous scholars, regardless of academic orientation, therefore interacted to a great degree.

The year 1920 marked a new phase in Bengali folklore. This phase was influenced once again by scholars from the Occident such as Theodor Benfey, Max Müller, E. B. Cowell, Charles H. Tawney, and Norman M. Penzer. Each of these scholars, along with others, contributed to the broader field of Indology. Their interests were classical to the extent that they focused predominantly on Sanskrit texts, yet they were sensitive to folk literature. Many references to the folk roots of classical texts can be found in their work, and a number of articles and books appeared between 1920 and 1947 that even dealt with motif analysis from a historical-geographic perspective, complementing similar work being done in Europe at the same time. Their concerns were with the demonstration of the diffusionist pattern of tale types and how this pattern manifests itself in the classical literature of India.[15] I will have much more to say about these issues in chapter four.

As the fervor over nationalism grew in Calcutta, the government began to increase the frequency of attempts to create internal and ideological discord among Bengalis. Governmental tactics often divided scholars politically and ethically, but contrary to the expectations of politicians, these occasional schisms did not divide or scatter the sentiments of the nationalists. More often than not, these incidents strengthened and solidified diverse indigenous groups of people in Bengal. One incident, however, left a permanent impression on the minds of Bengalis.

Lord Curzon's 1905 attempt to partition Bengal into an eastern and western portion on the basis of religious majority accelerated the nationalist movement, and this in turn stimulated folklore studies. The experiment of partition did not work, and in 1911 Bengal was made one entity again. The brief period, however, shocked Bengalis into realizing that their unity was being palpably threatened. From that period until independence in 1947, nationalism became firmly rooted at the center of Bengali consciousness.

BENGALI ATTITUDES AND RESPONSES TO THE ENCOUNTER

If we look at the history of folklore in Bengal, we find, as I have related above, a strong nationalist trend. Nationalism had been growing ever since the Sepoy Rebellion, and the interest in folklore that was initiated by outsiders was incorporated into the movement. To understand why folklore was so important in this movement, it is necessary to situate the activities of those who were involved in it. I have stressed the role of the city and education because the development of ideas about the folk was a product of these two major factors. Arabinda Poddar (1970, 229). has stated emphatically that the progress of the Bengali intellectual movement cannot be extricated from the idea of the city, because the beliefs of the movement synchronized with the rapid urban transformation of Calcutta.[16] The development of education is also intertwined with urbanization. Prior to the advent of the British, the traditional locus of education in West Bengal was Navadvip-Krishnanagar in Nadia. In 1782, however, two years before the establishment of the Royal Asiatic Society in Calcutta, royal patronage of the Sanskrit *tola*s ceased as a result of the death of the *mahārāja* of Nadia, Krishnachandra. This marked the shift to Calcutta as the center of education (cf. Basu 1975, 114). But the kind of education practiced was largely defined in Western terms. Hindus were more successful in utilizing the newly defined educational system to their benefit, since Muslims were still embroiled in power struggles with the British and did not attempt to interact with them on the intellectual level to any significant degree.[17] Because of their willingness to receive Western training, educated Hindu elites were in the best social and economic position to become the spokesmen of the urban population. The movement for reform began in this urban environment, and the elite spokesmen represented the views of only a small minority of the total population. Much of what they had to say was filtered through a sieve of experiences that were conditioned by the ideology of the British establishment in Calcutta.

To a great extent, Calcutta developed on the model of London, and even though circumstances of life in urban Bengal did not allow for all the luxuries that London provided, an earnest attempt was made to replicate British fashion and lifestyle. Bengali intellectual elites thus began utilizing English as their major mode of communication. Linguistic barriers slowly erected fences between the elite and village folk, further alienating Bengal's urban population. The elite became estranged beings. Their radical new ideas could not spread beyond the periphery of the city because of the gulf that had been created when the government rejected a plan for statewide education in Bengali.[18] English thus remained the language of a small but powerful and influential minority.

Prior to 1860, many of the intellectual elite in Calcutta were considered anglophiles, drawing their inspiration as much from London as from Bengal.[19] Some intellectuals, such as the writer Bankimchandra, felt that placing the cultural center of gravity in England was good for the social progress of Bengal. Poddar even goes so far as to suggest that the so-called Bengal Renaissance was nothing more than a British Renaissance enacted on Indian soil (1970, 245).[20] After the closing of Fort William and the institutionalization of Macaulayism in Calcutta (c. 1830–45), the "apologetic mythification" of India's past began (cf. Bharati 1970, 267–87; Kopf 1969, 288). The identity crisis caused by the collapse of the college and the anglocentric attitudes of Macaulayism stimulated Bengali intellectuals to search for new meaning in old symbols, and old meaning in new symbols. To a great extent, the pattern of rhetoric was apologetic. In their new search for meaning, the Bengali intellectual elite consciously chose to divinize their cultural history in an attempt to keep alive the glorified image of their forebears.

The creation of new meaning took many forms: the redefinition of religion, educational and economic reforms, and cultural revivalism. Central to the nationalist revival of Bengali culture was the attempted reestablishment of the broken link of discourse between the rural masses and the urban intellectual minority. This, however, was not an easy task to accomplish, because the alienation that enveloped urbanites was so great that they had difficulty communicating with and mobilizing the rural folk. The revival thus began in the city and functioned largely as a medium of communication to dispel the illusions of those urban elites who remained anglophiles even after the nationalist movement was well under way. But once these Anglophiles realized that they were wavering between two cultures and fitting into neither, they joined the movement for independence wholeheartedly.

The revival of tradition emerged as an attempt to unite all Bengalis in response to the divisiveness of colonial rule. It took shape in many ways. One of the earliest manifestations of revivalism after Bholanath Chandra's initial call for *svadeśī* (indigenous) economics was the instigation of an annual *melā* (fair) in 1867 by the Tagore family. These *melā*s were very successful among Hindus, running for the duration of 14 years. The last was staged in 1880. The *caitra*, or *jātīya melā*, as it came to be known, was predominantly a Hindu phenomenon, excluding Muslims to a great extent.[21] The chief inspiration for it came from Rajnarayan Bose's Society for the Promotion of National Feeling, an organization that catered to the Bengali intellectual elite. In hopes of stimulating an urban awareness of traditional art, the organizers of the *melā* included an exhibition of folk crafts. It was also hoped that an urban understanding of these traditional modes of livelihood would revitalize these crafts and further establish *svadeśī* economics throughout the province. Other performances at the first *melā* were *jātrā* (itinerant street theater), *kīrtan* (devotional songs), secular singing, poetry recitation, bioscope demonstrations, lantern shows, and traditional forms of gymnastics (cf. Poddar 1977, 179). The major aims of the *caitra melā* were the propagation of folk culture and the religious and national unification of Bengalis. The *melā* succeeded in doing this for the Hindu population to a degree but resulted in further alienating Bengali Muslims from the mainstream of nationalist activity.

Rabindranath Tagore (1861–1941), winner of the Nobel Prize in 1913, was nurtured in this milieu. His upbringing in an orthodox Pirali Brahman household exposed him to the classical side of Bengali culture but sheltered him from the world beyond the gates of the family mansion at Jorasanko. As a child, Tagore was exposed to a great deal of traditional wisdom and verbal art in the form of proverbs, rhymes, riddles, dramas provided for him by family servants at home, and the staged performances arranged by his parents and relatives.[22] These early exposures and influences had a lasting effect on him and played a major role in his later attempts to unite Bengal.

Rabindranath Tagore. © The Granger Collection, New York.

Tagore went to England in 1878–80 and found that he identified with the colonial plight of the Irish. Although later in life he would see this period as insignificant (cf. Poddar 1977, 168), his Irish experience marks the beginning of his career in India's freedom movement. Tagore's career from 1880 to 1910 is a record of increasing social awareness, and by the last decade of the nineteenth century, Tagore was deeply involved in the freedom movement.[23] In 1890 he returned to England and began writing with a much more critical (i.e., anti-British) perspective. During this trip, he came to realize that any nationalist scheme had to be grounded in the tradition, language, and cultural climate of Bengal. This idea served as Tagore's personal paradigm for the Bengali identity quest (cf. Poddar 1977, 175).

Tagore was well aware of the rift between the rural folk and the urban elite, since he himself was a product of the tension. Krishna Kripalini quotes a seminal passage from Tagore bearing on this connection:

> The soil in which we are born . . . is the soil of our village, the mother earth in whose lap we receive our nourishment from day to day. Our educated elite, abstracted from this primal basis, wander about in the high heaven of ideas like aimless clouds removed from this our home. (1980, 155)

Returning home, Tagore took up the linguistic cause and pushed to have Bengali reinstated as the official language of political discourse in Bengal.[24] He felt that nationalist sentiment must lean toward a corpus of national literature as well. National literature was to be constructed on a foundation of folk traditions in order to link all Bengalis into one chain of "collective patriotic consciousness" (Poddar 1977, 177).[25] This theme was expounded in his 1894 lecture titled "Bengali National Literature."

That same year, Tagore, together with other prominent literary figures of Calcutta, established the Bengali Literary Society, an organization concerned with the preservation of the traditions and folklore of Bengal. The Society, along with its aforementioned journal, *Sahitya Parishad Patrika,* did much to infuse a strong sense of identity and unity into the Bengali population.[26]

Tagore's efforts in raising consciousness about folklore cannot be underestimated (cf. Sengupta 1963, 148ff). His own personal patronage of research, his journal editing, the prefaces he wrote to Bengali books on folklore as well as his own writing on the subject, and his personal artistic indebtedness to the itinerant mystic bards, the Bauls of Bengal (cf. Dimock 1959), have all stimulated and shaped the field much more than is normally acknowledged. In his own romantic words, Tagore stated the following:

> As the roots of a tree are firmly bound together with the soil and its upper part is spread towards the sky, in the same way the lower part of a literature is always hidden, being to a large extent imprisoned in the soil of its mother country. . . . There is a ceaseless inner connection between the lower literature and the higher one. (As quoted in Zvalebil 1961, 14)

From 1894 onward, Tagore himself was involved in the collection of verbal art. He collected rhymes in and around Calcutta but lamented the fact that the genre was dying out (1956–58, 6: 642–43).[27] A few years later he began to realize that the many forms of verbal art that he had enjoyed as a youth were rapidly fading into oblivion. Fearing that nationalist sentiment would fade along with the disappearance of traditional knowledge and lore, Tagore actively sought to revive genres of oral tradition. Among the genres he covered were folk ballads *(palligīti)*, itinerant drama *(jātrā)*, myths *(paurāṇik kahīnī)*, legends *(ūpakathā)*, and fairy tales *(rūpkathā)*. By rewriting the accumulated wisdom of India in his own style of literary Bengali, he envisioned the creation of a regional literature based on local folk tradition.[28] There is an ironic element in this fact. In his effort to revive Bengali oral tradition, Tagore relied heavily on works concerning Indian regions far beyond the borders of Bengal written in English by civil servants.[29] Tagore's invented and normative understanding of what Bengali *lok sāhitya* (folk literature) should be inadvertently brought together pan-Indian elements into an urban, aristocratic vision of the Bengali folk. As Poddar has pointed out, Tagore chose those elements of culture that he saw as universal, irrespective of time, space, and country (1977, 182). Tagore's universal position gradually removed him from the political arena. By 1910 he had moved away from nationalism in order to promote what he called world humanism, which would ultimately transcend all ethnic, cultural, religious, and linguistic distinctions.[30]

Tagore's contribution to the development of folklore cannot be underestimated, but all his attempts, though sincere and thoughtful, could not wrench him out of his class-oriented, urban environment, the inhabitants of which mostly saw folklore studies as an effort to salvage the past. He collected and wrote in the city, and he drew inspiration from its affluent residents. His reading of representative works by British ethnographers and civil servants shaped his conception of folklore. Moreover, his creation of the Bengali peasant emerged out of his own realization of the dichotomy between urban and rural. He himself experienced this estrangement, and in order to rectify it he imagined what the archetypal Bengali peasant should be. The literary creation of the folk was a necessary step in the history of Bengali nationalism. This is not only true of Tagore's works, but also of an entire generation that he influenced.[31]

The nationalist trend continued after Tagore's withdrawal from politics, and it remained a vital and integral part of the freedom struggle until independence in 1947. Each step along the way, the creation of the concept of folklore occurred in the shadow of British ethnology in India, or as a result of direct contact with British scholars in England. By the 1930s a true folk revival was well under way in Bengal. This latest revival was primarily due to Gurusaday Dutt (1882–1941), a Bengali civil servant residing in Sylhet (now in Bangladesh). Dutt was deeply influenced by Tagore and Kshitimohan Sen, a colleague of Tagore's from Calcutta. His political position on folklore was explicitly developed within the framework of Bengali nationalism, but his understanding of the concept of folklore was a direct result of his visit to England in 1929, where he met Cecil Sharp, a folk dance revivalist in London. In January of that year Dutt attended a folk dance performance at the Royal Albert Hall. Reflecting on that moment a few years later in 1936, Dutt fondly wrote:

> I was impressed by the value which was being attached to the almost extinct folk dances and folk songs of England by educated people. . . . It was on that occasion at the Royal Albert Hall that my memory went back with a fond long-ing to the village dances of my childhood, which had a great deal of similarity in respect of vigour and spontaneity with folk dances of England and I there formed a resolution in my mind to devote myself to the conservation of the village dances of my province on my return to India. (Dutt 1936, 26)

Dutt returned to Mymensingh (now in Bangladesh) and formed the Folk Dance and Song Society in 1932. But by far his most successful pan-Indian organization was the Bratachari Society (Vow-Taking Society), an eclec-tic movement modeled after the Scout movement of R.S.S. Baden-Powell (1857–1941) in England.[32] For Dutt, *bratacārī* came to mean "one who holds the view that all life is based on joy and should be pursued as a rhyth-mic ritual" (cf. Sengupta 1965, 136).[33]

That the movement was nationalist in orientation is attested to by the three vows taken by all bratacharins:

1. I am a Bengali.
2. I love the land of Bengal.
3. I shall serve Bengal.

As the movement spread into Bihar (1936) and south India (1940) the goals became increasingly pan-Indian. The training of the neophyte bratacharin was based on folk custom, and the songs they sung were arranged to the tunes of Bengali *lok saṅgīt* (folk songs).[34] This movement drew praise from all sectors of Indian society. Politicians, theologians, phi-losophers, and radical revolutionaries alike all praised the unifying progress made by Dutt. The Bratachari movement was a unique coming together of forces from numerous sources. Its eclectic nature made it desirable in India beyond Bengal, but its usefulness was limited to the romantic-nationalist context, and its success was largely due to the charisma of its inspired leader. The organization did not live out its usefulness, for it did not last after the death of Dutt, just a few years before independence. His legacy as a revival-ist, however, is an important chapter in the history of folklore studies in Bengal. The nationalist in Dutt saw that urban people could be brought closer to their rural roots through a common cultural revival. In his opinion, "the mission was to bring into clear perspective the robust and genial manners of the elements of folk culture and to make them known and popular among the urban people who have deviated from the main stream of the country masses."[35] Dutt imagined that if unified along an urban-rural continuum, they would be strong enough to withstand the destructive forces of colonialism.

The story is a long and complex one. The use and abuse of folklore for various ends are the defining characteristics of the history of the field in Bengal from 1800 to 1947.[36] The British attempt to divide and rule through the exploitation and manipulation of folklore worked effectively only on occasion. Conversely, the use of folklore as a nationalist tool worked well in Bengal, yet it retained an ambiguous social status in India generally, as Stuart Blackburn (2003) has suggested. Ironically, the very unity for which Bengal strove was destroyed on the eve of independence when East Pakistan (now Bangladesh) was born. This is understandable, given the minor role allotted to Muslims in Bengali affairs during the Renaissance. The distinction, however, was made along political and religious, rather than cultural, lines. Regardless of the fact that Bengal became two separate political entities, it remained one cultural unit in many ways. It is a historical fact that when the central government of Pakistan attempted to ban the songs of Rabindranath Tagore for their supposed anti-Islamic content, East Pakistanis rebelled (cf. Singhal 1972, 167–85). When a further attempt was made to eliminate Bengali as an official language of Pakistan, the outraged East Pakistanis began a new movement to become an autonomous nation. Since 1947 we have not been able to speak of the history of Bengali folklore: we must now speak of two separate histories divided along national and geographical lines.

FOLKLORE AS INVENTION

The development of folklore studies in colonial Bengal is bound up with, and runs parallel to, the urban creation of an unknown but hauntingly familiar other, the Bengali peasant. It was a dialogic response to an encounter with European Orientalists, who also had romantic visions of India. Those urban Bengalis who chose to observe British etiquette and propagate empirical science defined in European terms gradually became alienated from their own heritage. To a certain extent, they forgot their past. When they perceived that this was happening, a gradual realization occurred, which facilitated the search for new meaning. This new meaning was made up of faint memories and metaphors of revived beliefs, practices, and customs.

Upon coming to Bengal the British developed opinions, biases, definitions, and images, while the Bengalis reversed this process in turn. It was a case of dialectical invention, as Rudolph Agricola, the fifteenth-century humanist, would have called it.[37] Neither fully understood the other, and their encounter stimulated new modes of perception and thought. Every encounter is a transformation, as Roy Wagner has stated, with the unavoidable consequence of change (1975, 10). As Wagner notes, invention occurs whenever an alien or foreign set of conventions is brought into relation with one's own (1975, 10). Invention, then, is a necessary aspect of creative culture, but often it is intensified when a society undergoes rapid transformation, as Calcutta did in the latter portion of the eighteenth century.[38]

Invention should not be seen as undesirable or pejorative, for as Wagner has pointed out, it is a positive and expected component of human life (1975, xvi). Human beings cannot live in a world they do not understand. When we no longer understand our existential predicament, we must create new meaning, something that gives purpose to life. Invention is a medium of understanding that which was unknown prior to a cultural encounter. It is "knowledge by extension" (Wagner 1975, 27). The post-encounter *Weltanschauung* is never the same as it was prior to it. The philosopher Martin Heidegger touched upon this point when he stated that things could only be seen after they have been conceived. However, concepts must themselves first be invented before they can be perceived.[39] Cultural invention is thus a powerful use of metaphor to create common cores of meaning that enable alienated and estranged human beings to envision once again the world in a manner that intuitively makes sense. Meaning is thus personal and culturally shared at the same time. This line of reasoning further suggests that the given perceptions of a community may not actually depict or represent another given group of people or phenomenon. It is, in a sense, a relative value judgment or truth claim, approximating what sociologists à la Max Weber term an ideal type, a model of reality, rather than reality itself. This point of view enables us to understand the metaphoric invention of "the folk" and subsequently of a discipline called folklore.

Bengali intellectual elites could not see the peasants in Heidegger's sense, for they had never attempted to conceive of them. When the necessity arose, they exuberantly invented tradition, giving something new the aura of antiquity. Sometimes this happened consciously, as in the case of Tagore and Dutt, or unconsciously in the minds of the many Calcutta residents who participated in but did not plan the revival. The indigenous discipline of folklore did not exist in Steven Toulmin's sense until well after independence.[40] In fact, the concept, the term, and its definition did not become an issue until 1956 when the Calcutta-based journal *Folklore* consciously set out to draw the parameters of a field of study. That year S. K. Chatterjee suggested *lok yānā* (folk vehicle) as an equivalent term in a column that he contributed to the journal. Earlier attempts to do this by positivists such as D. H. Moutray Read and Sarat Chandra Roy in 1921 were prompted and guided by British members of the London Folk-Lore Society.[41]

As late as 1932 Roy still lamented that *students of history* did not take folklore and tradition seriously. But he happily acknowledged that tradition was gradually becoming a subject of investigation and discussion by the Indian Science Congress, the Oriental Conference, and the Bombay Historical Congress (1932, 353). Even with the domineering presence of the British scholars, the emphasis on the historical dimension of tradition suggests a pre-Thomsian definition of folklore as popular antiquities to be considered the object of study.[42] These pre-independence definitions were developed and applied by British researchers in India and utilized only by indigenous scholars who were trained by Orientalists and antiquarians who shared their vision of India's past generally and Bengal's past specifically. The romantic nationalists had no such conception. This is suggested by the fact that there are no equivalents for the term "folklore" in any of the north Indian vernaculars derived from Sanskrit. Trilochan Pande's 1963 claim that the term *lok vārtā* (folk talk) parallels the term "folklore" is unfounded. At best, the term is ambiguous.[43]

The term *lok sāhitya* was and still is more popular in north India. As I have suggested above, it gained currency in Bengal during the literary reconstruction of the folk that occurred in the era of Rabindranath Tagore. The term "folk literature," however, delimits the field of inquiry to those elements of lore that are deemed worthy of study by the literati. Prior to 1956 there was no concrete conception of folklore in Bengal. The discipline was invented along with the image of the rural masses. Numerous attempts were made to find an Indian synonym for the English term, but scholars gradually realized that contrived nomenclature only obscured the issues.[44] The debate over definitions continues to the present day, an example being Mazharul Islam's recent attempt to suggest that a Bengali–English hybrid term (i.e., *lok lor*) should be employed in the vernacular, because there are no exact equivalents to lore in Bengali (1985, 1–34).[45] All these uncertainties should suggest a distinct sense of ambiguity toward the stuff of folklore, the nomenclature that should be used to describe its study, and the *lok* themselves.

The invention of folklore in Bengal was a necessary process in the quest for new identity and nationhood. As a concept, it emerged out of a nationalist milieu that actively sought out new ideas that could be applied to old phenomena. The advocates who were the actors in the Bengali nationalist drama were primarily responsible for this creative process, a process hastily stimulated by British Orientalists. Their contribution cannot be underestimated, for as we have seen, the transformational process was mutual. The Orientalist in Calcutta, like the contemporary anthropologist, created a new and meaningful reality for him- or herself through Indological investigations. Wagner has stated that "in the act of inventing another culture, the anthropologist invents his own and in fact he reinvents the notion of culture itself" (1975, 4). Folklore, then, as an integral aspect of culture, can be viewed as an invention, albeit a quintessential one, alongside a number of other cultural products that lent meaning to a newly emergent sense of South Asian identity during the colonial period and continues to take shape in the postcolonial era.[46] This is not only true of what is now the province of West Bengal but the whole of India and its neighboring countries.

WHERE, THEN, DO WE STAND?

Given the constraints on terminology outlined in the previous section, what position can we take in terms of studying South Asian expressive culture? We can take our cue from Dan Ben-Amos when he writes the following:

> In our zeal for scientific methodology, we abandoned cultural reality and strove to formulate theoretical analytical systems. We attempted to construct logical concepts which would have cross-cultural applications and to design tools which would serve as the basis for scholarly discourse, providing it with defined terms of reference and analysis. In the process, however, we transformed traditional genres from cultural categories of communication into scientific concepts. We approached them as if they were not dependent upon cultural expression and perception but autonomous entities which consisted of exclusive inherent qualities of their own; as if they were not relative divisions in a totality of oral tradition but absolute forms. In other words, we attempted to change folk taxonomic systems which are culturally bound and vary according to speakers' cognitive systems into culture-free, analytical, unified, and objective models of folk literature. (1976, 216)[47]

What Ben-Amos is suggesting in this passage is the need for context sensitivity and an emphasis on indigenous taxonomic categories prior to making cross-cultural parallels. For example, in north Indian vernaculars, it is quite common to distinguish between different kinds of stories on the basis of whether they are true or false. In Bengali, Hindi, and other languages of north India, both *kathā* and *kahānī* translate to mean story, but *kathā* means a true story, whereas *kahānī* is a false story (cf. Chatterji 1985; Narayan 1997; and Wadley 1978). The English word "story" simply does not have the same implicit connotations, and assuming that it does leads us down the wrong interpretive path.

Another example of the need for ethnolinguistic context sensitivity can be gleaned from the proverb genre. Narayana Rao, for instance, points out that the English term "proverb" too transparently "seems to be a cover word for a complex cluster of folk speech forms" (1981, 23). After surveying a number of works written in English by researchers, both South Asian and foreign, Rao demonstrates how the term "proverb" masks a variety of vernacular terms:

> Some terms, such as *kahānia* (Gujerati) and *sōlōki* (Bengali), indicate a genre. *Kahānia* represents a song sung in couplets by women. *Sōlōki* means a proverb within a story. Words like *sāmeta* (Telugu) and *sāmite* (Kannada) point to the concept of analogy underlying the use of proverbs. Both of these terms are derived from Sanskrit *sāmyata,* "equivalence." The Bengali *pravād,* as well as the Tamil *paṛamuri* suggest the legitimizing function of proverbs. The words mean "words of the ancients" or "sayings of the community." Also, *sāstram,* used in Telugu, and *lōkōkti,* attested to in several languages, indicate a similar legitimizing function. (1981, 23)

Clearly, the English term "proverb" does not have the semantic suppleness to cover such a wide variety of genres, terms, and contextual uses. To complicate matters even more, the same proverb often has different meanings in different languages. For example, the proverb "It's dark under the lamp" is known in Kannada, a southern Dravidian language, and in Kashmiri, a northern Indo-Aryan language. Their sentence structure is the same, but they carry different connotations. In Kannada, it implies that a virtuous man is the lamp who has hidden (i.e., "dark") vices. In Kashmiri, however, the same phrase conveys a political sense; that is, a moral and ethical ruler has evil (i.e., "dark") counselors (cf. Ramanujan 1990, 6). But some ethical issues dealing with etiquette, such as the egg reprimanding the bird for chirping, seem to apply to multiple linguistic regions. The egg-bird proverb, for example, is used in the same performance contexts in Hindi-speaking and Telugu-speaking areas to scold a child for using proverbs in front of elders, which seems to be a pan-Indian phenomenon (cf. Rao 1981, 26).

Proverb speaking, it would seem from the Indian data, is socially hier-archical, in that the subordinate (the bird) does not chirp oral wisdom to the superior (the egg). It would be interesting to expand the investigation to other countries of South Asia to determine whether or not proverbial speech is hierarchical throughout the subcontinent. But the point here is that we cannot assume universal usage, cross-cultural meaning, or even terminologi-cal translation without first engaging in the ethnography of communication, the sociolinguistic study of language performance in everyday life.

To illustrate the importance of indigenous taxonomies, let me review an excellent example provided by Joyce Burkhalter Flueckiger (1996), in which she explores the rich traditions of an area in central India known as Chhattisgarh, a multilingual borderland populated by Hindus, Christians, Muslims, and various tribal groups. She approaches the study of local performance tradi-tions by providing detailed descriptions of various genres enacted, heard, and viewed in the region. Her approach, however, is holistic in the sense that she does not view each genre in isolation from the others. In this sense, she indicates the intertextual nature of a community's folklore traditions. She emphasizes the distinct but overlapping nature of genres to understand how genre terminology is understood locally and how the performance of such genres aids a community in constructing its identity. Flueckiger is sensitive to the fact that Western literary terms are inadequate for understanding the dynamics of genre in Chhattisgarh, hence her underlying logic for studying the entire indigenous genre system as an integrated whole.

Her first task is to see if there are any internal divisions made in the com-munity, which leads her to divide the local genres into ritualistic and entertain-ment categories. The ritual genres include *bhojalī*, *ḍālkhāī*, and *suā nāc*, while the entertainment genres include *kathānī kūhā*, *candainī*, and *paṇḍvānī*. The ritualistic genres are often gendered, she notes. *Ḍālkhāī*, for example, a rite of reversal marking the transition to womanhood, is traditionally performed within a specific festival context that marks the occasion. However, Flueck-iger points out that local men are usurping the ritual because they feel that it is too lewd and lascivious to be performed by females.

The author's sensitivity to context allows her to demonstrate how genres adapt to different situations and why they are not frozen but fluid categories of performance. She employs the term "revoicing" to discuss the implications of genre fluidity. A nice example of revoicing is the parrot dance *(suā nāc)*, an *ādivāsī* (tribal) dance performed for Hindu patrons to transform grain into the goddess of prosperity, Lakshmi. However, the same women also perform the dance in the non-Hindu context of their own tribal community to fulfill a vow. Here we see the same genre employed in two very distinct ways.

In her discussion of the entertainment genres, she further elaborates the contexts of performance while simultaneously exploring how local traditions interact with regional and pan-Indian ones. *Kathānī kūhā* is the term for professional storytelling. Because it is individualistic and not specifically linked to a distinct community of listeners, it can easily draw on pan-Indian themes. The *paṇḍvānī* narrative also draws on pan-Indian narrative themes found in the epic *Mahabharata,* but it draws on those episodes that have regional significance. The classical themes thus become transformed into a regional configuration. The same is true of the *candainī* epic, which can be found in the contiguous areas surrounding Madhya Pradesh, in which Chhattisgarh used to be located before it recently achieved province status. This vernacular epic is performed in various locations to suit the needs and sensibilities of a particular community. One region's *candainī* is thus not the same as the next region's *candainī.* Claiming the same epic tradition as "ours" as opposed to "theirs" is an adaptive strategy that allows performers to claim community ownership of a particular variant of the tradition, an important theme that will reemerge in chapter four when I discuss intellectual property rights.

Looking at folklore in context, as Flueckiger and many other folklorists now do, allows us to arrive, as Ben-Amos's quote above urges us to do, at a deeper understanding of a community's cognitive and aesthetic systems, thereby offering us yet another window into what makes a particular regional culture distinct. But it also offers us richer ethnographies of performance and communication, which ultimately allow us to do better cross-cultural studies. The more microethnographies we have, the more reliable cross-cultural studies we can produce. In so doing, the folklorist can contribute greatly to expanding the general anthropological study of human behavior. As we have seen, the previous generations of folklorists focused mostly on the decontextualized texts of folklore at the expense of the contexts of folklore. Therefore, the context of much folklore assembled during the colonial period is lost, and what we are left with is a paper trail that is only of limited use. The first anthropologist to point out that the meaning of a text lies in its performance was Bronislaw Malinowski (1884–1942) in his oft-cited 1948 essay "Myth in Primitive Psychology," in which he states the following:

> We are not so much concentrating our attention on the text of the narratives, as on their sociological reference. The text, of course, is extremely important, but without the context it remains lifeless. As we have seen, the interest of the story is vastly enhanced and it is given its proper character by the manner in which it is told. The whole nature of the performance, the voice and the mimicry, the stimulus and response of the audience mean as much to the

natives as the text; and the sociologist should take his cue from the natives. The performance, again, has to be placed in its proper time setting—the hour of the day, the season, with the background of the sprouting gardens awaiting future work, and slightly influenced by the magic of the fairy tales. We must also bear in mind the sociological context of private ownership, the sociable function and the cultural role of amusing fiction. All these elements are equally relevant; all must be studied as well as the text. The stories live in native life and not on paper, and when a scholar jots them down without being able to evoke the atmosphere in which they flourish he has given us but a mutilated bit of reality. (1992, 104)

In the next chapter, I provide some typical examples of decontextualized texts collected by colonial folklorists, about which we know only a limited amount. Nevertheless, they make for interesting reading while providing fodder for situating such texts in their ideological contexts of collecting (cf. Naithani 1996, 1997, 2001a, 2001b). They also allow for comparative literary studies in terms of themes and motifs employed. To provide some semblance of balance, however, I also include a few examples from my own field notes and the work of others to give the reader a sense of how contemporary folklorists working in South Asia now approach their material.

NOTES

1. For a development of this negative evaluation of Bengal, see Heginbotham (1975, 1–50). R.C. Majumdar (1960) also offers a good overview of European attitudes toward India. See also Sinha (1995).

2. On mutual comparison as a mode of understanding, see J.Z. Smith (1982, 19–36).

3. For a scathing critique of Jones's agenda, see Lincoln (1999, 76–100, 192–206).

4. A notable exception to this rule was Halhed, who emphasized vernacular languages and traditions. His *Grammar of the Bengali Language* (1778), which was published before the establishment of the Asiatic Society, was the first of its kind and is considered by S.K. De to be the "best introduction to the scientific study of the language" (1962, 72).

5. See his discussion of Carey in Kopf (1969, 93ff). Carey was not ashamed to admit that he was an advocate of the Bengali language. In fact, Carey designed a reader for Bengali students in 1801, which is still invaluable as a historical document depicting the various castes of eighteenth-century *rural* Bengal. Carey's colleagues at Fort William were vehemently critical of his emphasis on regional dialect and local custom, but this did not dissuade him from continuing his crusade for the study of rural Bengali culture.

6. For a good account of the goals and aims of missionary work in India, see Richter (1908).

7. I use the term "intellectual elite" in a manner similar to Toynbee's notion of intelligentsia as that group of urban-educated thinkers who mediate between cultures during times of social contact and crisis. See Toynbee (1962, 154–58). Kopf later expanded on the issue in 1969.

8. Shortly after the printing press was introduced, Serampore began utilizing it as a means to "cultivate" or "christianize" Bengalis according to the normative standards decreed by European society. In 1818 alone, the Serampore Mission released three separate journals and newspapers. The emphasis on mass literary production of European reading matter eventually resulted in the proliferation of popular literature, similar to the chapbook phenomenon in medieval Europe. See, for example, Pritchett (1986).

9. Witness Bhabanicharan Bannerji's book *Kalikata Kamalalay* (Calcutta, the Lotus-Abode, 1823), a sociological work describing the customs and manners of city folk. This book was intended for a country audience that had no prior urban experience. It was designed to acquaint the villager to life in the metropolis. For a summary, see Kopf (1969, 209–213).

10. See Siddique (1966, 1–47) for a complete explication of this. Between 1886 and 1901, there was an increase in the number of college students. These were mostly Anglo-Bengalis who were there for pragmatic reasons (i.e., to attain a clerical post). More Indian students were also going to Europe to study. In 1894, 56 of the 308 total students studying in Europe were from Bengal. This was the highest percentage of students from any given province in British India.

11. Hastings himself gave two reasons why it was necessary to study Indian culture: 1) "it helps the natives of India to acquiesce in British domination" and 2) "it imprints on the hearts of our countrymen the sense of obligation and benevolence" (Embree 1976, 135). See also Marshall (1970, 187).

12. See Hartland's presidential address in *Folk-lore* (1901, 38ff).

13. See Dalton's *A Descriptive Ethnology of Bengal* (1872).

14. For a complete list of Mitra's work, see entries 4081–4275 in Kirkland (1966, 139–46).

15. For example, see Edgerton's *The Pancatantra Reconstructed* (1924). Of the indigenous scholars of the period S. C. Mitra has already been mentioned. Another scholar who stands out is Dinesh Chandra Sen. Sen's presence at Calcutta University was a primary inspiring force for the interest in folk literature and nationalism. Sen's *History of Bengali Literature* (1911) still stands as the classic work in the field, and his *Folk-Literature of Bengal* (1920), a compilation of lectures, is his most important contribution to the study of the Bengali folktale.

16. Even in the early portion of the eighteenth century, Calcutta was not recognizable as a distinct entity. It was nothing more than "an anomalous cluster of hamlets," according to Poddar (1970, 229).

17. As Western education became more widespread during the early decades of the nineteenth century, more and more Hindus were leaving the traditional Sanskrit

schools established by the Brahmans from Nadia who came to the city after the decline of Navadvip. More Hindus than Muslims were thus receiving a western education, since Muslims were more inclined to study in Islamic schools.

18. Vernacular education was not instituted until 1906. On March 11 of that year, the National Council of Education was formed to promote education in Bengali. The introduction of the movement closely corresponds to the appearance of homemade goods in urban marketplaces. These were explicit attempts by the urban intellectual elites to bridge the widening gap between city and village.

19. Poddar (1977, 1) defines anglophilism as the "bewitching but infructuous obsession of earlier generations of colonial intellectuals."

20. For a different point of view, see Kopf (1969, 181; 275ff). He feels that even though Bengalis responded well to foreign ideas and customs (280), they were not willing to completely disavow their own heritage (286). It may be more accurate to say that the Bengal Renaissance was the culmination and by-product of the Orientalist impact on Calcutta. It was certainly conditioned by the encounter but was not determined solely by it.

21. *Caitra* is the name of the Hindu lunar month that approximately corresponds to the Gregorian period of March–April. *Caitra* marks the beginning of the new lunar year and is traditionally a time of celebration. See Nicholas (1982). *Jātīya* in this context means national. It was later renamed Hindu Mela. The Muslim contribution to the Bengal Renaissance has often been underplayed. There was clearly a stream of Islamic intellectual thought in Calcutta that developed alongside Hindu movements. These two streams occasionally overlapped but remained separate. I cannot do full justice to this subject here, but see Qureshi (1971) and Furedy (1972, 125–46).

22. See Tagore's accounts of these early influences in his book *My Boyhood Days* (1945). The earliest songs learned by Tagore were rhymes. Rhymes became a passion for him, and later in his life he became the first to collect them systematically. Concerning rhymes, he wrote that they are the product of indigenous women, and that they convey the "dance rhythms" of Bengal's ancestors in their youth. See *Rabindra Racanābalī* (Tagore 1956–58, 6: 609). See also Haque (1967, 85–105), Sen (1996), and Siddique (1966, 148–57).

23. By this time Tagore had already published a number of articles on folklore. In 1883 he published his first folkloric article on folk songs (*lok saṅgīt*). See Haque (1967, 113ff).

24. He did not succeed in this until 1908, however, when he delivered his first official political address in Bengali. This became such an issue that some people took the argument to extremes. Dwijendranath Tagore, for example, pushed to have all foreign idioms completely removed from Bengali.

25. Later, in an address to students delivered in 1904, Tagore urged scholars to collect descriptive accounts of Bengali regional dialects, religious rituals, oral literature, folk customs, etc. See Tagore (1956–58, 3: 32). This, according to Tagore, would lead to the rediscovery of tradition.

26. See Tagore (1956–58, 3: 592) for his statement concerning what should be collected and published in this journal (i.e. epics, songs, rhymes, etc.) for the purpose of stimulating national spirit.

27. See also Haque (1967, 116) and Sircar (1997).

28. These retellings were published as two separate volumes in 1897 and 1898. Tagore firmly believed that by transplanting his versions of traditional material in Bengali oral literature, he could engender what he perceived to be authentic folk composers to do the same. Tagore's homespun theory of folklore was similar to Hans Naumann's theory of *gesunkenes Kulturgut* (i.e., the idea that cultural materials from the upper classes could eventually filter down into the stream of folk culture). Even though Tagore visited Germany in 1921, there is no evidence in his writings that he was familiar with Naumann's work. See Haque (1967, 127).

29. For Rajput material he relied on Tod's *Annals and Antiquities of Rajasthan* (1920), for hero tales he surveyed the twenty-three volumes of Cunningham's *Archaeological Survey of India* (1871–87), and for folk songs he studied Acworth's *Ballads of the Marathas* (1894).

30. Some Bengali intellectuals criticized him for this, but he did not let them dissuade him. His generally negative outlook on nationalism after 1910 is quite apparent in his book on the subject. See Tagore (1917, esp. 117–54).

31. For a list of indigenous folklore scholars and their works that were influenced by Tagore, see Haque (1967, 105–39).

32. Interestingly, Baden-Powell gained his martial scouting experience in India and Afghanistan. Could it be that his original interest was sparked in South Asia? If so, Dutt was simply bringing the tradition back home, so to speak.

33. The first Bratachari meeting was held in conjunction with the First All Bengal Folk Dance Training Camp on February 7, 1932, in Suri, Birbhum (now in West Bengal).

34. On the use of folk tunes to arouse motivation in *bratacārī* songs, see Mukherjee (1962). One notable exception was a rhyme to be sung to the tune of "Oh my darling Clementine:" "Oh Brother, becoming a *bratacārī*, see what fun life is" (my translation).

35. *Folklore* (Calcutta) 3 (1962): 424.

36. Similar stories could be told about other regions of India as well, as Blackburn (2003) has done for the Tamil-speaking region of south India.

37. Agricola defined invention as one pole of a process, the proposing of an analogy which can be judged in reaching a conclusion.

38. This point is forcefully made by Hobsbawm when he writes that "we should expect it [invention] to occur more frequently when a rapid transformation of society weakens or destroys the social patterns for which 'old' traditions had been designed" (1983, 4). There has been much good work done on the concept of cultural invention in recent years. In addition to Wagner, see, for example, Detienne (1981), Hobsbawm and Ranger (1983), O'Gorman (1970), and Schlanger (1970).

39. In his *Aus der Erfahrung des Denkens* (1954): "Only that which has been conceived can be seen; but that which has been conceived has been invented" (as quoted

in O'Gorman (1970, 3). Based on this, O'Gorman makes a convincing case that Columbus did not discover, but invented, America. See esp. part III.

40. According to him, a discipline is a communal tradition of procedures and techniques for dealing with a theoretical or an organized set of institutions, rules, and the people whose business it is to apply or improve those procedures and techniques. In this sense, a discipline is like a biological species, inhabiting its own self-defined biome or ecological niche. See Toulmin (1972, 142).

41. The authors state that "the [London] Folklore Society's Journal may serve as models of method for Indian students of the science" (1921, 46).

42. William Thoms introduced the word "folklore" to British academic discourse in 1846. He coined the term to replace "popular antiquities," which was used until that time. For a discussion, see Claus and Korom (1991, 7–10, 17–35).

43. *Vārtā* literally means "talk" in the sense of mediation or negotiation. In medieval sources, which Pande fails to identify, the term is used to denote a genre of hagiography about the lives of holy men and women. For his discussion, see Pande (1963, 25). Moreover, this term, coined in the 1920s by V. S Agrawala, was used predominantly in Hindi. It does not, to my knowledge, appear in Bengali sources.

44. Several examples are *lok vrata* (folk vows), *lok vijñān* (folk understanding, or the science of the folk), *lok saṃskṛtī* (folk culture), *jan sāhitya* (people's literature), and *lok śruti* (that which is heard by the folk).

45. See also his earlier article in Islam (1974, 25–53), where he first suggested the use of the hybrid term *lok lor*.

46. I do not wish to suggest that the materials of folklore did not exist in the world of lived experience and day-to-day communicative interaction. I do wish to state, however, that the mental construction of a concept known as folklore was indeed created to suit the needs of those involved in the reconfiguration of Bengali society and thought. While the real and the imagined are not diametrically opposed, they do constitute different categories of inquiry; each with its own set of intrinsic criteria for investigation. By delineating these criteria and establishing the bases of each, we may proceed to discuss the relationships between the objective materials of folklore and the subjective concept of folklore, as was suggested in the introduction.

47. See also Honko (1968) and Gossen (1971) for further discussion of indigenous genres, as well as Claus and Korom (1991, 168–72).

Three
Examples and Texts

VEDIC LEGEND

Sarama Retrieves the Cows (Rig Veda)

By command of Indra and the Angirasas (bards) Sarama found sustenance for posterity. The Lord of the Gods (Brihaspati) split the rock and found the cattle; the heroes shouted merrily in company with the cows (1.62.3).

Seven <u>rivers</u>, mighty and beneficent, from heaven (flow on earth), and (thereby) the knowers of truth perceived the doors of wealth. Sarama found the kine and also plenty of food, by which, indeed, mankind enjoys (sustenance forever [1.72.8]).

When Sarama discovered the fated (entrance) to the mountain, then Indra made great and ample provision (for her young), as previously promised. Then the sure-footed one, already familiar with their lowing, led (them: Indra and the Angirasas) to the presence of the imperishable kine (3.31.6).

When you rent the clouds apart, for the sake of <u>water</u>, O Indra, there appeared Sarama before you (bringing news of the cattle). Then, as the Angirasas extolled you, you, our leader, pierced through the mountains and, by providing us plenty of food, evinced great interest in us (4.16.8).

At this sacrifice the stone (set in motion) by the hands of the priests began to make noise, whereby the *navagva*s (subgroup of Angirasas) celebrated the ten-month worship, when Sarama, traversing the path of truth, discovered the cattle, and Angiras rendered all (the rite) effective (RV 5: 45.7).

When all the Angirasas, on the advent of the adorable Dawn, came in contact with the (discovered) cattle, then milk and the rest were offered in

A singer/storyteller and his costumed monkey perform tricks for tourists visiting the beach, 1992. © Corbis.

the august assembly, for Sarama had found the cows by <u>the path of truth</u> (5: 45.7).

- H. L. Hariyappa, *Ṛgvedic Legends through the Ages* (Poona, India: Bombay University Press, 1953, pp. 150–52.

Commentary

The Rig Veda is the oldest text (c. 1500–1200 B.C.E.) in South Asian literature and contains a number of narratives that are retold repeatedly in later texts, including the legend of Sarama included here, which is a composite drawn from several verses in the text. The entire drama is staged by the Angirasas, a team of seven brothers working in consort with Indra, the king of the Vedic pantheon, who, in the end, is the great hero of the narrative. The *Taittriya Brahmana,* another Vedic text, discusses the legend in the following manner: "Sarama, goddess in the guise of a dog, being deputed by Indra, once, to find food on earth, was proceeding the mortal world from the Meru mountain. There she saw the people starving for want of food. Then she created plenty of water, which is the preliminary aid for food and which flowed through all fields. Sure footed, she led forth water and then in front she knowing the lowing sound of the imperishable ones (cows) proceeded towards them" (Hariyappa 1953, 161). Elsewhere in the Rig Veda (10.108.1–11), there is general jubilation after the divine dog recovers the cows. Cows were important to the Vedic Aryans, for they provided sustenance, succor, and wealth for these nomadic people as they entered northwest India from the Iranian Plateau. In fact, they are quite often portrayed as cattle marauders. Such early legends concerning the economic and ecological value of cows forecasts the later apotheosis of the cow (see the praise poem below). The frequency of mention of the recovery of the stolen cows also suggests that this must have been a great event for the Vedic Aryans. Thus it is not surprising that the narrative appears again and again in later story literature.

This narrative is retold numerous times in classical Indian literature, including versions in the *Mahabharata* and the *Varaha Purana.* Other prominent legends originating in the Rig Veda that appear often in later Indian literature are those of Shunashshepa, Vasishtha, and Vishvamitra. In addition to providing a wellspring of historically based narratives, the Rig Veda also offers us a number of creation myths, the best known of which is provided next.

COSMOGONIC MYTH

Purusha Sukta (Rig Veda)

A thousand heads has Purusha, a thousand eyes, a thousand feet.
On every side pervading earth he fills a space ten fingers wide.
This Purusha is all that yet has been and all that is to be.
The Lord of Immortality which waxes greater still by food.
So mighty is his greatness; yea, greater than this is Purusha.
All creatures are one-fourth of him, three-fourths eternal life in heaven.
With three-fourths Purusha went up: one-fourth of him was again here.
Then he strode out to every side over what eats not and what eats.

From him Viraj was born; again Purusha from Viraj was born.
As soon as he was born he spread eastward and westward over the earth.
When Gods prepared the sacrifice with Purusha as their offering,
Its oil was spring, the holy gift was autumn's; summer was the wood.
They balmed as victim on the grass Purusha born in earliest time.
With him the Deities and all Sadhyas and Rishis sacrificed.
From that great general sacrifice the dripping fat was gathered up.
He formed the creatures of the air, and animals both wild and tame.
From that great general sacrifice Richas and Sama hymns were born:
Therefrom were spells and charms produced; the Yajur had its
birth from it.
From it were horses born, from it all cattle with two rows of teeth:
From it were generated kine, from it the goats and sheep were born.
When they divided Purusha how many portions did they make?
What do they call his mouth, his arms? What do they call his
thighs and feet?
The Brahman was his mouth, of both his arms was the Rajanya made.
His thighs became the Vaishya, from his feet the Shudra was produced.
The Moon was gendered from his mind, and from his eye the Sun had
birth;
Indra and Agni from his mouth were born, and Vayu from his breath.
Forth from his navel came mid-air; the sky was fashioned from his head;
Earth from his feet, and from his ear the regions. Thus they formed the
worlds.
Seven fencing-sticks had he, thrice seven layers of fuel were prepared.
When the Gods, offering sacrifice, bound, as their victim, Purusha.
Gods, sacrificing, sacrificed the victim: these were the earliest holy
ordinances.
The Mighty Ones attained the height of heaven, there where the Sad-
hyas, Gods of old, are dwelling.

- Adapted from Ralph T. H. Griffith, trans., *The Hymns of the Ṛgveda*, (Delhi:
  Motilal Banarsidass, 1963), pp. 602–3.

Commentary

This *sūkta* (good speech) is contained in Rig Veda (10.90) and is often
referred to as the hymn to the cosmic man. *Puruṣa* literally means "man" (or
person), and because his sacrifice allows for the emanation of the universe, he
is considered the primal man, who must be sacrificed by the gods to create
the universe. Although he is masculine, Viraj is his feminine aspect, and prior

to creation gender is indistinguishable. Late in origin compared to other Rig Vedic hymns, this one is considered to be a blueprint for Hindu society, for not only is the myriad of things created from Purusha, but the social order as well. Hence, included in the sacrifice of his body is a general outline of the hierarchical *varṇa* (hue) system. Often erroneously translated as "caste," a better rendering would be "spiritual class." The priestly class emerges from his head, the purest part of the body, the rulers and warriors emanate from his torso, the merchants and agrarians from his loins, down to the Shudra laborers associated with the feet, the most polluted portion of the body. We thus have a descending order of purity, which is central to rules of social contact in the Hindu scheme of things.

Also significant is the role of sacrifice here, which in Vedic times was the central ritualistic complex performed by the Aryans. The *yajña* (fire sacrifice) is conceived to be a microcosmic form of the universe, and performing it is a reenactment of the gods sacrificing the cosmic man for the purpose of creation. There is thus a micro-macro relationship between the ritualistic acts of gods and the acts of human beings, with the intention of creating cosmic order *(ṛta)*. In addition to Indra, the king of the Vedic gods, Agni, the personification of fire, is mentioned. He is significant because he serves as a mediator between humans and gods, since he carries burnt offerings to the heavens on behalf of the human sacrificers.

ANIMAL FABLE

The Unteachable Monkey (Panchatantra)

In a part of a forest was a troop of monkeys who found a firefly one winter evening when they were dreadfully depressed. On examining the insect, they believed it to be fire, so lifted it with care, covered it with dry grass and leaves, thrust forward their arms, sides, stomachs, and chests, scratched themselves, and enjoyed imagining that they were warm. One of the arboreal creatures in particular, being especially chilly, blew repeatedly and with concentrated attention on the firefly.

Thereupon a bird named Needle-Face, driven by hostile fate to her own destruction, flew down from her tree and said to the monkey: "My dear sir, do not put yourself to unnecessary trouble. This is not fire. This is a fire-fly." He, however, did not heed her warning but blew again, nor did he stop when she tried more than once to check him. To cut a long story short, when she vexed him by coming close and shouting in his ear, he seized her and dashed her on a rock, crushing face, eyes, head, and neck so that she died.

"And that is why I say:
No knife prevails against a stone;. . . .

And the rest of it. For, after all,

Educating minds unfit
Cannot rescue sluggish wit
Just as house-lamps wasted are,
Set within a covered jar.

"Plainly, you are what is known as 'worse-born.' The technical explanation runs:

Sons of four divergent kinds
Are discerned by well-trained minds:
'Born,' and 'like-born':
'Worse-born' morally subtracts.
"Ah, there is wisdom in the saying:
By whom far-piercing wisdom or
Great wealth or power is won
To lift the family, in him
A mother has a son.

Again:

A merely striking beauty
Is not so hard to find;
A rare gem is wisdom,
Far-reaching power of the mind.

"Yes, there is sense in the story:

Right-Mind was one, and Wrong-Mind two:
I know the tale by heart:
The son in smoke made the father choke
By being supersmart."

- Arthur Ryder, trans., *The Panchatantra: Complete and Unabridged* (Bombay: Jaico Publishing House, 1949), pp. 143–44.

Commentary

Like virtually all the tales in the *Panchantantra,* the central message of this one, number 28 from book one, is that wisdom and rationality are valued commodities not easily acquired. Acquiring them, however, is something that all people should strive for, first to please one's parents, then to create a moral and civil society. The monkeys represent "wrong mind" in that they mistake the firefly for heat-giving fire, and they deceive themselves by thinking that the insects warm them. The bird, on the other hand, represents "right mind." Out of a desire to educate the foolish monkeys, she attempts to teach them the true nature of the object they falsely perceive, but in so doing, she is destroyed. The fact that wisdom and knowledge are represented by only one bird, while ignorance is represented by a troop of monkeys, suggests that ignorance is rampant in society and can endanger wisdom when outnumbered. To advance the cause of wisdom and knowledge often calls for sacrifices that only the noble would attempt. Lastly, it is significant that the bird is a woman who tries to teach a male monkey, only to be reprimanded. In a patriarchal society, as much of ancient India was, this narrative could also be interpreted as a cautionary tale about excluding women from the public sphere in which knowledge is generated.

PARABLE

Fish Jataka (Jatatakatthavannana)

"'Tis not the cold." This story was told by the master while at Jetavana, about being seduced by the wife of one's mundane life before joining the Brotherhood. Said the Master on this occasion, "Is it true, as I hear, Brother, that you are passion-tossed?"

"Yes, Blessed One."

"Because of whom?"

"My former wife, sir, is sweet to touch; I cannot give her up!" Then said the Master, "Brother, this woman is hurtful to you. It was through her that in bygone times too you were meeting your end, when you were saved by me." And so saying, he told this story of the past.

Once on a time when Brahmadatta was reigning in Benares, the Bodhisatta became his family priest.

In those days some fishermen had cast their net into the river. And a great big fish came along amorously toying with his wife. She, scenting the net as she swam ahead of him, made a circuit round it and escaped. But her amorous spouse, blinded by passion, sailed right into the meshes of the net. As soon as the fishermen felt him in their net, they hauled it in and took the fish out; they did not kill him at once, but flung him alive on the sands. "We'll cook him in the embers for our meal," said they; and accordingly they set to work to light a fire and whittle a spit to roast him on. The fish lamented, saying to himself, "It's not the torture of the embers or the anguish of the spit or any other pain that grieves me; but only the distressing thought that my wife should be unhappy in the belief that I have gone off with another." And he repeated a stanza:

'Tis not the cold, the heat, or wounding net;

'Tis but the fear my darling wife should think

Another's love has lured her spouse away.

Just then the priest came to the riverside with his attendant slaves to bathe. Now he understood the language of all animals. Therefore, when he heard the fish's lamentation, he thought to himself, "This fish is lamenting the lament of passion. If he should die in this unhealthy state of mind, he cannot escape rebirth in hell. I will save him." So he went to the fishermen and said, "My men, don't you supply us with a fish every day for our curry?" "What do you say, sir?" said the fishermen; "Pray take away with you any fish you may take a fancy to." "We don't need any but this one; only give us this one." "He's yours, sir."

Taking the fish in his two hands, the Bodhisatta seated himself on the bank and said, "Friend fish, if I had not seen you today, you would have met your death. Cease for the future to be the slave of passion." And with this exhortation he threw the fish into the water, and went into the city.

His lesson ended, the Master preached the Truths, at the close whereof the passion-tossed Brother won the First Path. Also, the Master showed the connection and identified the Birth by saying, "The former wife was the female fish of those days, the passion-tossed Brother was the male fish, and I myself the family priest."

- Adapted from Edward B. Cowell, ed., *The Jātaka or the Stories of the Buddha's Former Births* (Delhi: Motilal Banarsidass, 1990), pp. 87–88.

Commentary

This parable exemplifies some fundamental Buddhist truths. The first of the Buddha's Four Noble Truths states that all life is suffering *(duḥkha)*. The second truth states that desire or thirst *(tṛṣṇa)* is the cause of suffering and needs to be eliminated to achieve *nirvāṇa*. The moral of the story is that the fish is suffering precisely because of his passion, which here is his amorous thirst for his wife. It is a metaphor for life in general: just as the fish is ensnared and suffers because of his passion, so too do all human beings suffer because of our attachment to the material world, which according to Buddhist and Hindu doctrine is merely illusion *(māyā)*. The Bodhisatta (or bodhisattva), here represented as a priest, shows his compassion for all sentient beings by liberating the fish and giving him a second chance to achieve freedom from suffering.

ESCHATOLOGICAL TALE

King Vipashchit the Wise's Descent into Hell (Markandeya Purana)

"Not in heaven, nor in Brahman's world, I think,
Does man find such bliss as when
He can give refreshment to beings in torment.

If through my presence, racking torture
Of these poor ones is alleviated,
Then will I stay here, my friend,
Like a post, I will not move from this spot."

Yama's servant spoke:

"Come, O King, let us go, do *you* enjoy
The fruits of your good deeds and leave the torments
To those who, through bad deeds, deserve them?"

The king spoke:

"No, I will not go hence, while these
Poor dwellers in hell are happy through my presence.
A disgrace and a shame is the life of a man
Who feels no pity for the tortured, poor ones,
Who implore him for protection—even for bitter foes.
Sacrifices, gifts, austerities serve neither here nor beyond
For his salvation, who has no heart for protecting tortured ones,
Whose heart is hardened to children, old men and the weak,
Not as a man do I regard him—he is a devil.
Even though, through the presence of these dwellers in hell
I suffer the torment of purgatory, the stink of hell,
And the pain of hunger and of thirst rob me of my senses—
Yet I deem it sweeter than the joy of heaven,
To give them, the tortured ones, protection and help.

If through *my* suffering many unhappy ones become glad,
What more do I want?—Do not tarry, depart and leave me."

Yama's servant spoke:

"Behold! Dharma comes, and Shakra, to fetch you hence.
You must go indeed, King: up, and away from here!"
Dharma spoke:
"Let me lead you to the heaven which you have well deserved;
Enter this chariot of the gods without delay—away from here!"
The king spoke:
"Here in this hell, Dharma, men are tortured a thousand-fold;
'Protect us!' full of agony they cry to me; I will not move from here."
Shakra spoke:
"The reward of their *deeds,* these evil ones receive in hell;
You, prince, must for your *good* deed ascend to heaven."

- Adapted from Moriz Winternitz, *A History of Indian Literature,* Vol. 1 (New Delhi: Munshiram Manoharlal, 1972), pp. 562–64.

Commentary

The *Markandeya Purana* is most likely one of the oldest and most important texts in this body of lore. It is named after the ancient sage Markandeya, a character who appears in the *Mahabharata* as one who has achieved eternal youth. The text contains a vivid description of *samsāra,* the illusory stream of life, and the subsequent consequences of *karma,* the deeds of one's actions, in terms of rebirth, punishment, and retribution. These descriptions occur in the context of a question-and-answer session between a father and a son. It is during this session that Vipashchit's story of descent and ascension is told. Vipashchit was extremely pious during life, but upon his death, a servant of Yama (here also called Dharma), the god of death, took him to hell. Astonished, the king asked why he was being taken to hell after living such a virtuous life, to which the servant responded by explaining that the king once did not cohabit with his wife at an optimal time for conception. For this minor transgression of religious duty, the king had to spend a little bit of time in hell. When they arrived in Yama's domains, the servant instructed the king concerning the consequences of good and bad *karma* and the agonies of hell. After Vipashchit's time was served, the servant prepared to ferry him to heaven, but suddenly blood-curdling screams filled the air, and the restless souls of the suffering began to beg him to stay for one more moment and console them. It is at this point that the above passage begins.

The virtuous king does not envision the sufferers of hell as sinners, but only as suffering souls that need to be liberated. His only desire is to free these souls, and due to the power of his good deeds while on earth, Yama/Dharma grants him his wish. As Vipashchit then ascends into heaven, all those suffering in hell are freed from their pain. This story parallels Yudhishthira's vision of hell prior to his ascent into heaven, which is narrated in book 18 of the *Mahabharata* and discussed in chapter five of this book.

VAMPIRE'S TALE

Of the Marvelous Delicacy of Three Queens (Vetalapanchavimshatika)

The Baital *(vetāla)*. O King, in the Gaur country, Vardhaman by name, there is a city, and one called Gunshekhar was the Raja of that land. His minister was one Abhaichand, a Jain by whose teachings the king also came into the Jain faith.

The worship of Shiva and Vishnu, gifts of cows, gifts of lands, gifts of rice balls, gaming and spirit-drinking, all these he prohibited. In the city no man could get leave to do them, and as for bones, into the Ganges no man was allowed to throw them, and in these matters the minister, having taken orders from the king, caused a proclamation to be made about the city, saying, "Whoever these acts shall do, the Raja having confiscated, will punish him and banish him from the city."

Now one day the Diwan (minister) began to say to the Raja, "O great King, to the decisions of the Faith be pleased to give ear. Whosoever takes the life of another, his life also in a future birth is taken: this very sin causes him to be born again and again upon earth and to die. And thus he ever continues to be born again and to die. Hence for one who has found entrance into this world to cultivate religion is right and proper. Be pleased to behold! By love, by wrath, by pain, by desire, and by fascination overpowered, the gods Brahma, Vishnu, and Mahadeva (Shiva) in various ways upon the earth are ever becoming incarnate. Far better than they is the Cow, who is free from passion, enmity, drunkenness, anger, covetousness, and inordinate affection, who supports mankind, and whose progeny in many ways gives ease and solace to the creatures of the world. These deities and sages believe in the Cow.

"For such reason to believe in the gods is not good. Upon this earth be pleased to believe in the Cow. It is our duty to protect the life of everyone, beginning from the elephant, through ants, beasts, and birds, up to man. In the world righteousness equal to that there is none. Those who, eating the flesh of other creatures, increase their own flesh, shall in the fullness of time assuredly obtain the fruition of Narak [hell]; hence for a man it is proper to attend to the conversation of life. They who understand not the pain of other creatures, and who continue to slay and devour them, last but few days in the land, and return to mundane existence, maimed, limping, one-eyed, blind, dwarfed, hunchbacked, and imperfect in such wise. Just as they consume the bodies of beasts and of birds, even so they end by spoiling their own bodies. From drinking spirits also the great sin arises, hence the consuming of spirits and flesh is not advisable."

The minister having in this manner explained to the king the sentiments of his own mind, so brought him over to the Jain faith, that whatever he said, so the king did. Thus in Brahmans, in Jogis, in Janganis, in Sevras, in Sannyasis, and in [other] religious mendicants, no man believed, and according to this creed the rule was carried on.

Now one day, being in the power of Death, Raja Gunshekhar died. Then his son Dharmadhwaj sat upon the carpet (throne), and began to rule. Presently he caused the minister Abhaichand to be seized, had his head shaved all but seven locks of hair, ordered his face to be blackened, and mounting him on an ass, with drums beaten, had him led all about the city, and drove him from the kingdom. From that time he carried on his rule free from all anxiety.

It so happened that in the season of spring, the king Dharmadhwaj, taking his queens with him, went for a stroll in the garden, where there was a large tank with lotuses blooming within it. The Raja admired its beauty, took off his clothes and went to bathe.

After plucking a flower and coming to the bank, he was going to give it into the hands of one of his queens, when it slipped from his fingers, fell upon her foot, and broke it with a blow. Then the Raja being alarmed, at once came out of the tank, and began to apply remedies to her.

Hereupon night came on, and the moon shone brightly: the falling of its rays on the body of the second queen formed blisters. And suddenly from a distance the sound of a wooden pestle came out of a householder's dwelling, when the third queen fainted away with a severe pain in the head.

Having spoken thus much the Baital said "O my king! Of these three which is the most delicate?" The Raja answered, "She indeed is the most delicate who fainted in consequence of the headache." The Baital hearing this speech, went and hung himself from the same tree, and the Raja, having gone there and taken him down and fastened him in the bundle and placed him on his shoulder, carried him away.

- Sir Richard Burton, trans., *Vikram and the Vampire or Tales of Hindu Devilry* (New York: Dover Publications, 1969), pp. 217–20.

Commentary

This is the *vetāla's* tenth story. It is the briefest, and perhaps least complex, of the 25 in the *Vetalapanchavimshatika,* but it is illustrative of the text's pattern: King Vikram continues his task of retrieving a corpse from a graveyard tree, in which the vampire lives. He begins to tell the king a story as he is being carried away. At the end, the *vetāla* evokes a response from the king, which allows him to slip back to the tree, only to be fetched again by the king.

The motif concerning the queen's sensitivity should be familiar to Western readers from the nursery tale entitled "The Princess and the Pea," in which the princess is so delicate and fine that she notices three peas under a straw mattress covered with four layers of down after lying on it. The first portion of the narrative also suggests competition between the classical religions of India vying against each other for devotees in eastern India, where the narrative is set. We also find mention of the sacredness and inviolability of the cow. The next selection is a praise poem in honor of the cow's sanctity.

PRAISE POEM

The Cow of Plenty (Ramayana)

The cow from whom all plenty flows,
Obedient to her saintly lord,
Viands to suit each taste outpoured.
Honey she gave, and roasted grain,
Mead sweet with flowers, and sugar cane.
Each beverage of flavor rare,
And food of every sort, were there:
Hills of hot rice, and sweetened cakes,
And curdled milk, and soup in lakes.
Vast beakers flowing from the brim
With sugared drink prepared for him;
And dainty sweet meats, deftly made,
Before the hermit's guests were laid.

- William J. Wilkins, *Hindu Mythology* (Calcutta: Rupa and Company, 1978), p. 167.

Commentary

The cow has achieved an unprecedented and inviolable status in Hinduism due, in part, to the Hindu, Jain, and Buddhist emphasis on nonviolence (*ahiṃsā*). This poem, from the *Ramayana*, praises the calf of an ascetic of great power named Jamadagni, which was stolen by Kartavirya, sovereign of the Haihaya tribe. A semidivine hermit named Dattatreya had earlier given Kartavirya the boon of great strength, 1,000 arms, and a golden chariot that went wherever he willed it to go. The chariot took him to Jamadagni's hermitage, where the ascetic's wife greeted him with great respect. But Kartavirya, intoxicated with his newly bestowed power, showed no gratitude for her hospitality. Upon leaving, he took the cow extolled in the above poem. When Rama, the hero of the epic, heard of the cow's plight, he became enraged and challenged the thief to battle. With his mighty bow, Rama cut off Kartavirya's 1,000 arms and ultimately killed him.

FOLK PROPHECY

Shon Gukur's Prophecy (Hunza, Northwest Frontier Province, Pakistan)

They say that in early times Shon Gukur, the Bitan, had made a prophecy. They say he had said as follows:

"After some years there will appear a handful of fair-complexioned men wearing short coats. They will do great justice and Hunza will become very prosperous. These fair folks will go where there are no roads. They will construct iron bridges. Moreover in the place of privies there will be stables. In the place of stables there will be privies." They say he said: "In those latter days the man who should hold his peace will speak, and the man who should speak will hold his peace."

That is all: the story is this much.

- D.L.R. Lorimer, trans., *Folk Tales of Hunza* (Islamabad, Pakistan: Lok Virsa Publishing House, 1987), p. 100.

Commentary

Hunza is located in northwestern Pakistan, and the language spoken there is Burushaski. In the West it has often been envisioned as a fabled Shangri-La, a utopian place nestled high in the Karakoram mountain range where everyone lives to a ripe old age, in peace and harmony with nature. This romantic image has made it a tourist destination, and rapid change has ensued there in modern times. Lorimer served the British there during the colonial era and collected lore in his spare time. This prophecy was retold to him in 1923. Although he provides no commentary, it most likely refers to the coming of the British (i.e., fair-skinned men wearing short coats). There is an ambiguity

Street corner storytelling in rural India. © Imagica / Alamy.

in the prophecy, however. On the one hand, the prophet declares that these newcomers will bring justice and prosperity. At the same time, he paints a world-turned-upside-down scenario in which rules of etiquette are broken. Etiquette *(ādāb)* is especially important in Pakistani society, so the second part of the prophecy foresees the breakdown of traditional values and customs, where people urinate in stables and speak out of turn.

CASTE FOLKLORE

A Story on Caste (Santal Parganas, Bihar, India)

There was once a village inhabited only by Musahars. Among them was a girl who was so beautiful that she seemed more than human. Her father and mother were so proud of her looks that they determined not to marry her to a man of their own caste. They were constantly discussing whom they should choose as a son-in-law; one day they began to consider who were the greatest persons in the world. The old woman was of the opinion that there was no one greater than Chando, the Sun God, and suggested that they should marry the girl to him. Her husband agreed and off they set and presented themselves before Chando. Chando asked why they had come. "O Chando, we understand that you are the greatest being in the world and we have come to marry our daughter to you." Chando answered "I fancy there is some one greater than I." "Who is he?" asked the parents. "The cloud is greater than I, for it can hide my face and quench my rays."

At this the father and mother hurried off with their daughter in search of the Cloud, and when they found him, told him that they had brought their daughter to give him to wife, as he was the greatest being in the world. "I may be great," said the cloud, "but there is a greater than I, the Wind. The Wind rises and blows me away in a minute." So they went in search of the Wind and when they found him, explained to him why they had brought him their daughter. The Wind said "I am strong but there are stronger than I: the Mountains are stronger. I can blow things down and whirl them away, but I cannot move mountains."

So they went to the Mountain and explained their errand. The Mountain said "I am great but there are more powerful than I. The ground-rat is more powerful, for however high I may be the ground-rats burrow holes in me and I cannot resist them."

The poor parents by this time began to feel rather discouraged, but still they made up their minds to persevere and went on to look for the ground-rat. They found him and offered their daughter in marriage, but the ground rat denied that he was the most powerful being on earth, the Musahars were more powerful for they lived by digging out ground-rats and eating them.

The hapless couple went home very dejectedly, reflecting that they had begun by despising their own caste and had gone in search of something greater and had ended where they began. So they arranged to marry their daughter to a man of their own caste after all.

- Cecil H. Bompas, *Folk Lore of the Santal Parganas* (New Delhi: Ajay Book Service, 1981), pp. 168–69.

Commentary

The Santals are a Munda-speaking tribe inhabiting the Chota Nagpur Plateau, which straddles the contiguous provinces of West Bengal and Bihar in eastern India. Tribal communities in general were under great pressure to convert from their nature-based religions to more acceptable ones. Under the British, Christian missionaries were very active, and they targeted tribal communities as the easiest to convert. Missionaries promised them not only salvation but also social equality in a hierarchical society where they were considered no better than untouchables. In many areas, they have been successful in their mission, but the Santals, while seemingly acculturated into Hinduism on the surface, still retain much of their customary practices. The moral of this story is that one should not try to be something one is not. It suggests a kind of passive resignation to the Hindu concept of the predetermination of caste based on one's *karma* in the previous life. Commenting on the tale, Bompas's storyteller goes against the missionary promise when he states that "He may wish to change his caste and become . . . a Mussulman or a Christian; but people will still know him for a beef-eating Santal" (170). But there is also a hint of resistance to caste hierarchy at the end of the tale, since ultimately the girl is wed to another Musahar, who is implied to be greater than all the previous suitors, despite his low caste status.

UNREQUITED LOVE SONG

It's Drizzling, Oh My Friend (Bangladesh)

It's drizzling, oh my Friend!
Why get wet outside?
Behind the house arum leaves sprout.
Oh, cut one to cover your head!
My heart cries, oh my cowherd friend!

The night is cloudy and dark.
Friend, tigers are on the prowl.
Use your sickle to cut the fence,
Then come quietly in.
My heart cries, oh cowherd friend!

I can't, I can't, oh my friend!
Friend, my head spins.
Go back home tonight, dear.
Don't be sad.
My heart cries, oh cowherd friend!

I've ferried the flooded moat, and made it through the marshes, dear.
I've broken the wooden boat, all for you.
If I have to return home tonight,
I swear you're my mother, dear.
My heart cries, oh cowherd friend!

The in-laws are awake, oh friend!
My husband's awake.

How can I come, friend?
Oh, the in-laws are awake!
My heart cries, oh cowherd friend!

The bamboo door, oh my friend,
Creaks in the wind.
Open it slowly, carefully.
Oh, the in-laws are awake
My heart cries, oh cowherd friend!

Brother-in-law and father-in-law are awake, friend,
Awake all of the time.
Oh, husband's awake,
With a cane in his hand!
My heart cries, oh cowherd friend!

There's a pot of water in the bathroom, oh friend!
Wash your feet and come.
There's a tray of betel by the bedside, oh friend.
Oh, chew some with lime.
My heart cries, oh cowherd friend!

- Shamsuzzaman Khan, *Folk Poems from Bangladesh* (Dhaka, Bangladesh: Bangla Academy, 1986), pp. 49–50.

Commentary

Retranslated from the original Bengali here, this is an example of *bhāoýāiýā*, a genre of song typically sung by elephant drivers, ox-cart drivers, and buffalo herders in northern Bengal, Assam, and Bangladesh, to wile away the time during work. Composed in a northern Bengali dialect, the songs are sung to the accompaniment of a *dotārā*, a four-string instrument that is plucked. As in this song, the most common theme is love, especially unrequited love *(biraha)*. As such, the songs are slow and melancholy in rhythm and tune. Although sung by men, the songs are often from the perspective of the woman, whose itinerant lover is rarely home. She addresses him by his occupation; here he is a *rākhāl* (cow herder). The lover is most often not the husband, as she is *parakīyā*, the wife of another. The genre is modeled on the love affair between the cow-girl Radha and her absent lover, Krishna, an incarnation of the deity Vishnu in Hindu mythology. But the pattern is readily found in South Asian Islamic poetry as well within the *ġazal* tradition, in which a male poet opines from the female perspective about unrequited love. In the Sufi tradition, this pattern is said to be metaphoric of a human's longing to be with the divine beloved.

ETIOLOGICAL TALE

How Dharmaraj Came to Goalpara (Harishankar Mukhopadhyay, Goalpara, West Bengal, India)

That which I have roughly heard from ancestors is this, that this very Dharmaraj *ṭhākur* (lord) has come down from the time of King Ballal Sen. And what else? I mean, that from those historic days, this very *pūjā* (worship) has started. And also it is said that this very Dharmaraj, I mean especially Birbhum District's, I mean the first place, I mean this very, I mean from our Goalpara, appeared. In those days there were Goyala (cow herder caste) settlements in our village.

At that time when there was a settlement of Goyalas, imagine that in those days, they used to keep many cows. Outside the village where the worship of *bābā* (father) happens and where the pig sacrifice happens, to that very place, people used to go to graze cows. I mean the Goyalas. There was one specific cow, a very fine cow that used to give four or five quarts of milk at a time. That very cow used to go there and give milk almost every day. By "automatic system" I mean that the milk would pour. I mean it would pour out, come out on its own, without anyone milking it. And also the Goyalas had one day beaten a laborer who takes the cows to graze. Because "the laborer milks the milk and you drink it up," said the boy who took the milky cow to graze in the field. First he thought, "What else? He milks the milk, and you drink it up."

So now the matter is that in those days the Goyalas were curious. I mean in order to learn more about what the boy said, they followed the boy to where the cows graze. Suddenly the boy sees the cow. I mean slowly, going exactly to that place, he saw the milk flowing onto the ground by the automatic system. In order not to let the others see that, *bābā* miraculously caused a *ḍāṅguli* (stick game) match to occur. I mean this Dharmaraj, he also, I mean, is of the highest caste. I mean, smallish. I mean his looks. And also I mean his hair and everything is white. In this state he also went and started playing *ḍāṅguli* with the others so that, that their gaze would not fall in the direction of the cow. I mean so that the cow could give its milk.

So the Goyalas see that in this sort of, you know, and after seeing that sight, their curiosity is even more aroused. "The milk falls because of this place. What is in this place?" This is what they wondered, based on what the boy said. That's why in those days the spades and hoes were used; and they still are. I think they took that hoe and went there and dug in that place. As a result of digging, I mean on *bābā*'s head, in that place, there's a wound, and still in that place there is a stone image, though. This can be found in it. A bloody spot of that, of the spade and hoe's cut. And also, it can definitely be understood that, yes, this is something like a cut.

After that, he gives them a dream. I mean, "perform my worship," for I am Dharmaraj." I mean the deity of *kali* (dark age). What else? I mean that *kali* age is our fourth age. Among them, the age that is now running at present, this one they call *kali kāl* (time of *kali*). So the king of *kali* is saying, "I am a deity! So you all do *pūjā* to me, and if you worship, your hearts' desires will be fulfilled. And from then on, one hears that our village's, I mean, those Goyalas, one after the other, I mean, began to die, probably because they cut the lord's stone. And from them dying off it came to such a pass, I mean, that the number of Goyalas had then almost just about vanished; there were three or four families left. So, at that very same time *bābā* gave one or two more people dreams, you know, those who had worshipped this Dharmaraj or else other gods and all that religious stuff.

Take, for instance, a certain person, our Hari, that Hari. You know the one who sacrifices the *barāha* (pig)? So the matter is that this sacrifice that his caste keeps doing, the reason for it is *ṭhākur* gave him a dream too. I mean, in those days this village of ours was brilliant as far as knowledge goes. I mean there were many *paṇḍit*s (scholars). The reason for this is, in those days, usually, we ourselves used to think that we were something biggish, which is why they didn't try to know the outside world, and they held on to this attitude in a watchamacallit kinda way. They got caught up in it and went along with this way of thinking.

And then there's another guy here, a person in the village. His name was yer watchamacallit, this Chand Ray. His name was Chand Ray, what else? He himself was a devotee back then. In those days, he used to, you know, drink that liquor the low castes consume. Drinking liquor, I mean it didn't mean that they would drink their own liquor and remain in a stupor. No, not that. He would call god, sort of, in this intoxication. Now due to him constantly calling god, slowly but surely, he was able to understand *bābā*'s will. Finally, when *bābā* appeared again, Chand Ray went and told him that "We will worship. So how can we do the worship? We have no means. We eat by farming, and the food that we eat, can that food be given to a *ṭhākur*? If *ṭhākur* doesn't tell us what, how can we give it?" So he gave another dream command *(svapnādeś):* "You guys, whatever you eat, if you offer me whatever you all eat, that's sufficient.

But give me that food after having fasted and becoming purified and performing a fire sacrifice or having eaten fruit and raw food. And by doing various ritual practices, see that you give me this food. And if you give these things, then I will be satisfied. And how did the 'publicity department' know that I had appeared in Goalpara?"

In order to make this known, this is what the deity did. In those times, those people who played instruments and stuff well, especially cylinder drums, cymbals, and bagpipe, these various types of instruments, Dharmaraj himself, I mean, in that ecstatic mood, went to their houses and met with every one of them. And having done so, he said, "You all! There will be a Dharmaraj worship on the full moon of *Caitra* that will be held in Goalpara. You all go there and play. Whether you play my tunes for food or not for food, your stomachs will get filled." It is still said that those who are born into the *bāyen* (drummer caste) lineage, who on *Caitra pūrṇimā* shall beat drums out on the village's eastern side, were visited by *ṭhākur*. And also, even now, in our village there are, say, about 150 to 200 drums and other instruments in our village. Thus there are different kinds of "putting on," you know, lots of noise and pomp and circumstance. These different kinds of instruments exist even now, and at the time of the festival our devotees said, "Then what will we give?" So those who are now called scheduled castes, that is non-Aryan, they do it. Even though we continue to do it on our own, I don't do it those four days. Because the thing about us is that we are *kulīn, kulīn* meaning the highest priestly caste. The things which people had done in those days, perhaps we cannot do that, or perhaps we don't conduct ourselves that way. But due to our pure lineage also, we don't worship during those four days of his annual worship. For those few days, now, another priest from another village who is less pure comes and does the *pūjā* for the low castes.

- Frank J. Korom, Field Notes, Goalpara Village, Birbhum District, West Bengal, India, 1990.

Commentary

This is the first version of a commonly told narrative that I recorded shortly after I arrived in the village of Goalpara. The version was narrated to me during a casual conversation with Harishankar Mukhopadhyay, the ritual specialist *(pūjārī)* who is responsible for Dharmaraj's daily worship service. Harishankar was 56 years of age at the time of our conversation. He comes from a *kulīn* Brahman family that has been serving Dharmaraj for three generations. Although high school educated, he took up the priestly calling to contribute money to his family's income. He became the main priest after his father's death.

Harishankar is respected in Goalpara as a quiet man of fine character and judgment. When I first inquired in one of the village tea stalls about who to see for information concerning Dharmaraj, I was told to go see the *sebākar* (service doer), meaning Harishankar. His house is located in the Brahman quarter *(ṭhākurpāṛā),* only a minute's walk from the Dharmaraj temple. When we first met, he began by giving me general information about the village, eventually slipping into the religious realm. "Dharma *ṭhākur,*" he said, "is our village deity *(grāmya debatā),* and we must worship him as the supreme deity in the village." He recounted some of the events that would occur during the annual worship and then, without any cue from me, spontaneously began the narrative concerning Dharmaraj's first appearance in the village.

The narrative is important to the raconteur's community because it explains the first appearance of the village's major deity, the origin of his worship, and why and how it must be performed. Each telling of the narrative, while following the same basic story line, is different. By surveying a variety of versions together, one gets a more complete scenario of the ritual festival performed annually for the deity during the month of *Caitra,* which marks the transition of one lunar year to the next. The narratives also give one a sense of the social dynamics involved between low and high caste worshippers, as well as something of Dharmaraj's character as an nonanthropomorphic deity worshipped in the form of a stone, but who can take human form at will.

Even though this core story serves as a master narrative for Harishankar's community, one must point out that the two predominant motifs found in the story, namely the self-milking cow and the bleeding stone, appear in a wide variety of contexts outside Goalpara. Similar narratives about cows letting their milk flow to determine a sacred location are found throughout India. Such stories all explain the justification for building a temple on the designated spot where milk originally flowed. These stories are labeled *sthala purāṇas* (place myths) in south India. The other predominant motif, the bleeding stone, is largely confined to the southernmost part of India, while the milk motif predominates in central and northern India. The milk motif appears primarily among pastoral people and the blood motif appears mostly in relation to clearing forests, hunting and gathering, and cultivation. This could explain the concurrent appearance of both motifs in the Goalpara narratives, since many residents depend on both herding and rice cultivation for their subsistence. Further, the narratives suggest that at the time of Dharmaraj's first manifestation *(ābirbhāb)* the area was dense jungle. It must have been cleared at some point in order to convert the site into a sacred grove, but no one in the village recalls when this might have happened.

The Goalpara narrative is related to, yet distinct from, hundreds of narratives found throughout India. In a very small-scale way, it structurally and functionally resembles the indigenous genre of *sthala purāṇa* because it justifies and legitimates the location and activity of worship. But because many *sthala purāṇa*s describe the origins of large temples with institutionalized systems of ritual and patronage, they must be seen in relationship to other narratives that have grown around large temple structures. This is not the case with the Goalpara narrative, for there are no other competing stories. The oral corpus of versions thus functions as a master narrative, a key text for the organization of people's lives and beliefs. In this sense, the master narrative is the only canonical source for the deity's worship. It explains why and how the ritualistic worship should be performed, wherein lies its significance.

PURPORTED MIRACULOUS BIRTH STORY

The Burong Girl's Lapse (Hunza, Northwest Frontier Province, Pakistan)

In former times there was a man of the Burong and he had a daughter. She had become marriageable, but she had not been married.

He used to make his daughter take the flocks to Irkishi to pasture them. She misconducted herself with a certain herdsman and became with child. Nine months passed and she was delivered at Irkishi and a son was born to her. She took him and returned home. Her father and mother said to their daughter: "Where have you brought this child from?" The girl said: "O Father, I found him in the thorn bushes."

When she said this they were much annoyed and said to her: "Somehow or other you have given birth to a bastard, and now you have made it impossible for us to go out (of the home for shame). Tell us the truth about it."

"I have seen no one with my eyes," said the girl. "Only one day I had taken the flocks to Irkishi and I became thirsty. There was (rain) water in a hollow in a stone and I drank it. (Now) a rutting ibex had come from Bululo and urinated into the hollow in the stone. Apart from that I have seen nothing."

They gave her son the name Bumbedi. They believed her and said: "Our daughter has become pregnant by the urine of the rutting ibex. She hasn't consorted with anyone."

Up to the present day there are some households in Burong in Baltit who are descendants of Bumbedi.

That is all.

- D.L.R. Lorimer, trans., *Folk Tales of Hunza* (Islamabad, Pakistan: Lok Virsa Publishing House, 1987), pp. 140–41.

Commentary

Studies of sexuality in South Asia have suggested that illicit liaisons are quite common in mountainous herder cultures and even occur among cultivators in the plains below as well. In Islamic cultures such an encounter could carry severe consequences, so a need exists to explain incongruities like the birth of a child to an unwed woman. One way to justify and explain it would be to attribute the pregnancy to some sort of magical or miraculous act, such as being impregnated by the urine of an ibex in heat. Miracles are accepted in orthodox Islam, so the promiscuous activities can be justified as a superhuman event. A variety of such tales exist throughout South Asia in which the young woman becomes pregnant through the consumption of some object not normally eaten.

FOLKTALE

The Seven-Legged Beast (Srinagar, Kashmir, India)

A certain king, who took especial pride in his troops and spent an enormous amount of money on them, wished to know thoroughly how strong and able they were. Accordingly he ordered the general in command to assemble the men in battle array on a large *maidan* (field) without the city. On the day of review His Majesty, attended by his *wazirs* and *diwans* (ministers and advisers), visited the place, and while they were watching the maneuvers, a beast having seven legs suddenly appeared and prowled around near them. On noticing it the king was much astonished and wished to kill it; but the beast got away. The king rode after it as hard as his swift horse could carry him, and when he had thus pursued it for about two miles, the beast stopped, shook itself, and changing into a great and terrible jinn turned round on His Majesty, slew him, and ate him.

The *wazirs* caused earnest search to be made for the king for eight days, and then, no tidings of him having been received, they fetched his son and proclaimed him king in his father's stead.

One day the young king was seized with an irrepressible desire to know the cause of his father's death. He forced the *wazirs* to tell him, and when he had heard everything he commanded another grand review of the whole army to be held in the same place where the review in his father's time had been held.

On the appointed day he and all the court attended to watch the proceedings. They had not been present very long before the seven-legged beast came again, and growling fiercely at them, walked away. When the chief *wazir* saw this he laughed aloud.

"What is the matter?" asked the king.

"I laughed," replied the *wazir*, "because this is none other than the beast that allured your late father from our midst."

"Is it so?" Then I must slay it, for I shall not have any peace till this enemy is killed." Saying this, the king whipped his horse and rushed after it. The beast led him on and on for some distance, as it did his father, and then stopping, shook itself, resumed its original shape, and prepared to spring. In his distress the king called earnestly on the great God to save him; and God sent an angel to direct him how to fight the jinn.

"This is a most powerful jinn," said the angel. "Should a drop of his blood fall to the ground, while life is in him, another jinn will be quickly formed therefrom, and spring up and slay you. But fear not. Take this double-headed arrow and pierce the two eyes of the monster, so that he fall down and die." Then the angel departed.

Thus strengthened, the king dashed forward. He fought with the jinn for forty minutes. At last he plunged the double-headed arrow into both of his eyes, and thus slew him. When he saw that his enemy was dead the king drew his sword and cut off his head, and fixing it on his arrow, took it with him to the palace, where he placed it in one of the twelve thousand rooms of that building; and gave his mother the keys, bidding her not to open the doors thereof.

But as he did not tell his mother what he had so carefully locked up in the room, she supposed that it was some special treasure, and being very inquisitive, one morning went to the room and unlocked the door. Nothing, however, was to be seen, for the king had thrown the head into a corner; but a laugh was heard, and then a voice, saying, "Your son is a jinn. Beware of him. He is a jinn. Some time he will kill you, as he killed me, your husband. Get him out of the palace if you wish to live."

"Whence comes this voice? What say you?" asked the king's mother.

"Pretend to be unwell, and beg your son to get the milk of a tigress. Bid him to go himself and try to get this," said the head.

The next morning, with a sad and heavy heart, the king might have been seen wending his steps in the direction of a certain jungle, wherein tigers and other wild beasts were known to roam. He soon saw a tigress, with her two cubs basking in the sunshine. He climbed a tree and aimed at one of the teats of the beast. This teat chanced to be one in which she had suffered much pain for several days, owing to the presence of a nasty abscess near the place. The king's arrow broke the abscess, and the pain was at once relieved. Grateful for this relief, the tigress looked up and entreated the king to descend and ask whatever he would like her to get for him. His Majesty told her he wanted nothing but a little of her milk for his sick mother, who had taken a strange fancy for it. The tigress readily filled the cup that the king had brought with him, and also gave him a tuft of her fur, saying, "Whenever you are in any difficulty show this to the sun, and I will at once come to your aid." Taking the milk and the bit of fur, the king returned to his palace.

When his mother received the milk of the tigress she felt quite sure that her son was a jinn, and determined no more than before to have him killed. She went to the room where the head was, and informed the speaker of everything, and heard again a voice saying, "Be assured thereby that this man is a jinn. None but a jinn could obtain milk from a tigress. Have him killed as soon as possible."

"But how can I get rid of him?" she asked.

The voice replied, "When your son visits you and inquires after your health, tell him that you still feel very weak and sick. The tigress's milk did not do you any good. But you have heard of a princess who lives alone in a castle on a certain high hill. If she could come and touch you, you would become well. Your son will go to this terrible castle, and be certainly killed along the way."

In the evening the king went to see his mother. "Are you better?" he asked.

"No," she said. "The tigress's milk has not benefited me in the least. But I saw in a dream a princess who lives in a certain castle, and heard that if she would come and touch me all would be well. Until she comes I will never get strong."

"Be comforted, mother. I will fetch this woman for you, or forfeit my kingdom."

Early in the morning the king started on his perilous journey. He had not forgotten the bit of charmed fur. As soon as the sun appeared he showed the fur to it, and immediately the tigress and her two cubs came running towards him.

"What is the matter?" asked the tigress.

"I have to go and fetch the princess who resides in yonder castle."

"Fetch her! You cannot do that. Several people have tried, for the princess is very beautiful; but nobody has succeeded in getting near her."

"I will try, though I lose my life in the attempt."

Saying this the king left.

The tigress could not bear to have her benefactor thus leave her. So she ran after him with her two cubs, and begged him to ride on her. They soon reached the castle.

"In this place," said the tigress, "there are three big doors, through which it is necessary to pass before a person can get to the princess. Near the first door is an immense block of iron, which must be broken by a wooden axe, or the door will not open. At the second door is an imitation cow, surrounded by real jinns. If any person can milk the cow, he will pass through; if not, he will be devoured by the jinns. By the third door sits the princess herself. If she is pleased with you, she will receive you; but if not, she will accomplish your death."

On hearing these words, the king became very frightened, and begged the tigress to help him.

"Very well," she said. "By a charm which I possess I will enter the block of iron, and when you strike with the wooden axe, I will cause it to divide into two pieces; and then the doorkeeper will think that you cleft the iron, and allow you to enter through the first door."

"And I," said one of the young tigers, "will cause the statue of the cow to give milk, and will keep the jinns who stand round it from hindering you in milking. Thus will you be able to pass through the second door."

"And I," said the other young tiger, "will put a charm into the eyes of the princess, so that when she looks on you she may think you to be bright and beautiful as the sun, and be so fascinated with the sight, that she will open the third door and do anything else you may ask her."

Faithfully they all three performed their promises. The king safely reached the princess, and she, overcome by his beauty and immense power, professed her great affection for him, and entreated him to make her his wife.

The tigress and her cubs returned to their lair. In a few days the king took the princess home with him to his palace. "Mother," he said, "I have brought the princess. Oh! What a fearful place it was, and how difficult and dangerous the way to it! I should have perished on the way if a tigress and her two little cubs had not helped me. Praise be to God that I am here safe and well!" Some other conversation leading up to it, he told her also about the head of the jinn—how it had first appeared to him as a seven-legged beast, and led him away to a certain place where it changed itself back into its real character, a great and terrible jinn, and prepared to jump on him; and how he would have been slain and eaten up, as his father had been, if God had not sent His angel and helped him.

His mother was much surprised to hear this. "My son," she said, "I have been deceived. On the evening of the day when you borrowed the keys of the palace from me I went round several of the rooms, till I came to the one in which I heard the sound of laughing. On my inquiring the reason of this a voice said, 'Take heed lest your son, who is a jinn, slay you. I am the head of your husband. He killed me. Get rid of him, or he will kill you also.' My son, I believed the voice, and at its advice I sent you to fetch the milk of a tigress, hoping you would be slain in the attempt. And I begged you to go and call the princess, knowing that the way to her abode was full of terrible dangers. But God has been with you, and He, who sent the angel to direct you has also caused the tigress and young tigers to be your helpers. Praise be to His name!" Then she embraced her son, and wept bitterly.

Within a short time of these things the king married the princess, and spent the rest of his life in peace and prosperity.

- James H. Knowles, *Kashmiri Folk Tales* (Islamabad, Pakistan: National Institute of Folk Heritage, 1981), pp. 1–7.

Commentary

This is a fairly typical tale in the sense that it involves an interdiction and a hero who must go on a dangerous quest to achieve some sort of objective goal. Along the way, he is provided advice and support by a helper, in this case tigers. The conflict or tense situation created in the narrative to drive the hero's actions is ultimately overcome and resolved to restore balance and harmony. Although the story contains the Hindu *raktabīj* (blood drop) motif contained in the *Devi Mahatmya* of the *Markandeya Purana,* it is distinctively Islamic, as is suggested by the central antagonistic role of jinn in the narrative. These spirits, along with angels and demons, are the three classes of creatures created in addition to human beings by Allah. Jinn can be traced back to pre-Islamic Arabia but were incorporated into Islam by the prophet Muhammad. In the West, they are best known as the numerous genies in *1,001 Nights,* but they play a central role in Islamic folklore throughout the world. According to popular belief, they are created from smokeless fire, and they have the ability to take a variety of forms and fly. Jinns are not always malevolent. Some are thought to believe and follow the will of Allah. But others clearly serve Satan and harass people by roaming at night, possessing or haunting them, or causing insanity and confusion. Another class of supernatural entities called *parī* function similarly throughout the mountainous regions of South Asia.

BAWDY TALE

Two Monkeys, a Mouse, and an Elephant (Anonymous Narrator, Islamabad, Pakistan)

Two monkeys were sitting high in a palm tree one day, minding their own business, when they saw a female elephant approaching below. As the elephant passed their perch, it suddenly became ensnared in a trap left by poachers. The elephant began wailing out loud, but to no avail. The monkeys watched on curiously without doing anything to help. After some time had passed, the elephant became tired of trumpeting and sat silently on the ground as twilight approached.

Finally, a mouse out scavenging for his evening meal comes across the scene. "Hey there," calls the mouse to the elephant, "how goes it?" The elephant tearfully responds, "Oh mouse, I'm caught in this trap! I've been here all day, but no one has come to my aide. Now I am tired and hungry. I only wish to be freed, so that I can return home peacefully and uninjured." The mouse, being a rakish character, thinks, "Hmm, maybe there is an opportunity here. Perhaps I can negotiate a bit of amorous pleasure as reward for releasing her." Then the mouse responds to the she-elephant, "Well, perhaps I could be of some service." The elephant perks up and says, "Oh, I'd be eternally grateful if you could help. I'd do anything to reward you." So the mouse says, "Okay, I'll help you out of your predicament on one condition. I haven't been with a woman in weeks, and here it is dark, quiet, where no one can see us. I'll release you if you allow me to (narrator makes some suggestive body gestures in silence for effect). The elephant, nervous but desperate, agrees to the condition.

In the meantime, the monkeys up in the tree notice the mouse mounting the elephant from behind. "Oh, that's disgusting," remarks one to the other. "A mouse and an elephant together is revolting." The other agrees, replying, "If there were only something we could do to stop them!" Just as the mouse begins to copulate with the elephant, the monkeys throw a large coconut at the elephant and hit it on the head. "Ouch," yells the elephant, to which the mouse responds, "What's wrong my dear, too much for you?"

- Frank J. Korom, Field Notes, Islamabad, Pakistan, 1985.

Commentary

This humorous tale was told to me by an educated, urban, upper-class Pakistani whose name will remain confidential here. The story was told to me in Urdu, with some code switching to Punjabi during the bawdier sections for effect, during a game of cards, with several other people in attendance. Later in the evening, I recorded it from recollection in English translation. This risqué story is an obvious satirical retelling of a well-known fable about a smaller animal coming to the assistance of a larger one who is suffering some discomfort. The theme appears both in western fables such as found in Aesop and in South Asian variants included in the *Jataka* texts and the *Panchatantra*. But the obvious gluttonous and self-serving motivation of the mouse is the opposite of what would be intended in the more religious *Jataka* stories. Here we see how traditional themes found in classical literature float in and out of the oral stream of culture, becoming creatively transformed in the process.

RELIGIOUS LEGEND

Mandap, the Son of Kushmand, Makes a Pilgrimage (Banaras, Uttar Pradesh, India)

Mandap was staying with the wicked members of society and sinned. One day, he entered the palace of the king and robbed it with some of his friends. After that, he took the money to a brothel and remained there in the company of a prostitute, delighting in the pleasures of the flesh. One day he was drinking wine when his friends arrived and demanded their share of the money. He didn't give it to them and was beaten by his cohorts. When he demanded his money from the prostitute she refused and also threatened him. Following this, he was forced to flee from her because of his *karma*.

When he arrived at his own house, his friends were there waiting for him. They told the whole story to Mandap's parents. After thinking about the dilemma for some time, the father decided that it would be better to take Mandap to the king and explain the circumstances, but the friends refused this idea.

A confrontation followed, ending in all of the youths being forced to leave by Kushmand. Before his departure, the father told his son that he must remove the accursed sin *(pāp)* if he were ever to become pure again. His friends accompanied him as he left the house. Mandap was confused and frightened, for he wasn't quite sure how to comprehend all that had happened to him. As they walked, they came to an isolated spot near Assi *saṅgam* (confluence). There they beat him until he lost his senses. His so-called friends thought that they had killed him, and they fled the scene. When he regained consciousness he saw some devotees doing the *pañcakrośī yātrā*. Dazed and confused, he decided to accompany them on their journey. Upon arrival at the first night's halt he even received *darśan* (auspicious sight) at Kardameshvar.

Even though he was well versed in the law books and other religious lore, he had no light in his heart. The whole night he stayed awake in front of the shrine at Kardameshvar doing deep meditation and *pūjā*. His fellow *yātrīs* (pilgrims) began to respect him for his great austerities after this.

In the past he looked quite gentle, but after he met with these good people he shone from within, became pure. Having seen the devotion of the devotees *(bhakts)*, he made the decision to take the path also. And in so doing he began to walk the path of truth, slowly attaining power and coming closer to unity.

He continued with the others the next day. The good folks gave him food to eat upon arrival at the second night's stop at Bhimchandi. There the devotees listened to the sacred history of the Goddess's residence. Mandap also did a lovely dance and sang devotional songs *(bhajans)*.

On the third day they reached the western gate of Kashi, the image of Dehali Vinayak. There he realized the intensity of his past *karma*. He became absorbed in deep contemplation. He silently prayed to the shrine within his mind. He prayed: "Oh Lord Shiva and Annapurna, keep me at your feet and save me from my sins." By the time he arrived at Rameshvara, the feeling and intensity of his devotion was quite changed.

After worshipping at Rameshvara and Somnath he danced fervently and sang devotional songs without eating any food. He became totally absorbed by his devotion to the deities.

When he arrived at Vrishabhadvaja he bathed in the Kapila pool and performed worship to Vishvanath and Annapurna. After doing this he asked the pilgrims how he could release himself from sin. They told him that upon completion of the pilgrimage he would be cleansed of sin.

After completing the journey he went to his father's home. When he arrived there he chanted, "Shiva Shiva Mahadev Mahadev." When he heard his son's voice the father sent his wife to greet the son. The mother asked why he came back without cleansing his sins. Mandap, ecstatic at seeing his parents, told them about his experience performing the *pañcakrośī yātrā*. He invited them to Mukti Mandap. There the father asked for proof that he completed the pilgrimage. They prayed to all the deities there, and were rewarded by the presence of all the gods as they manifested themselves in their true forms. The deities responded in union: "All those that do the *pañcakrośī yātrā* will be released from all sin."

- V. Upadhyāya, *Śrī Kāśī Pañcakrośī Dev-Yātrā* [The Sacred Kashi Five Krosh Deity Pilgrimage] Varanasi, India: Śrī Bhṛguprakāśan, n.d.), pp. 29–33.

Commentary

Translated from a Hindi chapbook and easily purchased along the route of the pilgrimage, this devotional tale tells the simple story of someone who errs but in the end achieves salvation by worshipping Shiva, the patron deity of the city Kashi, which is also known as Varanasi or Banaras. It is believed that dying in this city amounts to liberation from rebirth. But to live is to sin, so periodically performing the circumambulation *(parikrama)* of the city allows the individual to purify him- or herself by purging whatever bad *karma* has accrued over a given period of time.

Even the worst of sins can be removed by performing this pilgrimage, which normally takes five days to complete due to the 108 shrines that one must visit along the way. This is attested to by the belief that even Rama, incarnation of Vishnu and hero of the epic *Ramayana,* had to perform the circumambulation of the holy city after he killed the ten-headed demon Ravana, who was a Brahman by birth. Brahmanicide is considered to be the highest sin by Hindus, so before he could undertake his coronation, Rama had to expiate his sin by performing the pilgrimage. The main function of this narrative is thus to explain the great merit *(punya)* one achieves by performing this special pilgrimage.

MEMORATE

The Terror of the British (Anonymous Narrator, Cooch Behar, West Bengal, India)

When I was a young boy, I used to hear terrifying stories from older people about how the British would abuse Indians. We children grew up afraid of them, but we were also curious. Later, I studied medicine and even learned a little bit of English in college. I worked as a doctor until I retired. For part of the time, I worked in a British cantonment part of town; only the British were allowed to live there, but some Indian people worked in the cantonment. Even when I was an adult, I was afraid of the British soldiers, with their sabers and guns, and those uniforms with the pith helmets and shiny black boots. Sometimes I had nightmares about them. Well, when I got older the dreams got worse. British soldiers started terrorizing me in my dreams. One would come in the night and sit on my chest so that I couldn't move. I even tried to call out, but no sound came out of my mouth. He just sat there laughing, and I couldn't move. I was paralyzed for what seemed like a long time, when he suddenly disappeared. This happened to me on a few occasions.

- Frank J. Korom, Author's Field Notes, Cooch Behar, West Bengal, India, 1982.

Commentary

Memorate refers to a genre of first-person experience narratives in which a supernatural element is involved, making it something out of the ordinary. In this interesting example, however, the extraordinary power or force is a British colonial officer. As mentioned in an earlier chapter, the British are implicated in much contemporary folklore as a result of their colonial rule. This poignant example suggests what is elsewhere in the Anglican world known as hagging, which occurs when a demonic spirit, such as an old hag, comes and sits on the chest of a victim during the night, inducing paralysis. In medieval Europe, this was referred to as the incubus-succubus phenomenon. Incubus refers to a male demonic spirit lying on a sleeping woman for the purpose of sexual intercourse, while succubus refers to a female demon lying on a sleeping man for the same purpose of sexual gratification.

Dreams *(svapna)* play an important role in South Asian culture, both positive and negative. They can lead to performing some religious action, as we saw earlier in the etiological tale included above, or they can induce demonic possession that requires ritualistic exorcism to cure the individual. In this memorate, there is no sexual implication as in the incubus-succubus phenomenon; rather, the point is that British terror can and might bring about states of inaction. Symbolically, it suggests the overwhelming power of the colonial rulers over their perceived weaker subjects.

ROMANCE

The Marriage of Hir and Ranjha (Patiala, Punjab)

Firstly, I take the name of God; secondly, of the great Muhammad, the friend (of God). Thirdly, I take the name of father and mother, on whose milk my body throve; fourthly, I take the name of bread and water, from eating which my heart is gladdened. Fifthly, I take the name of Mother Earth, on whom I place my feet. Sixthly, I take the name of Kwaja (Khizar), the Saint that gives me cold water to drink. Seventhly, I take the name of Guru Gorakh (Nath), whom I worship with a platter of milk and rice. Eighthly, I take the name of Lalauwala, that breaks the bonds and the chains of the captives.

Ranjha was born in Mauju's house and Hir in Chuchak's. The prophets took counsel together and the Panj Pirs (five saints) were rejoiced. There are Five (great) Saints; the sixth is Miyan Ranjha; the seventh is the Holy Miyan Mir. Ranjha was born and the entire household rejoiced. Taking the cups the presents were made with the market-full of food. God wrote no labor (in his fate): he was to be happy with (tending) buffaloes.

The Mughals came from Kashmir by the order of God. Land was given to Miyan Ranjha, nine links and three chains. Others got good land; Ranjha got tares and weeds. Said (Ranjha): "O Nikku, you chief of the Blacksmiths, make me an axe, a sickle and a hoe. Let me have a hoe by daybreak and there will be no delay about your wages." Said he, "I will ply (the hoe), clear the weeds and make the land arable." (Said Ranjha): "Come, my heart, I will go and become a *faqir* [mendicant]; I am not happy here." As Ranjha sat (at his work in the field) he becomes hot, and Lali, his brother's wife, laughed at him. Ranjha left Takht Hazara, and the first night he found trying. At home he had cream and milk, now he could not even get stale leavings. He had had a bed and pillows to sleep on, now he dwelt on the sand. He could make no complaint to the Great God, for Fate had written it so.

It was midnight at the time for the Saints. "Why are you traveling at this hour of the night? Long your beard and long your moustache and your bedding under arm. If you seek your good go hence, or be pushed out." "Oh Qazi [judge]," said Ranjha, "I tell you the truth. Inns and mosques, O Qazi, are built for religious use; and you would turn away a saint, you infidel and without faith! You keep fasts and say prayers and know the words of the Quran; and you would turn away a saint, you infidel and without faith! I have left Takht Hazara of my fathers; I have left my mother and all my customs: May the city prosper where stayed the *faqir* for the night!" The youths brought him bread and cold butter-milk: (Said he): "Live for ever, you youths, with whom the *faqir* stayed for the night!"

"O you wanderer to the right, go to the left, put not your feet toward the right: For hither to the left the lions roar and to the right the horrors. I live upon my own earnings, do come in and eat with me. My red bed and my white bedding do I gladly share with you." "I have left Takht Hazara of my fathers, and have left my weeping brethren. Sooner or later troubles fall upon us all." "One thing I say to you and I tell you the truth. My sons are earning well and my daughters take them their food to the fields. I have two virgin daughters in the house and I will marry them both to you. I adjure you by the Quran not to spoil this match." "One thing I say to you and I tell you the truth. Your sons shall dig me neither wells nor ponds. If you seek your good go back, or I will push you away. I am Ranjha and am going to Jhang Siyal and you shall not stay me." "On water I am Lunan, on land I am Lunan, I am Lunan the haughty. Where I Lunan place my feet the earth trembles. Spend the night with me that the city may prosper. For your sake have I come here, that never (before) left my palace." "One thing I say to you and I tell you the truth. I take a *man* [a measure] and a quarter of poppy juice (daily) and drink an endless quantity of *bhang* [marijuana milkshake]. I take a *ser* and a quarter [two and a half pounds] of opium and a whole cup of wine in one draught. I drink the milk of brown buffaloes (only) and eat cakes of sugar and butter." "O carters and camel-drivers, take up your loads: O porters take cups of wine to my palace. If your wages are one *lakh* (of rupees) I will pay two *lakhs*: I will keep nothing back. Ranjha has come to my city: a holy saint has come."

"I, Ranjha, have come from Takht Hazara, the son of Mauju the Jatt. When I, Ranjha, was five years old I was put to mind buffaloes. Tending the buffaloes for twelve years, I look upon my father like a king. When my father died I fell into trouble and my brethren cheated me. I, Ranjha, will go to Jhang Siyal and will not be stayed by you. I have left many women behind me and Lali loved me much."

"I will beat you, I will bind you, I will hang you up at once. They asked me for one *lakh* (of rupees) and I gave them two *lakhs;* the labor of none (of them) was unpaid for. You have gone back on your word and all your life I will not let you go. For your sake did I come here, that never (before) left my palace." "Your sticks will break and your ropes will snap; you cannot hang the *faqir.*" "It was in laughter and fun that I upbraided you; so load up your bags, my friend. You are like a madwoman wandering in the burning-grounds and quarreling foolishly. Turn your head and see: the palace is on fire!"

{On the road to Jhang}

"One thing I say to you and tell you the truth. The Saints have sent me and I have come to you. I want to offer five *sers* [quarts] of milk to the Saints and have no more to waste." Then said Ranjha: "I tell you: Your goats shall die and none of your sheep shall escape. Your lambs shall die in the fields, and your old mother at home. Your wife shall die and you shall be a widower and shall be ruined!"

The Five Saints and the sixth Ranjha took counsel (together) in the wilds: And beneath the Saints was spread a black blanket full of holes. Ranjha sat and played on the flute and the sound of it reached the Court (of God). Indra heard the flute and sent a brown buffalo from heaven. He had patience and took a large pitcher and the buffalo gave milk. The first spurt Ranjha gave to Mother Earth, and the second went into his cup. He filled cups and gave them to the Saints and the Saints drank and gave their blessings, (saying): "Go, Ranjha, Hir has been given to you on the authority of Mecca and Medina." Ranjha left Takht Hazara in low spirits; (And said): "I have no friends now, nor do I know of any (friendly) town!"

Night overtook Ranjha at the ferry and the sting of sorrow entered him: (said he): "For God's sake, O (ferryman) Ludan, give me a boat, for I have to go to Jhang Siyal." "It is midnight and the hour for the Saints: why are you traveling at such an hour? This river runs violently and runs afar: It frightens holy men and saints and you shall never cross it (now). Better stay now and lie down under a bush, and cross in the morning."

Ranjha played the thirty-six tunes and played in the wilds: On pipes and then on drums and then he made (creatures) dance. And then the cock crowed and the peacock screamed: "For God's sake, Ludan, give him a boat;

he is some holy man or saint." (Said Ludan): "This is no time for saints and holy men, but for thieves and pick-pockets to roam. Large fish and waterfowl and crocodiles roam (the river). If he were a saint or holy man of Mecca he would find a boat for himself. I have seen many a vain fellow like him."

It was the hour of early morn; (said Ludan): "From where have you come alone? A staff is in your hand, a blanket over your shoulder, and a kerchief on your head. Other rivers flow gently, but the Chandai boils along, sweeping away the mud walls and throwing down brick ones. There are endless fish and tortoises in the world. I have a boat ready for you; but why drown, O heedless Jatt?" (Said Ranjha): "I that have been loved and petted at home have (now) Ludan for my lord! I am dwelling in the house of a fool and am throwing away my life in tears. It was no fault of my parents, but the barbers and Brahmans deceived me. May your boat sink and your oars break! I have found a ruby from Khwaja."

"I, Ludan, have come quickly, have come to the lofty bank. Say: have you stolen any one's cattle? Say: is any one pursuing you closely? Make your choice (of the boats) and take the good one according to your desire. Take one and leave one, that Ludan's house may not be ruined." "Quickly have you come, O Ludan, have come to the lofty bank. Neither have I stolen any one's cattle, nor is any one close behind me. If you are a (true) boatman's son, Ludan, quickly get the boat. May you be happy in both (worlds), that saved my life in this one. The bed is red, the bedding white;—that noble's boat is this? Let me rest a moment here, O Ludan, that I may be at ease."

Ranjha gave him a bribe, and becoming his sworn brother, went to sleep (on the bed). (Said Ludan): "There is a lofty palace of the Siyal's near the Khera Quarter. The red bed and the white bedding and the boat are Hir's, the Siyal (lady) Daughter of Chuchak, sister of Pathan, a very maiden of love. If even a bird flies over her bed (Hir) the Jatt woman will take away my life!" But Ranjha gave a bribe and went to sleep, and made Ludan drunken with *bhang*.

As (Hir) lay asleep she had a dream that someone had ruined (lain down on) her bed (in the boat). (Said she): "I tell you the truth, I tell you that this will not leave my mind. I had a dream in the night; a black snake came and frightened me." Then said she: "I must meet Ranjha, or I shall be driven into the grave. Open your books, O Tulsi, and see what is written in your books." "I open my books and I tell you truth: Your lover has slept on your bed; I will tell you no lies." The maids met together and consulted, and sent Fatti up a tree. (Said she): "I swear by the Saints; I swear by the *Quran*; I tell no lies. Your lover has slept on your bed; I tell you the truth. Go and seize Ludan the boatman, that has taken a bribe and destroyed (the honor of) your bed." "The heart is deeper than seas and rivers: who knows the heart? It has boats and oars and boatmen within it! The Fourteen Quarters (of the World) are in it, stretched like a canopy! He who knows the dictates of the heart will be happy every moment! You strike a naked body and my eyes are weary. If one such blow as you give me were to reach you, you would understand! O wicked, tall and handsome youth, you have lain on a jasmine bed. As you have lain, awaken now and pluck the jasmine flower."

Sawan had come and Hir's heart inclined (to love) and the herbs began to spring. Beautiful were the rings in her ears and bracelets on her arms. (Said Ranjha): "What if I lay on your bed for awhile? Do you fear shame from your family? Like the lines on the palm (of the hands) you and I have been lovers from the beginning." The peaches were ripe in Jhang Siyal and the sweet grapes in the gardens. Said Hir: "Ranjha, tell me truly: what is the relationship between us?" (Said he): "When I, Ranjha, was in the house of Indar, you were a maiden there. When I, Ranjha, was Namanand, you were my wife Gorkhan. When I, Ranjha, was born in Takht Hazara, you were born in Mihar Chuchak."

"You have a beard and your hair is grown; how is it that you are still a bachelor? Either your mother's or father's relatives are low people or your brethren love you not. Either you are born of an inferior mother, or you are a dealer in rubies. In some way there must be a fault in you that you are a bachelor." "There is a beard on my face and hair on my head, but I am no bachelor. My mother was well born and my father well born and lordly in Takht Hazara. I am not born of an inferior mother and am much loved by my brethren. I have seven sisters-in-law and many women at home; I am a dealer in rubies. I have heard of Hir in Chuchak's house and her will I marry. I set not my heart on good or bad (women) and am much loved by Lal."

The sun and moon ceased to rise and the stars to shine forth. The water dried in the ponds and the grass dried up in the wilds. Mohammad formed the marriage procession and Brahma set up posts (of the marriage canopy). The maids of heaven sang songs of rejoicing and fairies brought the henna. The Panj Pir performed the ceremony and Khwaja (Khizar) was witness. Hir and Ranjha met together and God was favorable to them.

(Said Hir): "Father, I have brought a herder, a Jatt, to graze the buffaloes. Whichever of them he touches with his staff will surely bear a (cow-) calf. Hitherto you have sent twenty-one herders; this one will graze them alone. The beauty of the herder is like the moon and his habits shall not depart. The herder has one bad habit, that Hir must take him food (to the fields). He will himself draw, curdle and set the milk." "O Hir, the herder you have brought: will he graze any one's buffaloes? Ranjha's heel has the sign of royalty (on it) and he has a mighty staff, three-fourths of a *ser* of clarified butter he puts on his locks, which fall to the ground. Ranjha's teeth are pegs of gold: whose buffaloes shall he graze? The houses that this youth shall visit will be ruined. His work shall never prosper, but he shall wander (begging) from door to door. My cattle graze at midnight, but he passes the night in sleep. If you wish your good let the youthful servant go: I am pleased with my former herders."

(Said Ranjha): "At home I was a nobleman, but going abroad I have become of no account. O Hir, you have made me lighter than a straw that was as heavy as a mountain, the son of a nobleman is called a servant. Your brother Pathan is angry with you, and your father reproaches you. Let go of my robes that I may go back home, and let me, the helpless swan, fly away. Let me go of your own free will, that I may mingle with my brethren." "I tell you one thing, Ranjha, and I tell you the truth. If you remain I will remain, or I will go with you."

(Said Chuchak and he speaks the truth): "Hear, friend Ranjha, drive the buffaloes from this paddock and the cows from the other." Before seventy Khans and seventy-two nobles Chuchak betrothed Hir and Ranjha (saying): "As long as you shall live she is yours, and when you are dead she will not deny it. If any one tears Hir from you I will bear witness (against him) in the Court (of God)." When Ranjha was told this he drove off the buffaloes and the cows.

(Said Ranjha): "Your father has given me, O Hir, cattle that will only graze at night. They pull out their pegs and they break their ropes; these buffaloes are very vicious. My company is with the serpents and my friendship with the lions. You sleep in the painted palace and I cannot pass the night." "With joined hands I beseech you and I tell you the truth. On one side of me (sleeps) my father Chuchak and on the other side my mother Julli. On one side sleeps my brother Pathan and near him his wife Kodi. Drive the buffaloes to the forests, I will join you at daybreak."

"The buffaloes have come, but my servant has not come; what pleasures is he enjoying? Neither have I spun, nor have I plied the needle, but I have come with food for Ranjha. When I shampooed my Ranjha I found his body hot. Nine buffaloes do I vow to (Sakhi Sarwar) Sultan, and the tenth shall be a (cow-) calf. I will give him my skirt and the kerchief from my head: To him will I present them that shall make my Ranjha well. For him that shall make my Ranjha happy, will I be a pilgrim to Mecca. I, Hir of the Siyals, was ruined for you, when you (Ranjha) pushed off your boat.

The buffaloes have come, but my servant has not come, and I search for him in the forests. I will rub his feet and knead his hands, he who is my favorite. My youth is fleeting and none can stay the flowing waters. When I go abroad my father Chuchak scolds me, when I return home my mother

Julli does the same. When I go to the mosque Fatta the Qazi scolds me and at home so does my uncle Kaidu, the cripple. The maids jeer at me in the spinning place and even women in the lanes. My youth declining has gone far away and seems far off. Had I known that I would fall into such trouble I would never have been born among the Siyals! The buffaloes have come, but my servant has not come: how have the buffaloes come?" Today Ranjha has not come to Hir's house and there is no news of him in the forests. Milkmen watch their milk and Gurus watch their disciples.

"(I) Hir am an elephant and Miyan Ranjha is my driver: you can use me as you will. Friends take leave of friends, as Gurus do of their disciples. Our four eyes met, as spear against shield. Wandering in the forests my kerchief is torn, and ripped up is my red scarf. If the separated meet again, happy will be the meeting! Hear O saintly Khwaja, my errant servant is under your care. Let no snake bite him, no lion frighten him, no thief trouble him! The rains have come and my heart rejoices and the earth brings forth." Parents shall find husbands for their maids and the Panj Pir for Hir.

"Hear, O you stream, I know you well: why do you throw down the trees? Do you rival the great rivers, you who are not even equal to the ponds? Such a ford can buffaloes cross, such a passage can cows. Such a ford can Miyan Ranjha cross, the lord of Hir, the maid. If a *faqir* curses you, you shall no longer flow. Hir shall surely meet Ranjha, though she might lose her life. The night is dark and the lanes muddy and the lightning frightens me: But Hir shall surely meet Ranjha, if God is favorable. God's earth does sleep, but I the wretched am pierced with the arrows (of grief).

The milkmen have collected the milk and the call (to prayer) resounds through the city. If you will meet me, Ranjha, meet me, or my life will depart in tears. Serpents and lions come to destroy me and the waters have risen on high. All call them buffaloes, but the buffaloes are spirits and fairies. The buffaloes' horns are beautifully curved and their buttocks are fat. The buffaloes' milk is sweet as sugar and their butter is like sugar-candy. Going out they beautify the fields, coming home the lanes. Come, my Lord Ranjha, let us play *chaupur* [board game] and let the buffaloes go home." The story of lover and beloved is known throughout the world.

(Said Pathan): "A low set are servants and bad to the smell. Have you stolen some sweet perfume, or is Hir embracing you? Raise up your arm, Ranjha, for you smell of sandalwood." Hir was under Ranjha's arm, but God hid her. (Said Ranjha): "You call me a low man and have no shame! I have stolen no sweet perfume, nor is Hir embracing me. A sandal-tree had been cut in Kashmir and floated down the river: The buffaloes (in crossing it) ran against the sandal-tree and the scent stuck to the buffaloes." Then Ranjha raised up his arms and there was no sign of Hir! And God preserved the virtuous Ranjha, the son of Mauju, from shame.

(Said Ranjha to Hir): "I speak the truth and I tell you truth: Take your brown blanket and the cow-buffaloes that are standing (waiting). You rich can find many servants, and we servants many a place. The flying swans cannot be stayed, and fly to the heavens. The betel-fields have many a keeper and flowers have many a bee. Your brother Pathan threatens me and it is not well that I remain. O Hir, to fall in love with you, is to awaken lions and black snakes. It is a stake of heads and bodies and you do not know how to play."

She tore the hair of her head and her locks nurtured on butter (and Hir said): "You wretched herder, you would desert the daughter of Chuchak at the first reproach!" Said Kaidu, "I speak the truth and speak it to you. I have come as a pilgrim from Mecca, O Ranjha to you. Three days have I been hungry and had no bread at all. Give me bread for God's sake, you servant, and may you live forever. I, Kaidu, have come as a pilgrim from Mecca to Ranjha."

"Who can light a hearth in the wilds? Who can put a cauldron (on the fire) here? I am the herder of Mihar Chuchak and get my bread once in the eight watches. If you are very hungry make your way to the Siyals." "Give me half of half a piece or a quarter of a piece (of sweetmeat). Give me first all the bread, so that you may receive double in the next world." When Ranjha heard Kaidu's speech, he put some cakes into Kaidu's wallet. Taking the cakes Kaidu went and cried out amid the Siyals: "I have seen Hir and Ranjha in the forests, and I tell no lies. Ranjha will take Hir away, and there will be shame for the Siyals."

When the Siyals heard this, they sent Hir to be taught by the Qazi. (Said the Qazi to Hir): "This is not like the Siyals: follow the way of your parents. Be wise, O Hir, and go the way of the Kheras. The Kheras will take you away in marriage and will bind your arms with a rope. That Ranjha on whom your heart is set is but a worthless herder." Said Fattu, the Qazi, to Hir: "Do not go from Heaven to Hell." (Said Hir): "Hear, O holy Qazi: men call you, 'Lord,' and men call the True God 'Lord,' that gives sustenance to all! I, Hir, am the earth, and Miyan Ranjha is my plough that continually ploughs. Like opium he has entered my bones, and I cannot live without drinking (him). How can your heart brook that you take me from Ranjha and give me to the Kheras? O Qazi, if you so love the Kheras, give them your own daughter in marriage!"

"Be wise and give up your pride, and be humble, and be the maid of the Kheras. Attach yourself to false silver and leave the true silver of the Kheras. You will become like a *faqir* with bare head and naked feet. Your shoes will be worn out and your skirt tattered and the dust of your feet will fly to your head. In the lattices of the lofty palace of Sida the cool air plays. To leave the Kheras and to seize the skirt of Ranjha is to go from Heaven to Hell."

"Hear, O holy Qazi, who writes on the white papers: May fire seize your house and burn all your books! May your son die and let his wife be a widow and let your daughter suffer! If you give Ranjha right to the Kheras: may fire burn your grave!"

(Said the Qazi to the Siyals): "I tell you the truth, and I, the Qazi, claim your protection. Hir does not listen to me, nor can she be made to listen." The heads of the Kheras gathered together and held a meeting. Said one: "Give Hir in marriage to Mabbu, the goldsmith, who has no lack of wealth." Said another, "Give Hir in marriage to Raja Adali, who has a great empire." Said Chuchak: "Give Hir in marriage to Ranjha, the herder of my house." Said Kaidu: "Give Hir to the Kheras; it is the truth that I say." When this had been said at the meeting, Hir was betrothed to Sida, the Khera.

(Said Ranjha): "The strong currents of the rivers have risen and the eyes of me, Ranjha, are troubled. They are greatly troubled, as I wander after the buffaloes. Who shall know the trouble of a stranger, but his own mother? Neither did I take any money, nor did I receive any pay. Have I gathered any wealth by coming to the Siyals? But I have endured a thousand reproaches! When Sida takes you away as a bride, how shall I meet my brethren?"

(Said Hir): "Who shall bind on the marriage bracelets? Who shall stain you with henna? Into whose house shall you marry? Who shall make you a son-in-law?" "Mohan, the Brahman, shall bind on the bracelet; Fatti, the barber's wife, shall bring the henna. The maidens shall anoint me with oil and place the (marriage) throne beneath Ranjha. I will marry into the house of Chuchak; I will be the son-in-law of the Siyals. Twelve years have I grazed their buffaloes and have taken no pay. It was in the assembly of Mihar Chuchak that Hir was given to me. If any one takes her away now I will complain to the Court (of God). Sixty maidens collected to see the marriage procession of Sida. Sida had three rings in his ears and a large turban like a boatman. He was one-eyed and bald-headed and no match (for Hir)."

(Said Hir): "I belong to Ranjha, the herder of our house!" (Said Ranjha): "For your sake I put the drum and the goods of the Kheras on my head. I left Takht Hazara of my fathers, and my beloved brethren. I left my brother's wife Lali, who kills flying birds (with her glances). The (stony) hills would weep for Lali, and what am I but a man? I, the son of nobles, am called a servant, and who cares for a servant? Dismiss me so that I may go home and mingle with my brethren."

(Said Hir): "Without feet anklets are useless, and bracelets without arms. Mothers are useless without sons, though covered with wealth. Sisters are useless without brothers, who wait beside the roads. Women are useless without husbands, be they spirits or fairies. I, Hir, am useless without Ranjha, though thousands of Kheras surround me. If Ranjha turns away his face I suffer in the midst of hell."

(Said Ranjha): "There is no good thing in the *reru* tree, and the bees roam around it thirsty. For twelve years you made me graze buffaloes and now you make promises! I left Takht Hazara of my fathers and my weeping parents. I left my dear brethren and my uncles. Ranjha, the swan of God, is wandering in the lanes, while Sida, the crow, is called to your side. There were days when you fed me with sugar and clarified butter and put no curds into my cup. Remember, too, the day when you yourself came into the forests. When you go in marriage to Sida, the Khera, with whom shall I dwell in solace!"

(Said Hir to Ranjha): "You are the lord of my head. Go and graze the same buffaloes; go and graze the same cows. Let me spend twelve months with the Kheras and in the thirteenth month I will come to you. Let me take an oath on the Quran: I shall not go back on my word." Leaving Hir Ranjha returned and played his flute among the Siyals. When Ranjha played his flute all the people collected, (and said): "Before, when you played (on your flute) you did deceive the foolish Hir, now you deceive no one. Why do you play the flute, boy? Better go back to Takht Hazara!"

Ranjha left the Siyals and took the road to Takht Hazara. Said Lali: "Come, my maids, let us go together to see the bride my brother-in-law has brought. She must have stayed at the well, too shy to enter the village: One-eyed and so slender, that she bends times! She finds fruit in the poisonous *ak* plant and plucks and eats it. The daughter of Chuchak and sister of Pathan, the Jatt maiden is brought here."

(Said Ranjha): "Lalo, Hir has been torn from me, why do you tease me? You thrust a spear of steel in my breast. Leaving Hir I have come back to live. I will become a follower of Gorakh Nath and return to Takht Hazara no more." "The glory of your eyes has entered the palace. Your lips are dates, and your teeth pomegranate seeds, and your speech sweetmeats. I have seen many proud men like you brought to ruin. If you regard Takht Hazara come or go back." "We should slay our pride and become saints and be called people of God. Sitting on the seat of patience should we not complain? Carats will never be rubies, though washed in seventy waters. The redness of the ruby will never depart, though rubbed in seventy ashes. The base will never be noble, though you try seventy plans. The cygnet will never be a crow, though it stands upon a dunghill. He who rides an Arab horse, will he admire your pony? When unrequited love is gone a *lakh* of rupees is gained."

It was the hour of early morn when Ranjha found the road to (Gorakh Nath's) Tilla. As he approached the Tilla its glory increased. The lions roared and he could not see the hill, nor spoke Ranjha when he called. The way was difficult and the road was steep and Ranjha walked with care. Asta and Masta, the mendicants, were sitting there, and Ranjha bowed his head to them. He offered them five rupees and betel leaves (and said): "I, the son of Mauju and grandson of Matta, have come to take sainthood. Bore my ears and put in the rings, so that my beauty may increase."

(Said they): "Have your parents scolded you? Is your living so hard, that you are standing by renunciants? Of 24,000 (departed) breaths you cannot recall one. If a merchant suffers loss that merchant weeps. If you become a disciple of Gorakh Nath you will lose the chiefdom of Takht Hazara." Gorakh sitting at his Tilla was very gracious.

(Said Ranjha): "Bore my ears and put in the rings and give me the deer-skin cloak. I will beg through the whole city for you and tend your fire and water. The other followers are here and there, I, Ranjha, will ever be your servant." (Said Gorakh): "There is gold and clarified butter in your house, and you enjoy at home the pleasures of the world. Gazing on strange women you are bringing misery on yourself. My son, when you have become a *faqir*, your face will not be as now. Hear the words of Gorakh, sainthood is a difficult thing."

"Hear, my Lord Gorakh, I have come from Takht Hazara. I am the son of Mauju and the grandson of Matta, think me no wanderer. Put the garment of sainthood round my neck and shave my head. With joined hands I pray and place my head at your feet." "The name of greatness brings blows, and sainthood is a difficult path. I live among the stones and potsherds: Is this the sainthood you want from me? If I bore your ears and put in the rings, drops of blood will fall. If I rub ashes into your black locks, I shall destroy your pride. Mothers cook and sons eat, but I have no cities and lands (to give you). I sleep on the ground and warm myself at the fire: I have no bed and covering."

Ranjha descended the Tilla and stole Gorakh Nath's conch. Escaping the eyes of the Nine Naths Ranjha went to the Chenab River. He buried the conch in the sand and made his seat above it. He put it in the care of Mother Earth and meditated on the Saint Kwaja (Khizar and said): "Do not give up this conch to any one, if a mendicant should come for it." Burying the conch Ranjha returned to Gorakh's fire. Said Gorakh: "My son, the plans of libertines and thieves withstand not, however wise they may be. The cooked food is becoming cold and the time for eating is passing away. Waiting with nine hundred bowls the helpless mendicants will die of hunger. Bring the conch here, my son, that they may eat their food."

"Calling me a thief and bad names! You have lost your sense! I am the head of Takht Hazara, think me no low man." Said Kanipa, the follower: "Hear, my Lord Gorakh, Ranjha, the Jatt, has stolen your couch: No one else has stolen it. The sand has eaten your conch, and cows and buffaloes rest upon it. He gave it to the care of Mother Earth and made the Saint Khwaja (Khizar) witness. You shall never recover your conch, for the Jatt has buried it deep. This Jatt is a wizard and will never give you your conch."

"I, Gorakh, am sitting on my Tilla; I, Gorakh, am a great magician. I can throw the twelve and move men (accordingly) and will win the game from you, Ranjha. If I use my strength against the seventy saints they will all fly hence and none will remain. I will strike the earth with my shoe and make her sink, and will dry up the waters of Khwaja (Khizar). If you desire good, then give up the conch, or I will use you as the Lord of Lanka. Listen to my words, Ranjha, for I tell you the truth."

Then, said Ranjha: "Gorakh, bring no false charges against me. I am the son of Mauju, the grandson of Matta, and lord of one hundred heads. If I make a jackal's call then all my brethren will come: And all your mendicants will fly hence and none remain! If you seek your good, Gorakh, go hence, or you will be thrust away. Bring the whole force of the world, and yet I will not give up the conch until I have sounded it."

On the right Ranjha sounded the conch, on the left he played the flute. There was no end to the music in the conch. Hearing the music the Mother Goddess came riding on her lion. Three quarters of a hundred followers of Macchandar Nath came together. Hearing the music Raja Adali came with his court. Hearing the music the followers of Gorakh Nath were happy and the saints were happy. Hearing the music Gorakh Nath was pleased and made ready to bore (Ranjha's) ears. Into Ranjha's right ear he put a *pakka* (baked) ring, and into his left ear he put a *kacha* (unbaked) one.

(Said Gorakh Nath to Ranjha): "My saint, call the young women 'sister' and the old women 'mother.' Beg throughout the whole city and bring no shame to my (profession of) begging." (Said Ranjha): "Have you lost your sense that you bore the ears of runaways and fugitives? Make whole my ears and take your rings, I will be no yogi. How shall I call her 'mother,' for whose sake I would be a mendicant? If I become a yogi my family will become disgraced." "Hear, Ranjha, I, the Lord Gorakh, speak to you: The thing you desire cannot be granted by a *faqir*. Go, Ranjha, Hir is granted to you on the authority of Mecca and Medina. Hir is yours and you Hir's, and don't look at another."

Ranjha took on sainthood, but did not forgot Hir. (Said he): "Sir Guru (Gorakh Nath), send your black crow to bring news of Hir." Said Gorakh to his crow: "Fly to the Kheras, where Ranjha's Hir is, and bring news of her." The crow flew from the Tilla and entered Khera. He looked into every house, but found not Hir. The crow went to the house of Sida, and called out Ranjha's name (and said): "Ranjha has sent me, O Hir, and I have come to you. If you are still faithful, then come with me. He has become a yogi and is ever calling your name."

"Come, friendly crow, come to me (said Hir): I make a hundred salutations to you, you servant of Ranjha. I will make you cakes of fine sugar and mix butter in your food. If you bring Ranjha to me this shall be your food." "I say the truth to you and I tell no lies. Ranjha has been dead there for three days and his grave is on (Gorakh Nath's) Tilla. I and Ranjha were disciples together, the brother-followers of one Nath. You are his wife and my sister-in-law." When Hir heard these words she could keep no patience (and said): "Fly hence, you black crow! For if Ranjha is dead, then I will stab myself with a dagger."

"It was not true, O Hir, what I said to you just now. Ranjha has become a yogi and rubbed ashes on his body. Gorakh has been pleased with Ranjha and given you to him. Let me fly hence with a message for Ranjha." "Fly, O friendly crow, fly, O black crow. My first message is for my mother Tuli that bore me in her womb. My second message is for my father Chuchak, from whose head I was born. My third message is for the village elders, that gave me in marriage to Ranjha. My fourth message is for Fatti, the barber's wife, who used to dress my hair so well. My fifth message is for Fatta, the Qazi, who taught me in the mosque. A message from me is for the spreading tree, beneath which I was married. A message from me is for the sweet *pipal* tree, where I used to swing in the rains. A message from me is for Ludan the boatman, who spread my bed in his boat. Give all my messages to my lover Ranjha, whose Hir I call myself."

The crow flew away from Khera and came to Gorakh's Tilla. It sat down beside Ranjha and told him the entire story of Hir (saying): "Hir has become a dry reed, I have seen her with my own eyes. Go quickly, Ranjha, to Khera," said the crow to Ranjha. Ranjha came down from the Tilla sounding his conch. Stage by stage he came and entered the Khera's garden. It was early morn when Ranjha went to the Kheras to beg alms. Ranjha made cakes and put them in his wallet. And when the village children collected, he distributed the alms among them. Ranjha called *alakh* (formless god) before the door of Bhuga, the Khera Jatt. And sounding his conch he demanded alms of Bhuga. The young calves tore at their ropes and the cows lowed. They overset the milk-pails and spoiled all the milk. Said the Kheras: "What is this disturbance? From where has this wizard yogi come?" Ranjha entered the home of Hir's father-in-law, sorrowing like a hungry falcon. Hir was sitting before him on a painted couch, and throwing down his wallet he became frantic.

When Ranjha sounded his conch Siti brought him some millet as alms (and said): "Where do you come from, yogi? And what is your story? Take your alms and go; why create a disturbance? This is Sida's house: why have you come?" (Said Ranjha): "A yogi comes from Gorakh's Tilla, and a comely yogi too! Coming to Khera he calls out 'alakh' and sits at Sida's threshold. No (wheat) flour is given to him in alms, but what is given to the Nath is millet! Were it (wheat) flour the saint could cook it: your millet, Siti, will not even parch in an oven." "What is born will die, what is made will be broken: man is a creature of God. Merchants are robbed of their wealth and goods: why are you grieving over a broken bowl? If you want an earthen bowl, go to some potter's house. If you want a wooden bowl, go to some carpenter. If you want a bowl of silver or gold, go to some great merchant. I will get you a bowl made and fill it, Nath, with wheat and millet. This house belongs to no low man, but to the Lord Sida. When Sida comes you will be frightened and then where will you find Hir."

When Hir looked toward Ranjha she got up and sat down, and was rest-less: When lover meets beloved the flesh grows moist and (then) dry. Then Hir and Siti made a plan for (Hir's) meeting with Ranjha. (Hir) cut a finger of her right hand (and said) a snake had bitten it. (Said Hir to Siti): "O sister, I have seen a yogi, a yogi beyond belief. A yogi can make the dried forest green and make leaves bloom on every branch. He has come to the Khera's house and called 'alakh;' why send him away empty-handed? Make the yogi a dweller in Khera, or, Siti, I shall run away." (Said Siti): "O Kheras, a snake has bitten Hir, a young snake has bitten her. A finger long it was and of golden hue, and it has put her in sore trouble. It has bitten the little finger of her right hand and the poison is strong. There is a wise yogi on the hill that knows about serpents."

Sida went to the yogi and Siti went with him. Said Sida with joined hands: "Listen my revered yogi, they call me chief of the twenty-one Khera (clans) and there is no lack of wealth in my house. In the night a snake bit (my wife) Hir and she will not be saved." "I tell you the truth. I cannot go there. I cannot leave my seat without losing my virtue. If you are in great trouble bring her to me. Even if she is dead of the snake-bite I myself will give her breath." Siti and Ranjha together made a plan. Sida sitting beside them had no knowledge of it. (Ranjha) took some ashes from his fire and poured them into Siti's hand (and said): "Give her the incense of my smoke and God will make her well."

Siti went back and sat beside Hir. And did all that the yogi had said. Hir then fell into great trouble and cried out with a loud voice: "If you do not want me to die in an hour take me to the yogi." They put her into a litter and bearers carried her. The yogi charmed her with his (fire) tongs and took out the poison. The separated met and the lover met his lass. (For) God preserves the honor of lovers and thieves! The yogi came down from the hill and went with Sida. And going to Sida's house took up his abode in the upper story. Giving the people herbs and medicines he cured (those possessed of) goblins and sprites.

When many days had passed (Ranjha) made a plan to carry off Hir. Then said Siti: "I tell you the truth. As you two love, so do I love Murad. If you take off Hir alone, I will demand redress. I adjure you in the name of Gorakh Nath to bring me to my love." Ranjha sounded his conch and meditated on Gorakh. The sound of the conch reached to Mecca and Murad, the Baloch, had a dream (that) his love remembered him and that he should go quickly to Siti. As Punnun went to Sassi, so Murad went to Siti. It was on a Sunday night in June that Ranjha carried off Hir. He took Hir off into the wilds and the Kheras knew nothing of it. Nor Siti knew, but she followed them and caught them up on the road home (and said): "I adjure you by Gorakh Nath leave me with Murad." Ranjha called Murad, who came in the twinkling of an eye. He mounted Siti on a camel and waded across the Chinab.

Afterward Chhatti gave news to the Kheras, (saying): "Ranjha has carried off your Hir and Murad has taken Siti." When they entered the palace and did not find Hir, they saddled their mares, (and said): "Come, let us slay the yogi that has disgraced the family." (Said they): "Hear, O servant, drinker of skimmed milk, you have no sense. You wander about eating stale bread, wandering in the wilds. You herdsman of young buffaloes, you have stolen Hir of the Kheras. The Siyals whose buffaloes you graze are after you." The five hundred bay and gray mares of Sida raise the dust along the path of the Kheras!

(Said Hir to Ranjha): "I have not ascended the dark mountain, nor crossed the Chenab River; nor have I seen Gorakh Nath's Tilla, nor reached Takht Hazara; nor have I seen the beautiful city of Raja Adali, where he sits in his court. Let us give Raja Adali a bribe and save both our lives. They will slay you and take me away bound, and we shall both die together."

The Kheras came up and caught Ranjha, for one man's power is to no avail. Said one: "Let Hir and Ranjha go; Hir is of no use to us." Said another: "Let us go to Raja Adali: do not release them here." They bound Ranjha and took him to Raja Adali, while he meditated on Gorakh (Nath). Said Raja Adali to the Kheras: "What is this quarrel? Has he stolen your mares, or money?"

"We say to you the truth, O Adali: Kalua and Tulsia set out from the Siyals and came to Rangpur of the Kheras. Before the whole assembly they sat Sida the Khera and put sweets into his mouth. Making a marriage procession Sida went to the Siyals and there found that Ranjha was Chuchak's herder. Fattu, the Qazi, performed the ceremony and Hir was married according to the law. A *lakh* of rupees was given to the Siyals and money was scattered in the forests. The drum was placed on Ranjha's head and he played it in every village. When Ranjha reached Rangpur of the Kheras beautifully and ravishingly he played the flute. Hearing the flute the city collected and all the people came to see. The married girls would not go to their husbands and maidens would not wed. So we thrust Ranjha away and he went to Gorakh (Nath's) Tilla. There he stole the saint's conch and (obliged him to) put the ring in his ears. The (new) yogi went to Dhaka and Bengal and studied and learned the ways of holiness. Returning later he came to Rangpur Khera and made his (yogi's) fire in the garden. He made the dried up garden green and brought leaves to every branch. During the eight watches of the night, the Jatt went a-begging and called out 'alakh' at the Khera's houses. Passing over ten houses he begged at two, wandering and begging like a thief. The simple Siti did wrong in giving millet as alms to Ranjha. So that he let drop his begging bowl and took a firm seat in the courtyard: And picked up the millet with his nails, praising (the virtues of) patience, (saying): 'Never leave the scattered corn; thus did Gorakh teach me.' He could take the stings from snakes and scorpions, and called Hir to Siti in the garden. The wily yogi carried off Hir and no one knows what has happened to Siti. If you desire your good, O Adali, you should hang him, since he should not to live."

In the midst of the court Adali said to Ranjha: "If you want service take a rupee a day; take as far as two (rupees). If you want to marry take slaves and maids; you cannot keep Hir. If you want buffaloes, take half (nine); you cannot take them all. If you want servants, take mine to tend the buffaloes of your house. If you want your good, leave the court, lest you be thrust out." Then spoke Ranjha and said to Adali: "I am son of Mauju and grandson of Matta and lord of a *lakh* of heads. I have a greater empire than you; think me no mere wanderer. If you would give me service pay me with the ruby of seven kings; I have no need for rupees. If you would give me buffaloes give me all and leave none. Give slave girls and maids to some poor man; slave-girls are of no use to me. If you would wed me among the Kheras, give me Siti and Chatti. First of all give me your own daughter Niwazan, to put into my wallet. For the sake of God and Muhammad the Prophet give Hir to me, the wearer of the blanket; spoil not the match between us. If you take Hir from me, you will be ruined and disgraced."

Kaidu called out in the Court: "I speak the truth. We were three brothers in our father's house: three own brothers. Chiefship was written in Chuchak's fate, and lordship in Mihru's: In my, Kaidu's, fate was written sainthood: it was the writing of God. Since this servant (Ranjha) came to the Siyals 360 maidens have refused to marry. If you want your good (O Adali) hang him; he is not fit to live."

Said Raja Adali to Chuchak: "Tell me the truth. Show me to whom you have given Hir; tell me no lies." In the court said Chuchak: "I tell no lies. Before seventy Khans and seventy-two nobles I gave Hir to Ranjha. Ranjha grazed my buffaloes for twelve years and took no pay at all from me. My brethren thrust him away, and seizing Hir married her to the Kheras. If there be a lie in this ask Hir: she is in your court. If there be a lie in this may I be punished in the Court (of God)."

Without a veil and on foot came Hir into the court. (Said she): "Kings and queens have suffered ill: I too am fallen into trouble. First trouble fell upon Ram Chandar, whose Sita the ten-headed (Ravana) stole. Then the ten-headed came to trouble, whose golden Lanka was stolen. Afterward trouble fell upon Mansur, for whom God allowed gallows to be erected. And then trouble fell upon Shams Tabrez, whose skin was flayed. Now has trouble come upon Hir, O Adali, that she should come into your court. Taking bribes you side with the Kheras, and my uncared-for herder is all alone! For wealth you side with Sida; to collect coins to put into your treasury! Sida clings to me like a stray thorn, like ink to clean paper. Ranjha is a rose flower to me: I am to him as a waterfowl on the water. My wings are wet and I cannot fly: I am not ashamed of my love! As Niwazan is a daughter to you, O Adali, so am I daughter to Mihar Chuchak. I am Ranjha's by right, give me to him, and spoil not the match."

When Adali heard these words he called Hir and sat her beside him. When Adali saw Hir's face he lost his wits and wisdom. He sent Hir to his own palace and put away the Kheras. Said Adali to Ranjha: "You too are a liar: Hir was first of all betrothed to *me!*"

Raja Adali committed sin and had Hir's bed placed on the upper story. When it was evening, Adali came to Hir's bed. (Said she): "O Raja Adali, you did no justice, and blemish your face for money! May rot destroy your walls, O Adali, and fire your gates. May you die, O Adali, and your queens moan for you, and the Qazi perform your funeral service. May your city become a heap of bricks and may iron harrows be dragged over it. Better fill your brick reservoirs, for they will be of service to you. Know me for a (true) disciple of Gorakh, when my words do not fail."

It was the hour of dusk when Adali came to Hir. Raja Adali did no justice when he put his foot on Hir's bed. When Adali lifted his foot Hir thought of God. Fire seized Adali's body and he threw water over it. Horses and ponies began to die; Hir and Ranjha performed this miracle! When Hir summoned him, Gorakh came (to help).

Raja Adali committed sin and seizing Hir took her into the upper-chamber. He thrust Ranjha from the court; the beautiful herder went away weeping. He lighted a (sacred) fire in the garden and played on his beautiful and ravishing flute. The sound of the flute reached to Mecca and a company of seventy saints came up. The sound of the flute reached to Multan and the Five Saints came in majesty. The sound of the flute brought the Mother Goddess (Durga), on her lion to Ranjha. At the sound of the flute came (Sakhi) Sarwar the Warrior, riding on (his mare) Kakki. At the sound of the flute came Hanuman, the leader, with his army. The army cut down the garden of Adali and left not a tree remaining.

All the saints collected and asked Ranjha: "Say truly, you youth, what evil has befallen you? Tell us the truth." Said Ranjha: " Before you all Adali has seized Hir and taken her to the upper-chamber." They took burning logs and set fire to Adali's city. Burning went Adali into the reservoirs and water was thrown over the people. And when the water reached the fire it blazed forth twofold!

Said his Minister to Raja Adali: "Ranjha has used his power. If you want to be saved give up Hir to the youth Ranjha." When he heard this Adali called Hir to him. When Hir approached Adali God himself cooled him. Messengers ran to search out Ranjha, but nowhere could they find him. Searching they found him in the garden beside a beautiful fire. (Said they): "Come, Sir Nath, Adali calls you and by him sits the daughter of the Siyals." Said Ranjha: "A curse upon your Raja Adali! What do I know of the daughter of the Siyals!"

(Said the messenger): "He comes not, O bribe-taking Adali, you should go to him." On his bare feet went Adali to Ranjha, (and said): "O Ranjha, you have shown me the miraculous power that is in you. With such miraculous power in you, why did you give up the rule of Takht Hazara? With such miraculous power in you, why did you tend the fire of Gorakh? With such miraculous power in you, why were you Chuchak's herder? I will marry you to Hir!" Then thus spoke Adali: "If you doubt this in your mind, O Ranjha, I will make Hir my daughter by law."

When Adali spoke thus to Ranjha, Ranjha went to the court, (and said): "Live forever, O Raja Adali, you have preserved my honor and my rights!" When Ranjha sounded his conch, Indra caused rain to fall; and all the people in Adali's city lived in happiness. Ranjha and Hir came together, for God favored them. Raja Adali did justice and turned away his face from bribes. (Said the people): "May sandalwood cleave to your walls and a sweet scent to your gates!"

Raja Adali held his court and prepared for Hir's marriage. The entire city and its dependents collected together. (Said Adali): "I give Hir to Ranjha; she is now my granddaughter! Behold, if anyone speaks evil of Hir, his whole city shall be buried!"

First Chuchak gave Hir to Ranjha and now Adali properly married her (to him). Ranjha took Hir and left on the road to Mecca. Ranjha of Takht Hazara and Hir of Jhang Siyal were helped in their love by the Five Saints. Ludan, the boatman, made this lay with much ability. The Jatt sings it to the drum and fiddle, and the *faqir* begs from door to door.

- Adapted from Richard Carnac Temple, trans., *The Legends of the Panjab,* Vol. 2 (Islamabad, Pakistan: Institute of Folk Heritage, 1981), pp. 507–80.

Commentary

This well-known *qiṣṣa* (enchanted romance) is one of the most popular stories of both the Hindus and Muslims of the Punjab, a fertile area straddling an eastern portion of Pakistan and a western portion of India. Originating in the Punjabi oral tradition, it became part of the literary tradition after Damodar Ghulhati (né Namodar Patwari) of the Jhang region first recorded it. He is believed to have lived during the reign of the Mughal Emperor Akbar, who ruled from 1556 to 1605. The Punjabi poet Waris Shah memorialized the love story in a poetic version around 1766. Today, numerous versions exist in Persian, Punjabi, Hindi, and Urdu, and it has been the subject of a number of films and comic books. It is often referred to as the Punjabi *Romeo and Juliet,* in which Hir is the daughter of the Siyal chief of Jhang who was betrothed to the son of the Khera chief of Rangpur. Ranjha, the youngest of eight siblings, was the son of Mauju, a nickname for Muizuddin, a Jatt chief of Takht Hazara in the Gujranwala district. Ranjha is disinherited and begins an itinerant life until he meets Hir, who falls in love with him at first sight. Because the Jatts are of lower caste than the Siyals, he is sent away and she is quickly married off. In Damodar's version, which is what the above oral version follows, the couple live happily ever after, but in Waris Shah's version, Ranjha returns to his natal village to reclaim his inheritance and prepare for the wedding. Hir's uncle Kaidu then tells her that Ranjha has died, after which she collapses and faints. The uncle then poisons her, and she is buried. When Ranjha receives the tragic news he returns to Jhang. Upon seeing her grave, he drops dead.

The narrative is interesting for a number of reasons, not the least of which is its syncretistic nature, where Hindu and Muslim identities are fluid, and where both Hindu ascetics and gods as well as Muslim saints play significant roles in shaping destiny. The narrative represents the religiously pluralistic nature of Indian society prior to the partition of the subcontinent on the eve of independence, after which a greater polarization of religious identities occurred. The fluidity of religious identities was especially pronounced on the two peripheries of the subcontinent (i.e., Punjab and Bengal), where the worship of the five saints *(pãc pīr)* of the narrative still continues. The syncretic nature of the borderlands is apparent also in the following narrative from neighboring Sind province.

SAINT'S HAGIOGRAPHY

Jhulelal, Lal Sai, Uderolal, Varun Dev, Doolhalal, and Zinda Pir Are One (Sind, Pakistan)

During the days of *Sapt-Sindhu* (land of seven rivers), the mainstream Sindhu and its tributaries were considered life-givers to the people who lived on its banks and drew sustenance from its waters. It was precisely the lure of plentiful water that brought invading hordes of Muslim rulers from neighboring kingdoms to Sind. Having conquered Sind and its adjoining territories, they spread Islam. In the 10th century C.E. Sind came under the rule of the Samras. The Samras, being converts from Hinduism to Islam, were neither bigots nor fanatics. However, there was an exception in the Samra region. Being far away from its capital, Thatta maintained its separate identity and influence. Its ruler Mirkshah was not only a tyrant but also a religious extremist. And as in the wont of many a tyrant, Mirkshah was surrounded by sycophants also. These friends advised him one day: "Spread Islam and you will be granted *janat* or eternal bliss after death."

Swayed by the promise, Mirkshah summoned the *panch*s (representatives) of the Hindus and ordered them: "Embrace Islam or prepare to die." The terrified Hindus begged Mirkshah for time to consider the *shahi firman,* or royal edict. The zealous Mirkshah relented and agreed to give the desperate Hindus forty days to plead with their God.

Faced with imminent death, the Hindus turned to Varuna, the god of the river, to come to their aid. For forty days, they underwent penance. They neither shaved nor wore new clothes, praying and fasting and singing songs in the praise of Varuna. They beseeched him to deliver them from the hands of their persecutor.

On the fortieth day, a voice was heard from heaven: "Fear not, I shall save you from the wicked Mirkshah. I shall come down as a mortal and take birth in the womb of Mata Devki in the house of Ratanchand Lohano of Nasarpur." After forty days of *chaliho,* the followers of Jhulelal even today celebrate the occasion with festivity as Thanksgiving Day.

The oppressed Hindus now anxiously awaited the birth of their deliverer. After three months, on the second *tithi* (day) of Asu month, they got confirmation of the news that Mata Devki had indeed conceived. The river god had incarnated himself in her womb. The Hindus rejoiced and praised the Lord.

On Cheti Chand, two *tithi*s from the new moon of Chaitra, Mata Devki gave birth to a bony boy. A miracle hailed the child's birth. The babe opened his mouth and behold, there flowed the Sindhu with an old man sitting cross-legged on a *pala* fish. The *pala* fish as everyone knows is a tasty fish that always swims against the current.

To welcome the newborn *avatar*, out of season clouds gathered and brought down torrential rains. The child was named Udaichand. Udaichand was to be the light in the darkness. An astrologer who saw the child predicted that he would grow up to be a great warrior and his fame would outlive the child. Udaichand was also called Uderolal, the "one who has sprung from water." Inhabitants of Nasarpur lovingly called the child Amarlal, the "immortal child." The cradle where little Uderolal rested began to sway back and forth on its own. It is because of this that Uderolal became popularly known as Jhulelal or the "swinging child." Soon after the child's birth Mata Devki passed away. A little later Ratanchand remarried.

News of the birth of the mysterious child reached Mirkshah who once again summoned the *panch*s and repeated his royal threat. Hindus, now quite confident that their savior had arrived, implored him for some more time informing him that their savior was none other than the water deity himself. Mirkshah scoffed at the very idea of a child saving the Hindus. "Neither am I going to die nor are you, people are going to leave this land alive," he jeered. "I shall wait. When your savior embraces Islam, I am sure you will also follow suit." With this remark, the haughty Mirkshah threw a challenge to his Hindu subjects.

The *maulvi*s (clerics) pressed Mirkshah hard not to let the Hindus off the hook. But the very thought of the child proving more than a match for him amused the conceited ruler. He therefore told the *maulvi*s to wait and watch. As a token precaution, he asked one of his ministers, Ahirio, to go to Nasarpur to see things first hand. Ahirio did not want to take any chances, so he took along a rose dipped in deadly poison.

At the very first glimpse of the child, Ahirio was astonished. He had never seen a child so dazzling or more charming. He hesitated, then mustering courage offered the rose to the child. The child gave a meaningful smile while accepting the rose. He then blew away the flower with a single breath. The flower fell at Ahirio's feet. Ahirio watched stupefied as the babe changed into an old man with a long beard. All of a sudden the old man turned into a lad of sixteen. And then he saw Uderolal on horseback with a blazing sword in his hand. There was row upon row of warriors behind him. A cold shiver ran down Ahirio's spine and he bowed his head in reverence. "Have mercy on me Sindhu Lord," he prayed, "I am convinced."

On his return Ahirio narrated the miraculous happening to Mirkshah. But Mirkshah was not convinced. He hardened his heart even more. "How can a little baby turn into an old man?" he mocked. "It looks like you have been fooled by simple magic." But in his heart, Mirkshah was afraid. That night he dreamt a dreadful dream. A child was sitting on his neck. The vision changed to an old man with a flowing beard and again to a warrior with a drawn sword confronting Mirkshah on the battlefield. The next morning Mirkshah called for Ahirio and gave him orders to counter the threat posed by the child. Ahirio, however, advised Mirkshah not to rush matters.

Meanwhile, the child Uderolal grew in stature and spirit performing miracles and comforting the sick. Residents of Nasarpur were fully convinced that God had come to save them. Uderolal also received the *guru mantra* of Alakh Niranjan from Goraknath.

To earn money for the family, Udero's stepmother would send him to the market to sell baked beans. Instead of going to the market, Uderolal would go to the banks of the Sindhu. There he would distribute half of the beans among beggars, the poor, and the *sadhus* (mendicants). The other half, he would offer to the Sindhu. He would then spend the rest of the day speaking to little children and the elderly about spiritual wealth. In the evening when it was time to go home, Udero would fish out from the river a container full of fine quality rice. This he would take home and give to his stepmother.

Growing suspicious about her stepson's behavior, the stepmother one day dispatched Ratanchand to follow him. When Ratanchand witnessed the miracle, he bowed to Uderolal from a distance and accepted him as the Savior.

Mirkshah on the other hand was being pressured by the *maulvis* to bring Hindu infidels into the fold of Islam. They gave him the ultimatum. "Order the Hindus to convert or be branded as associate of *kafirs* [infidels]." Fearing the wrath of the clerics, Mirkshah decided to meet Uderolal face to face. He asked Ahirio to arrange for a private meeting with Udero.

Ahirio who had in the meantime become a devotee of Daryashah, went to the banks of the Indus and pleaded with the water deity to come to his rescue. To Ahirio's amazement, he saw the same old man with a white beard floating on a *pala* fish. Ahirio's head bowed in adoration and he understood that Uderolal, the water god, was in fact the other form of Khwaja Khirz. Ahirio then saw Udero leap onto a horse and gallop away with a sword in one hand and a flag in the other.

Udero appeared before Mirkshah and explained to the stubborn ruler: "Whatever you see around you is the creation of only one God, whom you call Allah and the Hindus call Ishwar." The *maulvis* urged Mirkshah not to pay any heed to the infidels' talks and to arrest him. Mirkshah, dithering as usual, ordered his soldiers to arrest Udero.

As the officials of the court moved towards Udero, great waves of water leaped forth inundating the courtyard and crowning Mirkshah and his courtiers. Fire too broke out and flames consumed the palace. All escape routes were sealed. Udero spoke again, "Mirkshah, think it over. Your God and mine are the same. Then why did you persecute my people?"

Mirkshah was terrified and begged Udero, "My Lord, I realize my foolhardiness. Please save me and my courtiers." All at once the water receded and the fire died away. Mirkshah bowed respectfully and agreed to treat Hindus and Muslims alike. Before they dispersed, Uderolal told the Hindus to think of him as the embodiment of light and water. He also told them to build a temple in memory of the transformation of Mirkshah. "Day in and out," he said, "light a candle in the temple and always keep available water for *daat,* a holy sip."

Uderolal named his cousin, Pagad, as the first *thakur,* the priest of the religious sect that believes in the water god. Pagad followed Uderolal wherever he went. Uderolal gave seven symbolic things to Pagad. These seven form the essential elements of the Daryahi sect. Uderolal asked Pagad to continue the sacred work of building temples and spread the message.

Selecting a place near the village of Thijahar, Uderolal gave up his earthly form. Both Hindus and Muslims were present in large number to witness this mysterious happening. Mirkshah's representatives were also there. No sooner had Uderolal's soul left his body, than they took charge and wanted to build a *turbat* (grave shrine) at the site according to the dictates of Islam. The Hindus wanted to erect a *samadhi* (saint burial site) according to Hindu custom. While the debate continued, heavy rains came down, and a voice said: "Behold! You shall make my shrine acceptable both to Hindus and Muslims. Let its one face be a temple and the other a *dargah* [saint shrine]. I belong to all of you."

- Satnam Sakhi and Khavo Makhan Makhi, *Virtual Bera Paar,* "Story of Jhulelal," 2003, http://mysite.verizon.net/satnamsakhi/jhulelal/story.html

Commentary

Numerous legends of this sort, in which a local charismatic figure bridges the gap between Hindus and Muslims by establishing mutual faith, circulate throughout South Asia. In this case, faith has established Jhulelal as the community deity of the Sindhis, an ethnic group straddling both sides of the border between Pakistan and India. His birth date is auspiciously celebrated the world over in the Sindhi diaspora. The legend of Jhulelal has its origins in Sind, which was once a part of the Indus Valley Civilization, later a province of India during colonial times, and now a state of Pakistan, where he is known as Zinda Pir, the living saint. There are numerous Zinda Pirs throughout the subcontinent, and they refer to charismatic Sufi saints who were revered after their death by both Muslims and Hindus. This version of the legend is Hindu in nature, but one also hears the same story from a Muslim perspective. The point, however, is the same: that Hindus and Muslims worship the same God, which is a common theme among the many devotional communities that emerged in medieval north India as a result of a confluence of Sufism and popular Hindu religion among the lower castes.

ETHNIC STEREOTYPE ANECDOTE

Kacharis and Assamese Don't Go Together (Assam, India)

A Kachari man married an Assamese girl and he was given food in his mother-in-law's house. His hospitable mother-in-law asked him to eat what in his language meant "tie me." So he bound her hands and feet. Then she laughed, seeing that he supposed her to be speaking Kachari. So he told her in Kachari, but this time it also meant "go away" in Assamese, and he left the place.

- Recounted from James D. Anderson, *A Collection of Kachári Folk-Tales and Rhymes* (Shillong, India: Assam Secretariat Printing Press, 1895), pp. 1–3.

Commentary

Stereotypical jokes about ethnic groups living most closely to the joke-telling community are quite common throughout the world. This one, from Assam in northeastern India, not only puns on bilingualism but targets the Assamese "other," people of tribal origin, in this case the Kachari people. In upper Assam, for example, jokes about the Mising (Miri) and Naga tribes are most prevalent, while in lower Assam, Kachari (Boro) jokes are most common. However, in urban areas in which people from throughout the state reside, all varieties are common. Such jokes are part of a discourse of exclusion, in which the distinction between tribe and caste is reinforced, even though the political push is to dissolve the division in areas where there are large tribal populations. Such ethnic jokes inevitably target the tribal person as inferior to, thereby not as smart as, the caste person. Not only do they point at exclusion but also subordination. However, it is important to keep in mind that the subordinate groups also have their own jokes about caste, as implied in the earlier Santali caste tale above.

In his preface to the volume from which this anecdote is taken, Anderson states that Assamese and Kachari languages share a close affinity. Kachari adopts Assamese grammar and syntax but retains vocabulary, making such bilingual puns all the more inevitable. In a multilingual environment such puns are commonplace, and an example of a bilingual joke is also included at the end of this chapter.

PERSONAL EXPERIENCE NARRATIVE

My Encounter with a Big Bear (Robin Adair, British Officer in Colonial India)

"When I was in the Santal Parganas, I got news from a local planter who lived fairly far out. This chap was another indigo planter who, like many British people out in that part of India, had settled down to do *zamindari* work—the equivalent of a farmer. They had large tracts of land that they used to cultivate. There was a bear worrying villagers. This particular one had come in from the outlying area and I think several children had been mauled by the bear and the villagers were most anxious that something should be done about it. So he contacted me as Deputy Commissioner to see if I could arrange anything. So I went out there—this was a place very much out in the wilds really, very poor roads to get to it. I had a jeep in those days so that I was able to cope with pretty rough tracks. So I got out there in my jeep and I stayed the night with this chap. He had a very nice bungalow out there. The next morning we got the local Subinspector of police to come round with a couple of large bore guns. I had my own rifle, of course, and this chap also had a gun.

"So we set out in a party to try to round up the bear. The villagers knew where it was roughly. It had got into a small patch of jungle not far from the village, very thick, scrubby jungle on a fairly steep sloping hillside with a bit of fairly clear ground around. They said the bear was definitely in this bit of jungle. So we tried to scare it out with noises, beating the bushes with *lathis* [bamboo staffs], but to no avail. Eventually, we sort of surrounded this clump of jungle, getting closer and closer in. I saw what looked like a sort of dark patch. It was obviously the bear, but I couldn't make out which part of the bear it was. I thought, well, we've got to flush him out somehow, so I gave him a shot and he came roaring out. Instead of running away as one would have expected, he charged me, came straight at me.

"It was quite a frightening sight, actually. Pretty big creatures these bears. They stand, I suppose, over six feet high; they run on their hind legs waving their front paws; the paws have claws as long as one's fingers, razor-sharp claws. They slash at you with these claws, which is their method of attacking. I suppose he'd been wounded only fairly slightly; it hadn't impaired his action at all. He was clearly annoyed and he came out roaring with these big, slavering jaws and long teeth. It was quite a frightening sight. Very fortunately I had another barrel and I gave him a second shot and this knocked him down—didn't kill him but knocked him down and he rolled over down the hill and then we were able to close in and give him a final quietus. It was quite an exciting experience. I had been particularly invited in by the villagers to cope with this local menace."

- Rosan A. Jordan and Frank de Caro, eds., *British Voices from South Asia* (Baton Rouge: Louisiana State University Libraries, Special Collections, 1996), p. 9.

Commentary

One overlooked genre of folklore that has recently drawn much attention is the personal-experience narrative, an artful story told in the first person about some event that had a lasting effect on the storyteller. Sometimes the stories are embellished to create a more dramatic sense, allowing the narrator to construct his or her own past in a way that is meaningful from a personal perspective on how one wishes to be remembered in the future.

British folklore has been virtually ignored in South Asian folklore studies, except for South Asians recounting the cruelty and oppression of the British soldiers, such as the memorate included above. Here we get a unique example of a British soldier speaking for himself about "the good old days" of empire building. Many British soldiers and civil servants wax poetically and romantically about their experiences in colonial India. Often they paint themselves in the role of liberators or fixers of problems, as if Indians could not rule themselves or manage their own affairs without British colonial intervention. For the most part, many of the British in colonial India were seeking either adventure or fortune, or both. Many would serve their term of duty then retire in England, but some expatriates remain in South Asia today, residing in the Himalayan hill stations built by the British to escape the scorching heat of the plains during the dry summer months before the monsoon. Places such as Dehra Dun and Darjeeling still attract many tourists, both Indian and foreign, but the generation of British expatriates is quickly coming to an end. It is thus important for folklorists to document the oral history of the British raj while time still remains to record the words of those who experienced that significant but turbulent period of time first hand.

JUMBLE

Dog, Pudding, Spinning Wheel, Drum (Amir Khusrau [1255–1324], Urdu Poet)

Baked the pudding by burning the wood of the spinning wheel. A dog came and ate the pudding. Now you have nothing to do, but beat the drum.

- K. M. George, ed., *Comparative Indian Literature,* Vol. 1 (Madras, India: Macmillan India, 1984), p. 145.

Commentary

This genre is known as *anmīl* in Urdu, a statement composed out of incongruous elements. It pits the wits of a poet against the perplexing jumble of words presented by audience members. In this celebrated example, attributed to the thirteenth-to-fourteenth-century folk poet Amir Khusrau, four persons suggest four unrelated words that the poet must combine to create a coherent line of thought.

RIDDLE

Snakes and Coconuts (Punjab, India)

See a farmer eating sugar with snakes.
Answer: vermicelli

He lives at the treetop but is not a bird;
He has three eyes but is not Shiva;
He gives milk but is not a cow;
He has hair but is not a Sadhu [mendicant];
He is full of water but is not a pitcher.

Answer: coconut

- K. M. George, ed., *Comparative Indian Literature,* Vol. 1 (Madras, India: Macmillan India,1984), p. 116.

Commentary

In an influential article, Georges and Dundes (1963) defined riddle as "a traditional verbal expression that includes one or more descriptive elements, a pair of which may be in opposition; the referent of the elements is to be guessed." Riddles can be as simple as one sentence, such as the first item included above, or more complex, such as the second item, which provides an entire list of descriptive elements that seemingly have nothing to do with one another. Yet in both examples above, all the descriptive elements clearly refer to the answer. Vermicelli, eaten sweet, resembles baby snakes, while all the descriptions given in the second riddle characterize a coconut. Riddles can also take the form of a story, as in the example that follows.

RIDDLE STORY

Did You See My Pack-Saddled Ox? (Karnataka, India)

The one like myself went in search of his eloped wife. He met, on the way, a person digging for water on the tree, while having it on the land itself. The one like myself asked him "You wise man, dipping for water on the tree having it on the land itself, did you see my pack-saddled ox?" (i)

He answered, "Sorry, I don't know. On the road there is a girl, sitting cross-legged, shaking the heads and sprinkling the water, go and ask her." "O, clever lass, sitting cross-legged, shaking the heads and sprinkling the water, did you see my pack-saddled ox?" (ii)

"Sorry Sir, I too don't know," she said, "by the brook side there is one standing on the dry tree and cutting the green one, go and ask him." He went to him and asked "You, wise man, who cutting the green tree standing on the dry one, did you see my pack-saddled ox?" (iii)

"I too don't know, Sir," he replied, "there comes a pious lady who comes beating time with her feet, has an anus on the head, and hand upon the mouth, go and ask her." He went to her and asked "O, pious woman, who beats time with your feet, an anus on the head, and hand on the mouth, did you see my pack-saddled ox?" (iv)

I too don't know brother. There are two crooked banyan trees upon which is a pot of rice, upon that pot is a copper vessel. Ask the calf grazing in the pasture of the copper vessel," thus said that lady. He went and asked "O, the crooked banyan trees, the pot of rice on it, the copper vessel on the pot, and the calf grazing in the pasture of the vessel, did you see my pack-saddled ox?" (v)

Then the calf said, "I saw in the pulse market, the ox was lying and chewing the packs." (vi)

Answers:

(i)   The toddy-tapper in his occupation

(ii) A girl sprinkling water on betel leaves

(iii) A man standing on a ladder collecting betel leaves

(iv) A woman with toe-rings carrying water in a pot; anus on head = the mouth of the pot; hand on mouth = hand on the rim/lip of the pot

(v)   An old man minding a farm: crooked banyan trees = his two legs; rice = his pot-belly; copper vessel = his head; pasture = the few hairs on his head; calf = louse in his hair

(vi) Eating out of the lap of the lover

- Adapted from M.N.V. Panditaradhya, *On Riddles: A Definition and Analysis* (Mysore, India: Prabodha Publications, 1975), pp. 32–35.

Commentary

In Kannada, the major language spoken in Karnataka, different riddles can be grouped together to create a story. Although each riddle might have its own individual existence, when grouped together, they build up a combined effect that often ends with a witty or risky conclusion, here a couple engaged in flirtatious acts. Riddles may also take the form of rhymes, such as the following piece of metafolklore.

METAFOLKLORE

Folktale, Folktale, Riddle, Riddle (Santal Parganas, Bihar, India)

Folktale folktale, riddle riddle, where did you go cat?
I went to the flour pit.
Where have you what?
Look, here are my twigs; gulping audibly at the foot of the pipal tree.
Why, rain, do you not rain?
The frogs do not call out.
Why, frogs, do you not call out?
The *duluḍuṅ* snake swallows us as we call out.
Why, *duluḍuṅ* snake, do you swallow them?
These are our dinner and midday meal.

- P. O. Bodding, *Santal Riddles* (Oslo, Norway: A. W. Brøggers Boktryykkeri, 1940), p. 256.

Commentary

Metafolklore is "folklore about folklore" or folklore commenting on itself. It can occur in any genre, such as in the Kannada proverb "A pickle before a meal; a proverb before a speech" or the Malayali "There is no chaff in a proverb." Here, we see in this Santali nursery rhyme a *kudum* (riddle) commenting on itself and on the *gam* (folktale). Concerning this peculiar example, the collector and translator Bodding writes that it is "Not exactly a conundrum, but used together as such to amuse children. During the rainy season frogs fill the air with their continued and loud crying. The *duludun* is a very common and small non-poisonous snake, Callophislandii. Frogs are eaten by snakes" (256). This particular rhyme reminds us that it is often difficult to translate one genre into another when we use preconceived English categories.

PROVERB

Applied to Two Matters that Are Equal (Maharashtra, India)

ikaḍe bolaneñ nāhīñ tikaḍe tsālaneñ nāhīñ
(here no talking; there no walking)

- Alfred Manwaring, *Marathi Proverbs: Collected and Translated* (Oxford: Clarendon Press, 1899), p. 239.

Commentary

The above proverb is based on a well-known story told in Maharashtra, the state in which Marathi is spoken. The author relates: "A rich banker had a daughter who was dumb, and whom he wished to get married. Calling an old priest, he told him to look out for a suitable bridegroom. The priest happened to know another banker who had a son, but he was lame. He talked the matter over, and after many consultations finally arranged the marriage, but he said nothing to either party about the defeat of the other. On the wedding day they discovered that the bridegroom was lame, and that the bride was dumb. Both parties were greatly enraged with the priest, but he replied, 'Did I not tell you that everything was quite satisfactory; here was no talking, there

The final frame of Rabbani Chitrakar's narrative scroll painting titled *Fish Wedding*. The story is based on a Bengali fairytale about two fish getting married. Everyone is invited except the big fish, who get insulted, raid the party, and consume the guests in attendance. The narrative exemplifies the proverb "Big fish eat little fish," and is often told or sung to children for amusement or at bedtime. By permission of the Museum of International Folk Art, Santa Fe, New Mexico. Department of Cultural Affairs. Photo by Paul Smutko.

was no walking' After this the parties agreed together, and the proposal was duly carried out" (Manwaring 239).

NURSERY RHYME

Finger Rhyme (Nilgiri Hills, Tamil Nadu, India)

The little fingernail is small.
The finger for the ring is gold.
The middle finger loves coins.
The fourth is called Kotera.
The thumb is called Murutika.
And both are gone for cheese.

- Charles E. Gover, *The Folk Songs of Southern India* (Madras, India: Higginbotham and Co., 1871), p. 144.

Commentary

This particular rhyme comes from the Coorg tribal group that lives on the summit of a plateau in the western Ghats. However, other variants are abundant not only in India but throughout the world. One is quickly reminded of the English rhyme "This little piggy went to market." A Bhojpuri variant from Bihar goes as follows: "This one [little finger] says 'I'll eat, I'll eat.' This one [ring finger] says 'Where will I get it?' This one [middle finger] says 'Why not borrow money!' This one [index finger] says 'Where will I repay the loan?' This one [thumb] says 'Then no food to eat.'" In all three examples, the verse is accompanied by pulling on the appropriate appendage.

CAMPUS LORE

Parental Anxiety (Hyderabad, Andhra Pradesh, India)

Jamaluddin (of Hyderabad) was against giving higher education to his daughters. But one of them was anxious to go to college. Her mother had no objection but her father was adamant. After long and heated arguments, Jamaluddin gave in, and the daughter went to Lady Irwin College, in Delhi. She wrote home with rapturous delight about the exciting things in college. The food was delicious, the girls were affectionate, the teachers considerate and she loved ping pong immensely.

"There," exclaimed Jamaluddin, on reading out the letter to his wife, "I told you what would happen. She has fallen in love with a Chinese called Ping Pong."

- Judson K. Cornelius, *Campus Humor* (Hyderabad, India: Manikyam Mansion, 1997), pp. 47–48

Commentary

Campus lore can be folklore generated on a college campus, or humorous stories such as the one above about a campus. But this particular modern example is reminiscent of a similar pun on Chinese-sounding words often told by guitarists when they are tuning their guitars: "This next song is dedicated to the famous Chinese guitarist Tu Ning."

BILINGUAL JOKE

Bananas and Bachelors (Personal Recollection)

What do bachelors and bananas have in common?

Answer: They are both *akelā.*

- Frank J. Korom, Field Notes, Varanasi, Uttar Pradesh, India, 1982.

Commentary

During his acceptance speech on the occasion of receiving an honorary doctoral degree from Oxford University in 2005, the current prime minister of India, Manmohan Singh, commented that although British colonialists introduced English to South Asia, it is no longer a foreign language because it has become thoroughly indigenized. His perceptive comment suggests that English has become a kind of lingua franca for the polyglot nations of the region. The multilingual scenario of South Asia has given rise to a vast repertoire of bilingualisms, including jokes such as the one included here. The pun plays on words in Hindi and English in that *kelā* means banana in Hindi and *akelā* means alone. Given that bachelors are presumably alone they are *akelā,* but a banana is a *kelā.* Not only does the joke play upon bilingualism but also on an anticipated sexual answer, since the banana is a well-known phallic symbol. The force of the underlying humor rests in shattering the anticipation of the audience. We find similar jokes in English, such as "What goes in hard and dry and comes out soft and sticky?" The answer being "chewing gum," not the masculine organ before and after intercourse, is what makes the joke funny. Another example coming from Anglo-Indian lore poses the following riddle: "Women up front, cow behind." The expected answer is, of course, a part of the female and bovine anatomies but in actuality is the letter W, which begins the word "woman" and ends the word "cow."

Four

Scholarship and Approaches

CAVEAT

As we saw at the beginning of this volume, South Asia (i.e., the Indian subcontinent) is a vastly diverse geographical region in which the linguistic and cultural landscape is so variegated that any generalization only leads to misunderstandings. This is true of the South Asian folkloric materials that we study as well. Yet in a survey such as the present undertaking, I am called on to sort through the plurality of South Asian folk culture in order to describe prominent themes, tease out common strands, and point to universals. The results can be promising, if we keep in mind that our conclusions can only be tentative when we reduce a complex civilization into a series of formulaic statements. Reduction of this sort can, however, be a useful learning tool for gaining a cursory overview of how the expressive and aesthetic traditions of a region that has played a very significant role in the history of the cultural encounter between Europeans and their colonial others were used to generate folklore theory. But of equal importance, and more to the point of my present concern, is the critical place that pre-independence India inhabited in the early formulation of folklore scholarship. As adumbrated earlier, a number of academic theories emerged during the nineteenth century that placed India at the center of scholarly speculation and popular reflection.

The bulk of the folkloric data of Indic origin that we have at our disposal today is largely a product of the scholarly activities that took place during the colonial period of Indian history, including many of the samples reproduced in chapter three. Therefore, it must be seen as a unique by-product of European imagination and indigenous Indian creativity. The stuff of folklore must be viewed in specific temporal and spatial contexts, in the light of other pervading influences and forces that affected the cultural environment at the time of collection and analysis. The larger historical context of the development of folklore studies in South Asia is, of course, too complex to take up here, but some suggestions were made in chapter two. It is nonetheless worthwhile to bear in mind that the specific materials and ideas discussed below often lurk in the shadows of much larger issues and ideas that bring about sociopolitical consequences. It is necessary to draw attention to this point at the outset of this chapter because it is something that has often been overlooked by researchers of Indian folklore in the past, and because folklore is never apolitical.

A BRIEF OVERVIEW OF THE STUDY OF FOLKLORE IN SOUTH ASIA

No satisfactory intellectual history of the development of folklore scholarship in South Asia has been written to date. However, under the guidance of Richard Dorson, Mazharul Islam and Ashraf H. Siddique each wrote doctoral dissertations at Indiana University in Bloomington. During the 1960s, Dorson was attempting to internationalize American folklore studies, and the result was a strong push to blend historical studies with textual folkloric materials. Thus, two richly descriptive, albeit uncritical, dissertations exist as a basic source of information for the historical development of Indian folklore studies. Siddique's treatise, completed in 1966, focuses specifically on work done in Bengal, while Islam's study, completed three years earlier, is broader in scope, covering the development of the field throughout the subcontinent.[1]

Both studies roughly concur in terms of major temporal divisions but do not discuss any of the interesting literature on India prior to the British colonial period. Although the terms *loka* (folk) and *jana* (people) have been widely discussed by a number of historical figures in the Sanskrit tradition, very little has been written to explicate ancient indigenous concepts of the folk and their lore. Inquiries in this area of study would yield important information for an indigenous conception of folklore study during the precolonial period. There is also a further gap in our knowledge about folklore activities in India during the Islamic period of rule. In all fairness, however, it is safe to say that while some Muslim travelers and scholars such as al-Biruni (973–1048 C.E.) took an avid interest in recording the customs of the Hindus, their interest, like that of the Greeks before them (e.g., Halbfass 1988, 2–23; Kirtley 1963), was not widespread. Essentially, it was limited to fairly small groups of inquisitive intellectuals (cf. Lawrence 1976). However, the fact that ancient Hindu thinkers and medieval Muslim writers discussed aspects of what we consider to be folklore today does not imply that a germinal form of the academic discipline existed during the premodern period.

The conscious and objective study of a distinct configuration of aesthetic products could only flourish in a particular academic environment that encouraged and guided systematic pursuits in the field of folk culture studies. Such an optimal climate did not exist in India until well after the opening of Fort William College in Calcutta at the turn of the nineteenth century (cf. Islam 1979, 1–38; Kopf 1969; Siddique 1966). As demonstrated in chapters one and two, it is not completely inaccurate to state that a serious attempt to study Indian folklore from an academic point of view began well after the British incursion into the subcontinent, at a time when the general study of folklore was growing in Europe as well. It is only natural, then, that Bengal played a pivotal role in the development of Indian folklore research, and that much of the remaining external history of folkloric activities in India paralleled it to a great degree. It would be a mistake, however, to privilege Bengal as the wellspring of all Indian folklore studies.

Following Islam (1979, 39–175), South Asian folklore study can be broken down into three periods:

1. Amateurish collection (1838–78)

2. Professionalization (1879–1920)

3. Rapid expansion and indigenous involvement (1920–47)[2]

The researchers in each of these periods can be further characterized as belonging to specific occupational groups and adhering to identifiable academic methodologies as well as political and/or religious affiliations. Untrained amateurs undertook the bulk of the work completed during the first period. These amateurs coincidentally happened to be in India for a different set of reasons. Thus, civil servants, common British citizens, and a significant number of missionaries all amassed items of tradition in an encyclopedic fashion, paying very little concern to analysis. Many trained Indologists were already operating in Calcutta at the same time. Their research reflects a strong emphasis on textual studies.

The second period is marked by heightened anthropological awareness, increased attempts to refine fieldwork methods, and the establishment of the London Folk-Lore Society in 1858. Its journal, the *Folk-Lore Record*, provided a medium for the publication of popular items of tradition, as well as a good source of information for Indian students who were literate in English.

More and more professional ethnologists, both British and Indian, began to conduct research in India, as the folkloric field of vision expanded in geographic breadth but narrowed in theory and method. The period also reveals the subtle ways in which European ideological frameworks were constructed within an indigenous context. As we have seen, a number of Indian students who received British education became engrossed in the positivistic and evolutionary models being taught at Calcutta institutes of learning during that time. This is especially true after 1901, when the official British sanction for an ethnographic and linguistic survey was announced.

There was another increase in textually based research during the third period, but a slow merger of anthropological and literary approaches occurred as more and more scholars and students became interested in the contemporary forms of ancient narrative (see below). Indigenous student involvement is quite apparent during this phase, although a growing number of native researchers were voicing nationalist concerns as independence approached. Native research from the last few decades of the second period until the end of the third period thus suggests the presence of two overlapping schools of thought. On the one hand, those deeply involved in the freedom struggle attempted to utilize folklore as a means of ethnic unification and community mobilization. On the other hand, a number of indigenous social scientists continued to assert that their own investigations were objective and value free, untainted by romantic notions about the folk. However, it is incorrect to suggest that these two broad schools of thought were ever completely separate. Both developed and grew in the same environment, namely an urban one, in which unavoidable ideological contact was the norm of the day. This was one of the major points made in chapter two.

The post-independence period has seen a rapid expansion of American research in India, both in the areas of anthropological and literary studies. The establishment of a number of South Asia area studies programs in American universities shortly after the partition of the subcontinent allowed a number of younger American scholars to have a hand in developing the contemporary study of the region in the United States. Earlier, of course, Europeans had dominated Indology. As a result, a different set of ideas developed independently of European models, but these developments excluded folklore studies to a great extent. It was not until fairly recently that the study of Indian folklore was revived in America (see below). American ideas also stimulated indigenous folklore research in South Asia, thanks to the generous sponsorship by the Ford Foundation of a series of folklore workshops over a period of years in the late 1980s and early 1990s (cf. Claus 1998, 224–27; Claus and Korom 1991).

Max Müller, 1890. © Mary Evans Picture Library.

PROMINENT THEORIES

Max Müller (1823–1900)

As mentioned above, India held an enchanted spell over Europe during the formative phase of folklore scholarship. The occidental fascination with India can be traced back clearly to classical Greece, but a more accentuated romantic and philosophical interest began after Jones's eighteenth-century discovery that Sanskrit and Latin were linguistically related. The impact of Jones's finding cannot be underestimated, for the intensity with which Indological research began after his declaration has not been matched to date. Most of the textual research carried out in India during the British period, be it by civil servants, scholars, or missionaries, focused on classical Sanskrit literature and its derivatives. Scholars such as Theodor Benfey and Max Müller brought India into the European folkloric imagination by granting the traditions of South Asia a special place in the development of language and folk narrative.

Founder of the natural mythology school, Müller, a philologist and linguist by training, formulated the notorious devolutionary theory of the "disease of language" to describe the emergence of poetic speech, myth, and religion. Müller used this theory as a way of explaining the misunderstandings that are found in mythology. Because myths inspired by the sun were central to his thought, Dorson (1965) coined the term "solar mythology" to describe Müller's notion that Indo-European gods and heroes were mere solar metaphors of an earlier direct and intuitive awareness of the sun's power. Names of gods were thus originally names of natural phenomena, but due to the disease of the language, natural objects gradually became shrouded behind a veil of linguistic and mythological usage. Thus, Vedic hymns to natural phenomena such as the dawn later became enmeshed in mythological texts such as the Hindu *purāṇa*s. Müller therefore sees the Vedas as the oldest and most ideal form of religion, as summarized in the following passage from his 1889 Gifford Lectures:

> We see in the Vedic hymns the first revelation of Deity, the first expressions of surprise and suspicion, the first discovery that behind this visible and perishable world there must be something invisible, eternal or divine. No one who has read the hymns of the Rig-Veda can doubt any longer as to what was the origin of the earliest Aryan religion and mythology . . . [The deities'] very names tell us that they were all in the beginning names of great phenomenon of nature, of fire, water, rain and storm, of sun and moon, of heaven and earth. (As quoted in Morris 1987,93–94)

Primitive man, according to Müller, was awestruck by nature, and his primitive religion contained an underdeveloped concept of God. But for Müller, "natural" religion formed a substratum of all religion. Primitive religion, then, was a corrupted anthropomorphic form of the earlier (and higher) natural religion of abstraction. This idea is a precursor to Father Wilhelm Schmidt's (1877–1934) notion of *Urmonotheismus* (primal monotheism).[3] From human emotion arose speech forms such as language, myth, and poetry, as well as other nonverbal expressive forms. This essential emotional foundation later gave rise to anthropomorphic and polytheistic mythology, which were eventually transformed into a crude form of monotheism.

As a single God became responsible for the workings of nature and human destiny, and as scientific cosmologies became dominant, our understanding of nature became more abstract, even though a glimpse of elemental human thought could still be gotten from the myths and tales of the so-called primitive peoples. Since Müller was primarily a scholar of Sanskrit, India played a central role in his thought; the Rig Veda, arguably the oldest written Hindu text, thus proved to be significant in the formulation of his concepts by serving as the base text for comparison. But even though Müller's ideas concerning the development of language were influential for a short while, his theories were quickly abandoned in favor of more structural and generative linguistic models as mounting criticism from Andrew Lang (1844–1912) and others increased.[4]

Scottish scholar Andrew Lang. © Mary Evans Picture Library.

Theodor Benfey (1809–81)

Theodor Benfey's impact on the European study of Indian folklore was greater and longer lasting than Müller's. Benfey, also a scholar of Sanskrit, produced the first modern translation of the *Panchatantra* in 1859. Not only did Benfey's translation popularize Indian story literature in the European world, but it also raised new questions in academic circles concerning the diffusion of story themes. Unlike many of his contemporaries, Benfey was not interested in the primal source of narrative. Rather, he was looking for a "primitive" phase of story development that, in theory, constructed the foundation for all later variants found throughout the world. For methodological grounding, Benfey relied on the work of two French scholars: Antoine Silvestre de Sacy (1758–1838) and his disciple Auguste Loiseleur-Deslonchamps (1805–40) both of whom were interested in the diffusion of tales. Both took an interest in South Asian story literature as a possible generative source for European variants of Asian narratives.

Benfey was skeptical of Müller's hypothesis concerning the centrality of the Vedas. Instead of utilizing the Vedas as a representative sample, Benfey followed Silvestre de Sacy's lead and chose the *Panchatantra* as a likely candidate for the primary source of European popular narrative. His introduction to the German translation traces the routes of Indian tales through their many transformations in occidental literature. By tracing many of the *Panchatantra* stories back to Buddhist didactic literature, Benfey concluded that these tales must have been born in India, because her people were accustomed to parables and morality tales such as those found in the Buddhist *Jataka* texts (cf. also Lüdders 1904; Pierce 1969). Although he accepted the fact that certain kinds of tales in the *Panchatantra* corpus were of Greek derivation (that is, animal stories as variants of Aesop's fables), Benfey doggedly clung to his theory of an original Indian substratum.

Benfey further postulated that tales from the *Panchatantra* did not begin to diffuse out of the subcontinent until approximately the tenth century C.E. He characterized the migratory process as one in which the stories were extracted from written literature by the folk, retold and transformed by them, and again placed back into the ever-changing stream of written literature. He saw this process as a cyclical one that often obscured the original identity of a narrative, making it possible for the tales to adapt to regional cultures and take on poetic qualities imbued with nationalist sentiment.

Tale migration, he argued, began occurring as a result of contact between Indian and Muslim cultures after the tenth century. Increasing contact over time between Muslims, Hindus, and Buddhists resulted in a greater reliance on written variants to such an extent that printed versions of tales and fables came to overshadow oral ones. It was these written versions that spread westward, according to Benfey, into lands occupied by Muslims. He further argued that the *Panchatantra* tales ultimately entered Europe via the Muslim conquest of Spain and carried by Levantine traders doing business in Byzantium. He also postulated another migratory route via Central Asia. Along this route, Buddhist missionaries carried the tales to China and Tibet, after which Mongolians introduced them to the Slavs in the Balkans, from whom they were disseminated to the rest of Europe (cf. also Laufer 1898). It was thus, after the Mongol invasions, that the tales began appearing in European works such as Boccaccio's *Decameron,* a collection of one hundred tales published in 1353.

Benfey's migratory theory had a great impact on European scholarship, and folklorists have made extensive comments and critiques of his ideas. Benfey's German student Reinhold Köhler (1830–92), in an essay published in 1865, argued that the most important European tales were either directly Indic in nature or influenced by narratives originating in India (cf. Köhler 1898–1900). He compiled copious catalogues of then-known folktales, which always took him back to an Indian source for the origins of narrative. In Austria, Marcus Landau (1837–1918) studied the *Decameron* only to conclude that many of the fables included therein could be traced back to the Buddhist *Jataka* tales (cf. Landau 1884). Emmanuel Cosquin (1841–1919) in France was perhaps the most dogmatic proponent of Benfey's theory. He argued most forcefully that India was the indisputable home of European folk tales (cf. Cosquin 1922).

Each in his own way attempted to defend and modify Benfey's central thesis, while Aleksander Veselovskiĭ (1837–1906) in Russia and Julius Krohn (1835–88) in Finland each separately accused him of literary and Orientalist biases for his refusal to accept the possibility that Western narratives might have migrated eastward. In other words, diffusion is multidirectional, not a one-way process.[5] However, it was Joseph Bédier (1864–1937) who rather definitively silenced the controversy surrounding the Orientalist thesis. Based on a reanalysis of Benfey's original discussion in 1859, Bédier (1925) concluded that only 11 of Benfey's 147 tales could be traced definitively back to India. Based on the available evidence, Benfey's conclusions could therefore not be substantiated on empirical grounds. Bédier alternatively suggested that polygenesis, the independent invention of the same tale type, could be the cause of superficial similarities and parallels. There was no reason, according to Bédier, to postulate a comparison between two similar but culturally different tales.

In the end, Benfey was too dogmatic in his insistence on the Indic origin of narrative forms, but folklorists have learned at least two positive lessons from him. First, tales do indeed wander through time and space. Second, Benfey taught us to appreciate the interaction between oral and print culture in the production of folkloric texts. Benfey also emphasized the creative role that individuals play in the diffusion and transformation of lore, thereby foreshadowing the contemporary emphasis on human agency as a primary force in the transformation of cultural productions.[6]

Tale Type and Motif Diffusion

The diffusion of tale types and motifs to and from India continued to play an important role in folklore studies in the early twentieth century. It is significant that by the mid-1900s, India had achieved a major status in folktale research. This is especially true in light of the fact that Indo-European connections continued to be explored from a number of different viewpoints during this period. The comparative studies of Georges Dumézil (cf. 1968), for example, drew numerous data from Indic epic and legend in order to validate his theoretical premise pertaining to an Indo-European tripartite ideological and social structure.[7] India was so important to occidental folklore scholarship that the region became designated as the eastern border of the Indo-European world. Stith Thompson, for example, alliteratively canonized India's unique position by calling the second portion of his book *The Folktale* (1946) "The Folktale from Ireland to India."

As the Finnish method, and its focus on monogenetic diffusion, became more and more prominent, some of its proponents chose to focus their inquiries on India. Simultaneously, a proliferation of research that analyzed specific Indian themes, motifs, and types emerged among American Indologists in order to devise a theoretical anatomy of Hindu motif diffusion. Under the tutelage of Maurice Bloomfield (1855–1928), a scholar of Sanskrit at Johns Hopkins University, a number of students began to prepare case studies of popular literary themes, with the ultimate goal of creating a comprehensive encyclopedia of Hindu fiction. Unfortunately, the project was never completed, but many excellent thematic analyses of specific motifs were produced. These studies took into account variants from classical texts as well as those published by British ethnologists.[8] Bloomfield and his students, however, did not use motif in the specific technical sense later defined by Thompson as the smallest narrative unit of a story. Rather, they used the term simply to indicate any recurring narrative theme.

By midcentury, work in Europe and America was under way to create a number of Indic indices, further demonstrating the vitality that Indian folklore was perceived to possess (cf. Bødker 1957; Roberts 1961; Thompson and Balys 1976; Thompson and Roberts 1960). So important was India perceived to be that Stiff Thompson and Warren Roberts wrote in the introduction to their index that "the importance of India in folktale studies has been recognized and an objective study without theoretical assumptions is much needed" (1960, 3). Unfortunately, nonspecialists prepared these numerous indices. To do so, they utilized only European-language sources and focused predominantly on literary variants from classical texts. This has made their function relatively limited. Referring to the Thompson and Balys book, *Oral Tales of India,* for example, Heinz Mode asks if it is possible to create a reference work on Indian folktales based only on materials gathered from English-language sources. Much more serious is his correct accusation that Thompson and Balys's index consists of arbitrarily selected and analyzed biased sources (1961, 202–3). The arbitrariness of their venture has also inevitably led to the random deletion of important Indian *oikotypes* (types distinct to specific geographic locations) and motifs that are unique to specific provinces of the Indian subcontinent.

Most recently, Heda Jason (1989) has undertaken a project to update Thompson and Roberts (1960) by surveying post-1960 folktale collections. Of the 983 texts surveyed, she identifies 375 preexisting tale types and manages to create 28 new ones that are not found in any other regional index. The additions are welcome, but Jason's contribution is also constrained by the source material upon which she relied, a series of 21 amateurish English volumes published in India for a popular audience. We cannot rely merely on English translations to create a reliable South Asian tale type index due to the linguistic and cultural complexity of the region. To generate a more accurate index would require a survey of collections in the regional vernaculars. Exploring the vernaculars would also clear up another problem that arises in Jason's volume, namely, the notion that Indian narratives must be fitted into preconceived European genres, a problem with which I have dealt earlier in this volume. Thompson and Roberts were already aware of this when they compiled their index in 1960, but Jason still wishes to fit the new tales within her rigid structural typology.

Jason's taxonomy of genres is still the most sophisticated comparative system available, but she nevertheless seems unwilling to adapt her fixed categories to suit the specifics of the South Asian context.[9] Given such limitations, what is needed in the future is a team of indigenous folklorists who could survey the literature in each language to yield a richer and more localized database. The potential for multilingual tale and motif type indices is present today in a number of unpublished dissertations and texts in the vernacular languages of South Asia. It is hoped that a future joint effort between American, European, and Indian scholars will make these materials readily accessible in common languages of scholarly discourse.

The beginning of the twentieth century also introduced a new concern to complement studies of origin and diffusion. Scholars such as William Norman Brown and Murray Emeneau brought to light the dynamics of ancient stories in modern contexts. Both Brown and Emeneau published detailed accounts of modern uses and actual occurrences of incidents explicated in the *Panchatantra*. The sort of work that Emeneau and Brown produced was an attempt to cross textual-literary and contextual-anthropological approaches and exemplified the need to complement Indological studies with fieldwork-based inquiries. Emeneau (1940), for example, reported on a contemporary incident concerning a certain Kota man named Kalaypucn and his pet mongoose that parallels the classic tale called "The Brahman and the Mongoose" from book five of the *Panchatantra*. The tale is well documented in other parts of India and is known as far west as Wales, where it goes by the title "Llewellyn and His Faithful Hound Gelert." The characters in all the versions are different, but the progression of the core narrative is virtually the same in each. In the Kota case, the story has been modified and adapted for the local context. What is truly unique and remarkable about the version collected by Emeneau is that the Kota rendition was originally reported as a true event that took place 18 years prior to the recorded telling in 1937! Unfortunately, the potential for studying the social life of this particular tale was not exploited to its fullest, for Emeneau merely returned to the issue of diffusion in his closing argument by making a convincing case for independent invention. But his pioneering article remains suggestive of the insights that could be gained from an integrated study of both the textual and contextual social life of such classical stories (cf. also Blackburn 1996).

Brown's work on the *Panchatantra* is similarly suggestive (1919a). In the course of analyzing published versions of Indian animal tales that were presumed to be oral, Brown compared modern versions to Sanskrit parallels. This in itself is an intriguing exercise, but the conclusion that he reached shows a strong textual bias that skewed his final interpretation. Brown assumed that the modern versions must be derived from their literary Sanskrit relatives. Unfortunately, the direction that thematic borrowing takes is never unidirectional, as Benfey had already shown, and it is just as viable to assume that *Panchatantra* motifs could have circulated orally prior to their canonization in Sanskrit print. The more recent research of Frances Pritchett (1986) on Urdu-Hindi *qissa*, a Perso-Indic narrative genre of enchantment, clearly suggests that one cannot assume the priority of one medium of transmission over another.

The ultimate union of fieldwork-based and textual methods, which was suggested but not realized in the works of Brown and Emeneau, was delayed once again as academic interests in Europe and America moved away from the general study of Indian folklore during the years immediately following Indian independence. Literary scholars and Indologists from the West became increasingly absorbed in textual minutiae, and anthropologists continued to narrow their explorations of Indic kinship, social structure, and hierarchy, leaving the materials of folklore open for a new community of scholars. Indigenous academicians from South Asia began to utilize the concepts employed by their preceding European colleagues in positivist and/or romantic ways. The ever-widening gulf between literary and anthropological studies has not been bridged entirely, even though some exceptional attempts have been made from time to time. The reasons for the division are related to a similar dichotomy that has emerged between the ancient and modern languages of India.

The academic emphasis on the Sanskrit and Prakrit side of Indian culture unfortunately led to an artificial divide separating classical from folk streams of Indian culture, as I noted earlier in this volume. This has only recently been taken note of, and scholars are now taking theoretical steps to rectify the situation. The writings of Blackburn and Ramanujan (1986) and Ramanujan (1987, xvi–xix), make clear that folk and classical are mutually interdependent in India, and by extension, all South Asia. While a specific folk item might often not have a classical counterpart, or vice versa, the relationship still prevails in a majority of the narrative materials that are known to us. The popular north Indian *śīt basant* narrative, for example, has gone through a number of transmitting processes, but it is still difficult to determine exactly where the story fits on an oral-literary continuum. The symbiotic oscillation of folk and classical variants accounts for the mutual borrowing from oral to literary and back again, as well as the permeability of narrative forms in South Asia. This is a feature that certainly goes back as far as the Rig Veda which we normally think of as a classical text but has been shown to contain what is considered to be folkloric material in other contexts (cf. Bregenhøj 1987; Hariyappa 1953). After all, it was not written down for at least a millennium after its composition. Recent research in the field of Indian folklore studies has taken the folk-classical problem as a major issue and challenge for the future development of the field.

RECENT TRENDS AND DEVELOPMENTS

The last three decades have witnessed a revival of Indian folklore scholarship in North America, and with this renewed interest has come an increased methodological precision. While there has been a renewed interest in older issues such as the origin of frame stories (cf. Grinster 1963; Minkowski 1989; Witzel 1987), the analytical value of motif and tale types (e.g., Beck 1986), and a more contextual approach to the didactic value of religious narrative (e.g., de Caro 1970, 1988; Narayan 1989), the new approach is marked by a predominance of performance studies, which will be reviewed below. As mentioned earlier, the initial impetus for such an approach came in the late 1950s from the anthropologist Milton Singer (1961), who called for the study of cultural performances in interpreting complex civilizations such as India. By 1972, Singer had refined and published his performative interpretation of Indian culture in his landmark publication *When a Great Tradition Modernizes,* which analyzed cultural change by focusing in part on urban traditional performances in the south Indian city of Madras, now known as Chennai.

Singer's notion of cultural performance, however, has more recently been complemented by more specific sociolinguistic studies of performance as "verbal art" (cf. Bauman 1975). Blackburn's 1988 study of the Tamil bow song *(vil pāṭṭu),* for example, pays close attention to the text as well as the social context in which it is performed. The trend toward a fusion of textual and contextual concerns dominates current folklore study in India and is clearly the result of an interdisciplinary venture that encompasses scholarly work being done in both the social sciences and the humanities.

In a review article that summarizes the advancements made in Indian folklore studies, Peter J. Claus (1985, 198) points out that one of the obsessions of the current trend is with heroes. What this should suggest to the reader is a strong generic preference in favor of epic. Indeed, most of the full-length studies (and one anthology) of Indian folklore that have come out in recent years have dealt with the epic genre, a topic to which I will return below.[10] This trend suggests both the limitations of work done thus far, and the possibilities of future inquiries. On the one hand, the emphasis on epic allows us to explore the close relationship between classical and folk worldviews, for many local epics are based on the *Mahabharata* (e.g., Hiltebeitel 1999; Sax 2002) and *Ramayana* (e.g., Bose 2004; Richman 1991; Smith 1988). On the other hand, the focus on epics demonstrates the narrowness of current perspectives on Indian performance traditions. In fact, we know less about other prose narrative forms, such as folktales (but see Beck, Claus, Goswami, and Handoo 1987; Blackburn 2001; Ramanujan 1991, 1997), *vratkathās* (vow narratives), etc. Even less explored in the recent past are non-narrative and gnomic forms such as proverbs and riddles. The future direction of research in South Asian oral tradition should be directed toward the study of forms that have remained obscure to folklorists. With the current interest in ethnic

Bow singers routinely become possessed during ritual performance. © Stuart Blackburn.

categories, there is a great need for more taxonomic work. For example, the numerous types of performance traditions that are included in the current literature on Indian oral epics force us to reconsider static generic definitions in order to move into the realm of intertextuality (cf. Korom 1989), where genres are constantly crossing borders, colliding, and mixing.

South Asian folklore scholarship is currently at a critical nexus. A number of scholars in North America, Europe, and the countries of South Asia are presently engaged in research that should prove valuable not only to specialists in the area of Indology but also to those who are interested in cross-cultural and comparative studies of global folklore. The coming decades shall see the publication of a number of significant studies by younger scholars of South Asian oral traditions, which will continue to add to the growing vitality of folklore studies in this important area of the world.

PERFORMANCE STUDIES

The revolution that occurred in folklore theory in the 1970s was unprecedented. It involved radically redefining the academic discipline in a move to bridge the gap between literary and anthropological studies of verbal art. In addition, the study of material culture was also implemented to broaden the range of possibilities for folkloristic research. The new movement, heavily steeped in sociolinguistics (language embedded in social practice) and ethnomethodology (microanalysis and emic, or insider, interpretation), was guided, as mentioned above, by a performance approach that taught us to read performances as cultural texts, paying close attention to the aesthetic and communicative dimensions of not just framed performances but also everyday discourse (such as the poetic, everyday discourse of the Bengali *āḍḍā,* or gossip session). The new contextual approach, based on viewing life as performance, taught us to pay close attention to the words and actions of the so-called natives, something that Malinowski (1992) had urged us to do many decades before. At the same time it cautioned us of the need to maintain a comfortable distance that would allow for an objective analysis of the empirical data gathered in the field.

The performance approach, sometimes called the ethnography of communication (Gumperz and Hymes 1964), thus simultaneously provided insider (emic) insights and outsider (etic) analysis, combining subjectivity and objectivity into a seemingly seamless whole. In other words, the folklore revolution, so to speak, built on a foundation of linguistic particularity (i.e., the culturally specific medium of communication) and ethnographic observation (i.e., the description of the context of performance). We were taught that generalization was wrong, and that microstudies of performance phenomena were necessary in order to move the discipline forward. Many case studies utilizing the approach would then allow us to conduct better-informed comparative analyses across cultures to create universals out of a variety of culturally specific examples. There was certainly a burgeoning of case studies during this fertile period, but at the same time, it delimited the field of inquiry.

Not only was the methodology of studying folklore revised, but also the theoretical basis of its study. A folk group now referred to "any group of people whatsoever who share at least one common factor" (Dundes 1977, 22) while folklore referred to "artistic communication in small groups" (Ben-Amos 1972, 13), which came to be known as verbal art. Artistic communication, however, need not be confined to the verbal realm, since paralinguistic features and even material objects have the capacity to convey meaning. What an unorthodox revision this was from older definitions of folklore, which stressed the anonymity and spontaneous generation of the lore of the people! Now, social actors (i.e., the performers of folklore) and the audience (i.e., the hearers of folklore) were endowed with human agency, which forced us away from giving priority to the texts performed to consider the creative and interactive processes that go into the production and dissemination of folkloric texts.

Throughout the 1980s, the radical new vision resulted in the production of a voluminous set of monographs dealing with the performance practices of peoples throughout the world. One significant benefit that the reconfiguration of what was now being called folkloristics (i.e., the science of folklore) provided was precisely the internationalization of the discipline, for the late 1970s and 1980s saw a rebirth of interest in South Asian folklore studies among foreign scholars (cf. Claus 1998). It now remains to be seen if South Asian scholars will be bold enough to move out of their own cultures to explore the folklore of other nations. Indeed, the new approach, guided, as it was, by performance studies, led to a number of significant analyses of South Asian expressive forms by scholars residing outside the region, all of which were richly textured and theoretically sophisticated.

I have had occasion to refer to performance studies of South Asian folklore a number of times in previous chapters. In this section, I wish to consider briefly a few significant academic texts that have paved the way for the development of a truly performance-centered approach to the region's verbal art. After Singer's groundbreaking work, perhaps the text that signaled the current academic emphasis on performance more than any other was *Another Harmony: New Essays on the Folklore of India,* edited by Stuart Blackburn and the late A. K. Ramanujan. Incorporating, as the contributors do, semiotics, discourse analysis, ethnographic description, indigenous taxonomies, textual analysis, and a variety of other issues and perspectives, the volume demonstrates the truly interdisciplinary character that has marked contemporary folklore study in recent decades.

A few years after the publication of *Another Harmony,* many of the same contributors came together again to explore Indian oral epics in their social, religious, linguistic, and aesthetic contexts (Blackburn, Claus, Flueckiger, and Wadely 1989). Lastly, a year-long seminar convened at the University of Pennsylvania and organized around the themes of knowledge, performance, and transmission resulted in the publication of *Gender, Genre, and Power in South Asian Expressive Traditions* (Appadurai, Korom, and Mills 1991). What these volumes collectively accomplished was to set an agenda for future research in the area of South Asian folklore studies. Indeed, from the time that *Another Harmony* was released in 1986, a number of dissertations inspired by the essays in it have been researched and written.

During this same period from the mid-1980s to the mid-1990s, the Ford Foundation sponsored a number of folklore workshops in India and Bangladesh, which allowed many of the new North American performance perspectives to seep into the work of South Asian folklorists (cf. Claus and Korom 1991), so that what we notice today is not so much a unified theory of South Asian folklore based on a distinct methodology, but rather the emergence of a rich variety of contextual studies of verbal art that has enriched our understanding of the multifarious roles played by folklore in the lives of real people living in distinct locations.

While this trend has produced a rich body of scholarship, one criticism that could be raised is that the close study of performance configurations is too minutely focused on microethnographic contexts, which runs the danger of academic myopia, namely theoretical tunnel vision (cf. Limón and Young 1986). At the same time that performance studies started to peak in the late 1980s, a small but growing number of scholars began raising new questions revolving around the issues of globalization and transnationalism. In the following section, I conclude this chapter with some reflections on future directions that the study of South Asian folklore may take.

Frank Korom speaks during a Ford Foundation Workshop on Folklore held in Udupi, India, 1988. By permission of the Regional Resource Centre, Udupi, India.

GLOBALIZATION, TRANSNATIONALISM, AND POSTMODERN CONCERNS

In the remainder of this chapter, I do not want to dwell on what has been achieved, but what remains to be done. Indeed, for all its positive merits, there remain a number of "black holes" in folklore theory pertaining to South Asia that require our future attention. The proverbial criticism of the performance approach that began arising as early as 1986 was that it could not see the forest for the trees, meaning the study of folklore had become too ensconced in microscopic details, rendering it incapable of seeing the "big picture." But in a world that is constantly in motion, we need to break down geographic borders and boundaries to explore newly emergent forms that reflect contemporary global culture. In so doing, a number of themes emerge, the most important of which I outline below.

Subversion of Power Hierarchies

With some notable exceptions (e.g., Mills 1991), folklore scholarship remained apolitical for much of the period from the 1970s until the 1990s (with the exception of public folklorists, who worked outside academe to lobby for the rights of underprivileged and marginalized communities [e.g., Baron and Spitzer 1992]). A number of the scholars who pioneered new advances in the ethnography of communication during this period were politically inclined to the liberal left, and they philosophically advocated an academic form of Marxism (cf. Hymes 1999). Even so, complicated issues pertaining to human rights and other such pressing global matters were avoided to some degree in attempt to maintain a semblance of neutrality. Some significant exceptions notwithstanding, few such liberal scholars ventured to analyze the political dimensions of the uses and abuses of folklore in society. Very few dared to analyze the kinds of hierarchical and unequal power relationships that often determine the production and consumption of folklore on the popular level. How, for example, does censorship under a dictatorial regime impinge upon the free and creative expression of folkloric traditions? How does the totalitarian state conversely deploy folklore for its own ideological purposes (as was the case in the former Soviet-bloc nations of eastern Europe, where the term "folklore" still resonates with the tyranny of the state)? In response to the latter abuse of folklore by the state, what strategies are then devised and what mechanisms are put into place by the users of folklore at the ground level to counteract the oppressive dominance of the ruling class or government? Quite often, criticism of the reigning political order takes the form of jokes, which allows us to laugh while at the same time reflecting on the bitter irony of the humor. Subversion, it can be said, is a major function of the use of folklore by subalterns, and we need to pay close attention to its many manifestations.

To answer questions such as those raised above, South Asian folklorists must take their cue from social historians. In India, the cue would most notably come from the subaltern school, which was foreshadowed by the works of scholars such as E. P. Thompson (1966) in England and Carlo Ginzberg (e.g., 1983) in Italy. The common theoretical thread that weaves these scholars and schools together is the emphasis on the methods of resistance used by the oppressed to rebel, if only symbolically, against repression to incite individual freedom of expression. If nothing else, folklore is the freedom of expression. James Scott's 1985 term "weapons of the weak," for instance, has great potential to uncover what he would later call "hidden transcripts" in the use of performances to overcome social and political obstacles (cf. Scott 1990).

Weapons of the weak is a phrase used to refer to those items of expressive culture (a term I prefer over folklore because it is less restrictive and confining in its scope) that can be deployed by the masses minimally to provide psychological relief from oppression and maximally to secure liberation from it through disguised forms of resistance. As Scott writes about the Malay villagers he studied, "it seemed that the poor sang one tune when they were in the presence of the rich and another tune when they were among the poor. The rich too spoke one way to the poor and another among themselves" (1990, ix). Discourse, from this perspective, can be a valuable tool or "weapon" to cope with the contradictions of class and power relations (cf. also Scott 1985: 284–89). Hidden transcripts, on the other hand, refer to the implicit messages carried in performances that are known only to those who have been initiated into their secret meanings. To use a hypothetical example from India, a weapon of the weak might be caste mythology, which can be used to rewrite a low caste's myth/history in such a way as to elevate its status and thus symbolically defy the low caste position imposed upon it by the higher castes. We find evidence for this phenomenon in a variety of medieval and contemporary sources.

The hidden transcripts in such narratives are the coded messages that are sent out to members of the oppressed community when the weapon of the weak is performed outside public scrutiny in the course of everyday life. But often the hidden transcript exists in private to oppose the public transcript that justifies the domination of the ruling class. Scott notes that "subordinates in such large-scale structures of domination nevertheless have a fairly extensive social existence outside the immediate control of the dominant. It is in such sequestered settings where in principal, a shared critique of domination may develop" (1990, xi). Thus, the hidden transcript is a "critique of power spoken behind the back of the dominant" (Scott 1990, xii). Sometimes, however, such critiques are performed in public as an open display of defiance. What does it mean, for instance, for an untouchable to wear a sacred thread and claim twice-born status? This is precisely what the Satnamis of Madhya Pradesh did in their struggle for social justice in the nineteenth century (cf. Dube 1998). Surely we have a rich basis of analysis here, for the examples of oppression from India can be multiplied many times over.

Another Indian example would be the Holi festival, during which low castes receive social sanction to mock the upper castes that are the source of their oppression. I can say from personal experience that I have been doused by not only powdered color and water but also cow dung and other matters in both Banaras and Jaipur (where I was smeared with axle grease by an intoxicated rickshaw driver). Generally speaking, a foreigner would not normally be subjected to such abuse in India (although the temptation might certainly rest dormant in the Indian psyche as a result of colonialism), but Holi provides social sanction

Indian Sikhs smeared in colored powder throw dust at an annual fair during the Holi festival of colors in Anandpur Sahib, in the northern Indian state of Punjab, 2004. © Reuters / Corbis.

for turning the world upside down. In the topsy-turvy world, the oppressed can symbolically fight back against those who are normally perceived to be socially superior. Hence, to use just one example, a Dalit (untouchable) in Uttar Pradesh can smear color on a high-caste Brahman without the fear of social sanction. In this sense, performance has the power to reverse the dominant-subordinate social relationships that are endemic to society. Such socially sanctioned occasions, however, are not just events orchestrated by the dominant class to allow the oppressed to blow off steam; rather, they are moments of protest that can challenge or threaten such domination if only in a disguised fashion.

Globalization and Transnationalism

Scott's framework is useful for studying local culture, which is the primary concern of the subaltern school of Indian historians who study everyday resistance from the bottom up, and traditionally minded anthropologists who are still obsessed with the caste system, village India, and tribal culture. But what about the ever-increasing impact that globalization is having on culture in general? There is no doubt that we are living in a transnational world in which the idea of bounded culture developing in a vacuum, free from external influences based on cross-cultural encounters, is no longer useful. Culture today, as we as social scientists and humanists understand it, is what Arjun Appadurai (1996) would call deterritorialized (i.e., referring to the breakdown of national borders due to the impact of mass media, migration, cultural flow, and other interventions). In the light of deterritorialization that poses a new world order, we therefore need to ask ourselves whether it is at all possible to recover the past, as romanticists would have us do. Surely it is not possible to return to the past! Folklorists must therefore begin to tackle the problem of local-global interaction to determine who gains and who loses, both in the present and the past (cf. Korom 1999). Moreover, folklorists must look to the future to determine the course in which the aspirations of the oppressed will move. Where will they be 50 years from now, and what will their condition be?

The stakes are high. After all, we see how global influences condition the production and dissemination of folk performances all around us as a result of mass media and other impinging forces. Such external impingements upon the free enactment of tradition leave us no choice but to discern what the ramifications of such first world oppression on so-called third world cultures are. For instance, the traditional repertory of Bengal's narrative scroll painters/singers (paṭuȳās) is changing rapidly to suit the needs of new audiences and patrons. Some contemporary paṭuȳās are singing more and more about HIV/AIDS, the 9/11 tragedy, the brief war in Afghanistan to oust the Taliban, communalism in India after the destruction of the sixteenth-century Babri Masjid in 1992, and, most recently, even about the tsunami that devastated the southeastern coast of India in December of 2004. Some elitists might think of the shift from painting and singing about medieval religious stories known to most Bengalis and epic narratives from the *Mahabharata* and *Ramayana* to modern narratives as a degeneration of traditional folklore. However, such radical change is not just a quaint occurrence to be thought of in terms of a passing fancy.

Rather, as scholars, we need to situate our studies within the interface between the local and the global to understand precisely how and to what extent such change is occurring, and why. We must pay attention to the shifting terrain of global contours. Roland Robertson (1995) has cleverly coined the hybrid term "glocalization" to refer to the convergence of local and global concerns. Glocalization, as I use it, refers to the resilience of the local enacted in the shadow of the overwhelming powers of the global, as well as the rising appeal of the local in the global marketplace. Another question to ask is, to what extent does the global affect the local, and vice versa? I personally feel optimistic that the local can withstand the global through creative incorporation (cf. Korom 2003, 216–22, 232–45), but we need to pay attention to the oscillations between the two. There is no question that local culture must confront the challenges of a global culture dictated by the so-called first world. Scholars such as Akhil Gupta (1998), for instance, speak of the alternative forms of modernity that are emerging as a result of the local-global interface. Alternative modernity refers to the hybrid forms of knowledge that emerge as the result of local-global encounters. Such forms of knowledge are neither first world nor third world, neither East nor West. Instead, new forms of knowledge are to be located somewhere in between such dichotomous categories, a place defined by Homi Bhabha (1990, 1994) as a "third space," where culture is contested and negotiated by all parties involved in specific cultural, economic, political, and spiritual encounters.

Here I want to distinguish between globalization and transnationalism (cf. Kearney 1995). Globalization refers primarily to a territorially decentered geographic phenomenon in which the economic effects resulting from the global spread of technology stimulated largely by multinational corporations situated in the first world has far-reaching consequences. The dissemination of such technology moves largely from the economically privileged nations of the first world to the economically underprivileged ones of the so-called third world. Often the encounter leads to detrimental effects in the long run by implementing the unequal power relationships between the two. But we also have ample evidence of resistance to such oppression, and the folklorist needs to be aware of the historical and existential dynamics that determine the outcomes of global encounters between people, corporations, and nations that rarely know each other as neighbors do.

One contemporary example of this is the increasing number of suicides among farmers in south India, whose livelihood has been affected deeply by the spread of first world agricultural technology. In light of such desperation, we should not be surprised when we read about peasant attacks on the head-quarters of local multinational corporations in India by those people most victimized by the operations of such oppressive corporations. One could also add such events as the recent anti-American protests staged in Pakistan as a result of border incursions to uproot the perceived enemy in the ongoing war on terror. The scope of transnational study is so vast that it would be difficult to summarize in any meaningful fashion, but the folklorist needs to be aware of such issues if the discipline of folklore in South Asia is to make the neces-sary move from the village to the world. This transition is absolutely neces-sary in order to transcend the rural-urban divide that has plagued the study of folklore and anthropology for so long.

Protests against the World Trade Organization (WTO) in New Delhi, India, 2005. © AP/Wide World Photos.

Globalization, the negative effects of which have been described above, should be distinguished from transnationalism, which refers primarily to the flow of ideas, information, and people across national borders at an alarming speed. Transnationalism is grounded in the social, economic, political, and religious interrelationships between one or more nation-states. Transnational flow must be seen as moving in multiple directions, for it is difficult to say where it begins and where it ends. Having said this, we can posit some speculations. With the unprecedented introduction of the Internet, for instance, new forms of expressive traditions are emerging that were unthinkable even 20 years ago, allowing "virtual" folk groups to emerge (cf. Lal 1999; Rai 1995). The Internet is an especially interesting example because it provides the "surfer" with a veil of anonymity, which is empowering in the sense that it allows one to speak freely without fear of censorship or retaliation. Thus a woman who practices veiling *(pardah)* in Afghanistan or Pakistan can empower herself by expressing her thoughts anonymously and freely online (cf. Edwards 1994).

In both instances of globalization and transnationalism, however, unequal power relationships are implicit. Concerning the latter example, not everyone has access to the Internet, so how does this new technology benefit some people and exclude others? After all, using the Internet already implies the economic privilege of access and literacy. We need to interrogate such critical issues as we move forward into the twenty-first century. In India, the implication is that we are moving gradually away from a caste-based spiritual hierarchy toward one governed by economics and class. One could justifiably argue that this trend is what theorists call postmodern in nature, in which fragmentation of self and uncertainty of knowledge reign supreme.

Postmodernism

Transnationalism, especially, with its emphasis on international border crossings, implies yet another set of issues revolving around the concept of postmodernism. If modernity brought about a certain sense of certainty, as sociologists tell us, then postmodernism has issued in a distinct sense of uncertainty. Here I mean to use the word "uncertainty" to refer to the absolute refutation of any permanent form of knowledge. In short, postmodernity refers to the negotiation of culture and knowledge. Culture, from a postmodern perspective, is thus in the constant process of being negotiated by people living in the (sur)real world, a world-without-borders collage, what some theorists would refer to as pastiche.

Postmodern theory is both epistemological (i.e., study of knowledge) and ontological (i.e., study of being) in nature. It posits an uncertainty of knowledge, as mentioned above, for no knowledge, whether historical or fictional, in post-modern times is absolute, according to some cultural critics. Postmodernism also posits an uncertainty of self: Who am I? What am I, and why am I (cf. Heelas 1998)? How, for example, do members of a Gujarati family whose ancestors lived in Uganda for generations and who are then forced to move to the United Kingdom, eventually settling in Mississippi, understand themselves (e.g., the theme of Mira Nair's film *Mississippi Masala*)? The scenario of dispersal has produced a whimsical bit of South Asian diasporic folklore about mixed identities in the acronym ABCDEFG (American-Born Confused Deshi Emigrated From Gujarat). Such basic questions are deep points for reflection and interpretation. From a postmodern perspective, therefore, because knowledge is relative and subject to debate and negotiation, the individual self is fragmented, the logic being that there is nothing definitive and concrete to which the self can cling. We are all awash in a mesmeric sea of images, all competing in the marketplace of consumption. Selves, like sponges, thus soak up a variety of often conflicting and certainly ironic influences to create an unending variety of new identities and cultural expressions that mark the current era in which we are all living.

Denzel Washington and Sarita Choudhury star in Mira Nair's 1991 film, *Mississippi Masala*. © Cinecom / Masala / Mirabi / The Kobal Collection.

What inevitably results from this process is ever-increasing complexity, more heterogeneity, and more hybrid forms of the self and culture. This is contrary to earlier predictions of the global village, in which homogeneity was to pervade the world.

What all this ambiguous diversity suggests is that there are no clear answers. Some writers (mostly liberal) would have us believe that globalization is bad, while others (mostly conservative) would have us believe that it is good. But we are not confronted by an either-or proposition when attempting to determine the merits or demerits of globalization and transnationalism. Instead, what we are faced with is determining to what extent the generals apply to the particulars. Here is where we need to talk about mixed culture. Mixed culture in contemporary theory is often referred to as hybrid culture, a term that draws on a botanical metaphor referring to the grafting together of two species to create something new, a stronger and more agile variety. In other words, one plus one does not equal two, but three.

Hybridity

Hybridity refers to the mixed forms that emerge as a result of cultural encounter due to the ever-increasing flow of peoples and ideas across national borders. The term is used both for newly emergent forms of culture as well as for newly emergent forms of the individual. We can thus speak of hybrid individuals as well as hybrid cultures. An example of a hybrid form of culture is the kind of mélange of *bhaṅgrā*, dance hall, reggae, hip-hop, and rap music emerging from within the commingling of the South Asian and west Indian community in London. *Bhaṅgrā* lyrics composed in the United Kingdom not only mix genres of music but also a variety of languages, dialects, and speech forms, which provide succor to an emerging class of youths who no longer identify with one particular ethnic group or claim allegiance to one nation-state alone (cf. Baumann 1990). In other words, if I am Indian born, raised in Jamaica, and living in London, am I more Indian and less Jamaican, or more Jamaican and less British (cf. Werbner and Modood 1996)?

Take, for example, the musician Apache Indian, whose performances incorporate mixed lyrics of Punjabi and Jamaican English, with a bit of dialectal English thrown in for extra flavor (cf. Apache Indian 1992). His very name is a pun. "Apache," a Native American community in the western United States, and "Indian," a label mistakenly imposed upon the indigenous inhabitants of the New World by Columbus after his so-called discovery, are a pithy critique of the ironies of the modern world. His name, as well as his lyrics,

Bhangra, the traditional dance of Punjab, India. © Mehta / Indiapicture / Alamy.

is a critique both of the dominant Euro-American culture in which he was born and the norms that dictate his own position as a former colonized subject within a dominant English-speaking culture. Apache Indian's name alone forcefully suggests that he is not willing to be labeled in an either-or binary fashion. The Apache people, it should be noted, were fiercely independent, refusing to be labeled by the paternalistic rulers of colonial America. So where does mixture lead us?

Hybrid culture, as one might surmise from my comments above, is not one thing, but a mixture of things to produce something new. Just as *khicuṛi,* made from rice and *dāl* is neither rice nor *dāl,* or *garam masālā,* which is a variety of spices mixed together to bring about a distinct flavor, culture is a combination of ingredients that needs to be unraveled by the folklorist. Food metaphors are good examples to express hybridity because they are often indigenous folk metaphors. On the island of Trinidad, for example, the local culture, which is largely a combination of African and east Indian elements mixed with remnants of Spanish, French, and British colonial culture, is often described as *callaloo* by residents. *Callaloo* is a savory dish combining a number of local ingredients to create a national cuisine.

Old Wine in New Bottles?

The point here is that such cultural mixing is not something new. What transnationalism and globalization do is speed up the process of cultural transformation to create more and more cultural ironies, such as the pop star Madonna chanting in very badly pronounced Sanskrit in one of her songs, or Bollywood singers sampling American rappers. Lastly, hybridity does not just refer to verbal mixing but also to visual mixing and material culture in general. Ten years ago, for instance, it was very rare to see an Indian wearing an American baseball cap in South Asia, but now they are marketed in abundance throughout the region and worn by a variety of people in both urban and rural contexts. But we should not assume that the Indian citizen wearing a baseball cap in Kolkata or Karachi has any understanding of American baseball, just as we cannot assume that Madonna has any deep knowledge of Sanskrit, or that Bollywood composers are competent in the techniques of American rap. The point is that transnationalism is the vehicle for an unprecedented amount of cultural mixing, a creative mixing that takes place without cultural training. What folklorists need to do is straighten out the discontinuities and incongruities that prevail in the paradoxes imposed by contemporary culture. In other words, we need to disentangle what Frederick Jameson calls the "cultural logic of late capitalism" (1991).

Authenticity, Cultural Ownership, and Intellectual Property Rights

Hybridity, defined here simply as mixed culture resulting from transnationalism, is therefore dialectical in nature. It flows in many directions simultaneously. Ideas move just as freely from India and Pakistan to the United States and Europe as Euro-American ideas move to South Asia. But such rapidity of movement and flow raises serious issues about authenticity (that is, what is real?), cultural ownership, and intellectual property rights. Cultural ownership is a hotly debated topic in South Asia today. Think, for instance, of the self-proclaimed Bodo ethnic population in Assam, who wish to use Devanagari (i.e., Hindi script) as their ethnolinguistic script, rather than Assamese (which is based on Bengali script), as a method of defiance against the dominant powers that be. There is much reflection required here to sort out the future that language politics will take to deal with the contemporary flow of ethnic identities across cultures.

My reflections above suggest that intellectual property rights need to be examined much more closely, for they have international, legal ramifications (simply log on to the UNESCO Web site for details) that filter down to the very core of any given society in the world today. By invoking the phrase intellectual property rights, I mean to ask the question, who owns culture (cf. Brown 2003)? As culture moves across Europe, Asia, South America, North America, and elsewhere at unprecedented speed, is it morally and ethically correct for the American-born Madonna to chant verses from the Rig Veda without any culturally sensitive knowledge of their content and specific usage? Likewise, is it appropriate for Bollywood to borrow stories, themes, and motifs from Hollywood movies without crediting the proper sources of inspiration? Without elaborate comment, I will simply cite seeing a poster on a Kolkata wall recently (November 2004) that clearly appropriated a Hollywood motif of a young man being seduced by the lurid leg of an older woman, a well-known scene from *The Graduate.* The question I wish to ask is, does Bollywood wish to mimic Hollywood or create an Indian cinema that mixes Western influences with indigenous ones to create a cinema worthy of worldwide recognition?

Similar questions can be asked on the local level as well. As we saw earlier in chapter two, many communities in South Asia claim a specific tradition as their own, yet increasingly, these forms are being appropriated by others who claim the very same tradition as *their* own. Or what about the storyteller who claims a story or song as his own but then is saddened to learn that it has been recorded, published, and sold by another party without proper acknowledgement or financial reward? Such misappropriations occur at the most local level such as the village but also on the global level. How can we, for instance, meaningfully interpret multinational corporations usurping indigenous knowledge of plants to copyright new forms of medicines that are marketed worldwide without recognition of the original source, and with very little or no financial remuneration to the person or community that initially provided the information to them?

The Folklore of Power and Hierarchy

These complex issues once again bring us back to the quandary of power relationships. What chance does a Himalayan shaman have to win a legal battle in court against a multibillion-dollar corporation that is protected by the laws of its home country? Such issues are complex and need to be discussed openly and frankly on the international level. Folklorists, because they work closely with small communities (but need to expand), are in an advantageous position to provide expert opinion on such matters. Beyond advocacy and social justice, however, we need to make such problems part of our studies of South Asian folklore in the transnational world of globalization. Not only is there folklore about globalization, such as the current phrase "coca-colonization," but also the globalization of folklore, such as the Urdu slogan (marketed in Pakistan) *Kok hī to haiñ* (Coke is it) or the Hindi slogan (marketed in India) *Lāīf ho to aisī* (life is like this), both of which Coca-Cola uses for local advertising in South Asia. Again, we see the back-and-forth movement that provides metacommentary on the powerful influence that a multinational can have on local culture. At the same time, we witness a critique of that very same power structure.

Diaspora

The last frontier of folklore studies that I wish to discuss in this chapter is perhaps not the last but the first. It is related to the preceding discussion insofar as it deals with the global movement of people: diaspora studies. Diaspora studies as an academic discipline has grown in an interdisciplinary way, combining humanities and social sciences over the past few decades, and folklorists have much to contribute to it (cf. Braziel and Munnur 2003). Diaspora is cognate with the English term "dispersal," meaning to scatter, in the manner of dry leaves blown about on a windy open plain. Indeed, this area of concern is in the process of blossoming into a distinct subdiscipline within universities, as whole books are beginning to appear that address the phenomenon of global diasporas (e.g., Cohen 1997).

With the above in mind, we need to situate folklore studies within a broader scholastic context, one that interrogates the politics of space in a world rapidly being shaped by the unrelenting forces of deterritorialization and multiculturalism (cf. van der Veer 1995). While this process of deconstructing national borders to create a global culture seems to be symptomatic of postmodernity, the phenomenon of displacement is nothing recent or new, since populations have constantly been on the move throughout history (and even prehistory). However, a transnational perspective on migration might lead us to ask new questions about different kinds of movement and the hybrid forms of cultural expression that emerge in what Ulf Hannerz has termed the "global ecumene" (1989). Within the disputed terrain of the global ecumene, religion is a critical cultural factor (e.g., the role of nonresident South Asians in spreading fundamentalist strains of religion).

There are many critical questions that we can ask ourselves specifically about South Asia, which is one of the largest diasporic populations in the world, thanks to indentured labor initiated in the nineteenth century by the British raj after the abolition of slavery. What sorts of ritual syncretism or strategies of anti-syncretism might we locate within communities of South Asians living in a variety of circumstances throughout the world today? Do we have adequate methodological means for explaining and interpreting the influential role of religion in the formation of complex and multivalent ethnic identities; the economic and political impact that expatriates have on their countries of origin; and the rise of ethnic nationalism in diasporas, as well as the ongoing process of redefining the postcolonial nation-state in response to discourses occurring outside national boundaries and political borders? Moreover, how might we account analytically for the changing face of religion and culture on the local level while not ignoring the global communities to which local practitioners belong? These are just some of the questions one could raise in a general discussion of global diasporas. But like any geographical region of the world, a more specific series of questions could be asked within the South Asian zone.

From the folklorist's perspective, how do the experiences of South Asians abroad express themselves verbally and materially? Here, personal experience narratives can tell us much about the past and the present. Stories concerning arrival and departure provide us with ample data to document and analyze the narratives of pain and suffering on the one hand and the stories of success and jubilation on the other. In short, the study of diasporas is a fertile field for the folklorist. In terms of South Asia studies, we need to move beyond the borders of individual nation-states. We need to make inquiries into the lives of South Asians living in such diverse locations as Fiji, Mauritius, Guyana, Trinidad, Jamaica, and South Africa, to cite just a few of the nations to which South Asians migrated under British rule (cf. Korom 1995, 2000).

Concluding Remark

To conclude this chapter, the world is spinning around and around, and we are all caught up in its euphoria. All the areas of research mentioned above are fertile grounds for the future research of folklorists. We do not need to reject the particularities of the performance approach to accomplish such studies. Rather, we need to expand the field of inquiry to deal with the pressing issues outlined above that pose themselves to us in a shrinking world that keeps spinning relentlessly. The future of folklore studies hangs in the balance between continuing the study of the local while confronting the global (cf. Korom 2003). Only by attending to this critical juncture can we hope that folklore scholarship will move forward within the halls of academe.

NOTES

1. Siddique's dissertation was later published in the *Bangla Academy Journal.* The Bangla Academy also published Islam's dissertation as a book in 1970.

2. Blackburn and Ramanujan (1986b) update Islam by adding two more phases. For them, the fourth runs from the 1950s through the 1970s, during which time both South Asian and American scholars increased their interests in regional traditions. The fifth is the current one during which new theoretical models are being developed.

3. Schmidt speculated that monotheism preceded all forms of religion, since many "primitive" people had an idea about a sky-god father.

4. For discussions of Müller and Lang, see Cocchiara (1980, 277–95 and 430–45 respectively).

5. For more on Veselovskiĭ's contributions to scholarship, see Sokolov (1950, 100–8); for Krohn, see Cocchiarra (1980, 308–13).

6. A more extensive discussion of Benfey, his supporters, and critics can be found in Cocchiara (1980, 296–308).

7. For a valuable collection of papers assessing the contributions of Dumézil, see the "Symposium" in *Journal of Asian Studies* (1974): 127–68.

8. Some examples would be Bloomfield (1916, 1917, 1919, 1920a, 1920b), Brown (1919a, 1919b, 1920, 1921, 1922a, 1922b, 1927, 1937), Burlingame (1917), and Norton (1920). But the most comprehensive of this sort of study is still Hacker (1959).

9. For a more extensive critique of Jason's work, see Korom (1993, 235–36).

10. Some examples are Beck (1982a), Blackburn (1996), Blackburn et al. (1989), Gold (1992), Hiltebeitel (1999, 2001), Honko (1998a, 1998b), Lutgendorf (1991), Malik (2005), Roghair (1982), Smith (1991), and Wadley (2004).

Five
Contexts

NARRATIVE MATERIALS IN CLASSICAL LITERATURE

Hindu Indian culture has always greatly valued oral tradition, placing great emphasis on the anonymity *(apauruṣeya)* of *śruti* (that which is heard) and the imaginative creativity of *smṛti* (that which is remembered). The dual characteristics of hearing and remembering suggest a strong preference for the oral transmission of religious and ritualistic lore and also demonstrate a fundamental generic criterion of indigenous classification. For example, the earliest known religious literature of India, the Vedas, derive their authoritative force and canonical status precisely because they are classified as *śruti*—nonauthored revelatory sources. On the other hand, many works that are considered to be *smṛti,* such as the great Sanskrit epics (i.e., *Ramayana* and *Mahabharata*) give credit to the individual creativity of an author. Much of the Sanskrit *kathā* (story) literature that early European Indologists had taken as the major source for extracting folklore is characteristic of the latter. Taken together, the concepts of *śruti* and *smṛti* cleverly acknowledge theoretical points that folklorists have been making since the dawn of the discipline: the creative tension that exists between the anonymity of separate items of tradition and the individual bearer of those items. But Western scholars have tended to separate these two categories. Recently, Sheldon Pollock has scrutinized the distinction, forcing us to reconsider our understanding of their supposed division. He argues that the Sanskrit texts, when read properly, reject the bifurcation of revelation *(śruti)* and tradition *(smṛti)*. Pollock asks, "What are we to suppose to be the origin of what *smṛti* remembers? . . . If the term *śruti* is supposed to connote that certain texts are 'directly revealed,' does *smṛti* connote that other texts are somehow 'indirectly revealed,' or not revealed at all?" (1997, 400) He then concludes his nuanced argument by stating the following:

> *Śruti* means nothing other than "(Veda) actually now perceived aurally (in recitation)," i.e., extant or available; *smṛti,* nothing other than "(Veda) that is remembered," i.e., material that, having once been heard in recitation is inferentially recoverable from present reformulations (in language or practice), which once existed as part of a Vedic corpus. (1997, 408)

In other words, what Pollock implies is that both terms refer to the same thing; namely, the Vedas being recited or recalled. It is important for us to keep the interrelation between the two terms in mind as we proceed with the following examples, especially since so many texts claim to be a fifth Veda falling outside the classically defined four.

Beyond the ethnic classifications that were construed in ancient India, there also existed a simple enjoyment of good speech. Rig Veda (1: 18, 25) recommends that we should derive pleasure from words. The aspect of verbal and aural entertainment hinted at in the Vedas occurs repeatedly in the classical *kathā* literature, attesting to the vitality of storytelling in ancient India.[1] Indeed, many of the stories that originated in the epics and narrative literature are still vibrant today. For example, Gunadhya's *Brihatkatha* (ca. 600 C.E.), a vast collection of stories recorded in Paishachi Prakrit (once widely spoken in north India) and Somadeva's *Kathasaritsagara* (1081 C.E.) are wellsprings for contemporary storytelling traditions in north India, as is the *Hitopadesha* (ca. 950 C.E.) of Narayana in Bengal. But because of its vitality in the past and its disguised reappearance in the present, the narrative text that has received the most attention, both in India and abroad, is the *Panchatantra*. Indeed, more research has been done on the *Panchatantra* than any other corpus of Indian story literature, but because certain theorists speculated that the *Jataka* stories were the inspiration for the *Panchantantra,* I wish to begin my survey with the former.

Jataka

This class of early Buddhist texts concerns the more than 500 previous lives of the historical Buddha, who needed to be reborn many times before he could achieve enlightenment. It is often referred to as the "oldest collection of folk-lore extant."[2] The stories, fables, and riddles contained in this body of literature circulated in oral tradition, and itinerant monks used them to discourse upon the Buddha's teachings after his death. It can only be speculated when the stories were compiled in their present form, but a number of them appear in the canonical *piṭaka* (basket) literature revered by Buddhists of both the Theravada and Mahayana varieties. Two of the three *piṭaka*s are accepted by a number of scholars as predating the Council of Vesali, which was convened circa 380 B.C.E. to standardize the Buddha's teachings into what came to be known as the Pali canon, Pali being the language in which the texts were written. This is confirmed by sculptured carvings of the stories, in some cases even with clearly inscribed titles, on railings at such Buddhist shrines in India as Sanchi, Amaravati, and Bharhut.[3]

There are 550 "birth stories" included, which are arranged into 22 *nipāta*s (books).[4] The division is founded roughly on the number of verses *(gāthā)* quoted in each narrative. As the text progresses beyond 150 stories, the number of verses quoted doubles, then triples, and so on, until 80 verses or more are cited in a single tale. Each story begins with a "story of the present," known as a *paccuppannavatthu* in Pali. The purpose of these prefaces is to relate the narrative to be told by the Buddha. In other words, the preface sets the specific context of the Buddha's life that compelled him to tell the particular story in question. Each narrative then ends with the Buddha summarizing the identities of actors in the stories and their present birth statuses at the time of his discourse.

The *gāthā*s are significant because they represent the words of the Buddha in his previous bodhisattva (compassionate being) forms. They are proverbial in nature, and the language is much more archaic than in the narrative portions of the stories. This led Edward B. Cowell to speculate that the verses in pithy, proverbial form represent the oldest portions of the texts, around which narratives were later woven to make sense of the decontextualized sayings ((1990, 1: xxiv). The Theravada branch's traditional opinion supports this interpretation to a degree. Theravada's opinion is that the original *Jataka* book existed only as *gāthā*s, after which a commentary was commissioned in Singhalese, the language of Buddhists in Sri Lanka, to include the stories to which the *gāthā* referred. According to tradition, Buddhaghosa then translated the Singhalese commentary into Pali in 430 C.E.[5] Both Cowell (1990, 1: xxiv) and Thomas Rhys Davids concur that even if Buddhaghosa did not pen the commentary, it was produced shortly thereafter (1977, 1: xiii–xiv).

Although some of the themes in the *Jataka* corpus appear to be of non-Buddhist origin (i.e., part of a nonsectarian Indic conception), the majority of the stories are clearly a production of a Buddhist worldview. The main theme revolves around the concept of compassion, which is central to the mission of the bodhisattva (in Pali, *bodhisatta*), one who foregoes one's own enlightenment *(nirvāṇa)* for the sake of all sentient beings. Many of the tales are thus didactic parables of the bodhisattva figure moving about in the world and saving various creatures. As an overall narrative cycle, the aim, as mentioned above, is to set the stage for the birth of the historical Buddha, who must be reborn as a bodhisattva countless times before he develops the karmic capacity to become the Buddha, the enlightened one. This particular story is the culmination of an earlier prophecy embedded in the text, and it is told in grand style, with even the Hindu gods called forth to witness this cosmic event.

Panchatantra

The *Panchatantra* (five books), or the *Panchopakhyana* (five stories), is a collection of 84 animal tales first written down in Sanskrit. The work is accredited to an octogenarian Brahman known as Vishnusharman. It is a *nītiśāstra,* a treatise or law book of *nīti* (right, moral, and/or wise conduct). Ethical conduct and political wisdom are the central themes that the original author wished to convey to his audience, and he did so through prose narratives exemplifying patterns of proper behavior. Throughout the text, prose is interspersed with precepts in verse form that draw on older sources of knowledge, displaying not only Vishnusharman's conceptual grasp of traditional Hindu thought but also his marvelous ability to weave together numerous strands of story and verse into a coherent whole.

The *Panchatantra* is set within a frame story that is given in the introduction of the work. The overarching frame begins with a king in the south country named Amarashakti, and his three foolish sons (Vasushakti, Ugrashakti, and Anekashakti). The king compares his sons to a cow that "neither gives milk nor calves" because they are ignorant of (political) science and are not of any use to him. The king meets with his ministers to decide on a method to teach his foolish sons the science of polity, and he is advised to summon the sage Vishnusharman for this purpose. The king puts the three princes in Vishnusharman's care, and the teaching begins "under the guise of stories." It is for this purpose, according to the commentator, that Vishnusharman composed the five books.

Although there is this frame for the *Panchatantra*'s action, each of the five books is a separate dramatic unit with its own smaller frame story. Within each of these, then, there are a number of "emboxed" stories. Quite often there is a double emboxment, and later versions of the text go even further in this regard. The result is a marvelous panoply of story within story within story, which Franklin Edgerton has termed a "Chinese net" (1924, 2, 5). Through the gradual unfolding of each story, the task of educating the three princes is completed.

The frame story is a general feature of long Indian narratives, and considerable debate has occurred over the question of the device's origin and diffusion. Pavel Grintser (1963), for example, has argued that the *Panchatantra* usurped the literary frame from the *Mahabharata* via the *Brihatkatha* (cf. Minkowski 1989, 412; de Jong 1975). This has led a number of recent Vedic scholars such as Michael Witzel (1987) and Christopher Minkowski (1989) to return to older concerns by speculating on the early origin of the frame. The renewed interest in the frame story takes us back to issues that initially played a central and obsessive role in Indian folklore scholarship. It suggests the sorts of continuity that exist between the classical written and contemporary oral literature of India, but it also suggests the continuity of recurring issues and scholarly trends in research. Here is where the history of the discipline is most useful for understanding how we formulate opinions concerning the regions we study.

One of the earliest scholars to formulate an opinion on the *Panchatantra* was Johannes Hertel (1915), who first posited in 1908 that the text was produced originally in Kashmir circa 200 B.C.E., after which it diffused in a southern direction. He based this hypothesis on the oldest known version of the text, the *Tantrakhyayika,* which he identified as being of Kashmiri origin. Hertel felt that the Kashmiri version was the urtext (original text) from which all later versions were derived. Under mounting criticism from scholars such as Edgerton (1924), however, Hertel defensively changed the date to 300 C.E. Later, he retracted his claim that the *Tantrakhyayika* was the urtext, modifying his position to state that it was the oldest extant version, not the original. In his magnum opus, published in 1914, Hertel documented more than 200 recensions in more than 50 languages. Hertel was able to show that the text had a considerable geographic spread, from Iceland in the West to Java in the East.

Brihatkatha

The text, attributed to Gunadhya, does not currently exist, and what we know of it comes primarily from the frame story included in the *Kathasaritsagara,* in which we are told that, like much Hindu mythology, the narrative originated as a storytelling session between the divine couple Shiva and Parvati. Shiva tells the story to her but is overheard by one of his attendants, Pushpadanta, who in turn recounts it to his own wife. After a circle of retellings, the story returns to Parvati. She becomes infuriated that Shiva did not tell her an original story. The attendant is blamed and then cursed to be reborn as a human on earth. Malyavat, Shiva's other attendant who was cursed by Parvati, accompanies Pushpadanta to earth. Gradually, Pushpadanta tells the "big story" to a forest dweller named Kanabhuti, thereby breaking his curse. Malyavat's curse is then broken when he hears the story from the forest dweller. Malyavat in his human form is none other than Gunadhya, the purported author of the *Brihatkatha*. When all is duly explained, the bard is now able to release the narrative in its entirety to the whole world. He sends the 700,000 couplets to a king named Satavahana, who degrades it because it is composed in a lowly dialect inferior to Sanskrit. Gunadhya is crushed by the rejection and destroys all but 100,000 couplets. Upon hearing the news, the king feels remorse and accepts the surviving couplets, making them famous throughout the world. It is these surviving verses that comprise the heart of the *Kathasaritsagara*.

Kathasaritsagara

Somadeva's work, which means ocean of streams of stories, is a late eleventh-century compilation of more than 22,000 stanzas, which makes it twice as long as Homer's *Iliad* and *Odyssey* combined. The author admits that he is simply compiling and retelling the now lost *Brihatkatha* (big story). This is no mean feat in itself and allows us to judge the character of the lost text on the basis of Somadeva's rendering. The author tells us that he composed the work for the pleasure of the princess of Jalandhar, a certain Suryamati. Due to its massive size and graceful prose, the work is, perhaps, the most important compendium of Sanskrit story literature. Within its pages are contained the entire *Panchatantra*, all 25 vampire tales collected in the *Vetalapanchavim-shatika*, a concise summary of the Nala-Damayanti narrative popularized in the *Mahabharata*, and a variety of narratives that parallel Buddhist *Jatakas*, as well as narratives that come from outside the pale of Indo-Aryan culture. As the title suggests, the text represents the flowing together of a number of streams making up Indian narrative tradition. Evidence of this abounds, but one popular motif that appears repeatedly in the text is that of female pregnancy craving *(dohada)*, suggesting strong Jain and Buddhist influences (cf. Bloomfield 1920a; Penzer 1968, 1: 219–28). True to its name, the text is divided into 124 *tarangas* (waves) each of which is further divided into increasingly smaller narrative units.

The *Kathasaritsagara*, like the *Pancatantra*, is constructed around a frame story that recounts how the *Brihatkatha* was disseminated to mortals. The remainder of the text meanders here and there, like the streams of a river toward the ocean. Stories are interwoven in the same emboxed fashion discussed above with regard to the *Panchatantra.*

Hitopadesha

Of the many texts derived from the *Panchatantra,* this one is most popular in Bengal. The author gives his name as Narayana, and he readily acknowledges that he borrows freely from the *Panchatantra.* This text of "salutary advice" (Macdonnel 1968, 373) is essentially another collection of animal fables but also contains 17 original narratives not found elsewhere, including examples of fairy tales, tales of intrigue, and edifying tales (Keith 1928, 263). In fact, the *Hitopadesha* is based largely on the *Panchantantra,* since of the 43 fables in the former, 25 are found in the latter. The text is also framed as a *nītiśāstra,* but here the king's name is changed to Sudarshana, ruler of the ancient capital of Pataliputra. The text is divided into four books. The titles of the first two follow the *Panchatantra* in inverted order, so that it begins with winning friends then expounds on losing them. The third and fourth books are called "War" and "Peace," and the main story focuses on the conflict and reconciliation of geese and peacocks. Very little can be said with certainty about the treatise's author, but the earliest known manuscript is dated 1373 c.e.(Macdonnel 1968, 374). Based on certain terminology in the work, Arthur Keith (1928, 263) speculates that Narayana lived after 900 c.e. but before 1373 c.e.

Vetalapanchavimshatika

As mentioned above, this text is already found in the *Kathasaritsagara,* but it deserves separate mention, since a variety of recensions existed, and it continues to remain a popular set of stories, most likely of Buddhist origin (Macdonnel 1968, 375). Originally, it was probably part of a narrative cycle, but the vagaries of time have divorced it from any larger body of narratives. One version, by Shivadasa, seems to contain the original form of the narratives in prose and verse form (Keith 1928, 288). The title literally refers to "the 25 tales of the vampire *(vetāla).*" [6]

The frame of the stories, briefly stated, is as follows: The king of Ujjayini, named Vikramaditya, was in the habit of annually receiving fruit from a certain ascetic *(yogin),* which he would hand over to his treasurer. One year, the king accidentally discovers that the fruits contain jewels. Out of gratitude, the king offers the *yogin* a wish. The *yogin* instructs Vikramaditya to take down a corpse from a tree located at the cremation grounds and carry it to a ceremonial spot for a ritual that will lead to the attainment of high magical powers. The *yogin* warns the king not to speak a word while performing his task. The king then goes to the grounds, finds the tree, takes down the designated corpse, and throws it over his back, when he is suddenly startled to discover that a *vetāla* inhabits the corpse, but the king persists in his task.

To while away the time, the *vetāla* begins to tell the king a fairy tale. Embedded in the story is a riddle, which the king answers by mistake, after which the corpse disappears and returns to the tree. The king goes back to recover the corpse, and the same process occurs until the *vetāla* tells 25 stories in all. After the stories are completed, the *vetāla* begins the conclusion by revealing to the king that the ascetic is actually evil and wishes to slay him. Upon hearing this, the king asks the *yogin* to show him how he must prostrate himself during the empowerment ritual to follow. While the ascetic is lying on the ground face down, the king beheads him.

Shukasaptati

Another well-known text in this same vein is the 70 stories of the parrot, of which there are two extant recensions of uncertain date. This narrative is framed around a woman whose merchant husband, Madanasena, is planning to travel abroad. Before leaving, Madanasena's father gives his foolish son a parrot and a crow, wise birds that are to teach the mischievous son the virtuous path. Having been converted to the path of virtue by the wise birds, Madanasena plans for his journey and leaves the birds in the care of his young and promiscuous wife. Missing her husband, but being inclined to seek the company of other men to console her, she seeks the sage advice of her husband's parrot. The crow falters in advice, and the wiser parrot strikes a deal with the woman, agreeing to approve of her dalliances if she can extricate herself from the difficult situation earlier encountered by a certain woman named Gunashalini. The young wife's curiosity is aroused at the proposition. The parrot then tells her story after story, each time asking her how she would act if she were in the position of the heroine of each tale. In so doing, the crow engrosses the woman in story, thereby warding off infidelity until the husband's return.

Like the *Panchatantra,* this body of work was translated into several languages, most notably, Persian, in which it appears as two popular works in the fourteenth century. The earlier of the two is titled *Javahir Al-Asmar* (jewels of

Praying to Ganesha, from a collection of Sanskrit texts from the *Mahabharata.*
© Bildarchiv Preussischer Kulturbesitz / Art Resource.

evening entertainment), but it is better known in the second version, entitled
Tutinameh (the book of the parrot).

Mahabharata

The epic of the Bharata clan is the longest in the world, made up of over
100,000 verses. Tradition attributes the work to a sage named Vyasa, but
scholars have demonstrated that the text was compiled over a fairly lengthy
period of time, probably beginning early in the first millennium B.C.E. and
reaching a fixed form by the first century C.E. Some scholars speculate that the
text was composed in two phases. The first was a selection of approximately
7,000 *śloka*s (verses) composed by Vyasa himself. The second stage was an
elaboration on Vyasa's verses by Vaishampayana. By the Middle Ages, the text
was propagated in a northern and southern version, and both continued to
inspire regional poets to compose versions in their own regional languages. It
is also performed in a variety of folk forms, such as through ritual recitations,
popular theater forms, possession cults, etc. Lastly, it thrives in new media as
well, such as comic books and television adaptations.

The text is divided into 18 sections with no consistent length criteria. The longest section runs up to 14,000 verses, while the shortest contains fewer than 120. The 18 sections are further divided into 98 shorter subsections. The plot line probably has its origins in the bardic traditions of the warrior class, but the Brahmanic priestly class eventually appropriated it as the narrative gradually took literary form. This text, along with the *Ramayana* to be discussed below, is first and foremost a story of heroism and gallantry worthy of repetition. On another level, however, it is a morality tale intended to portray the constant struggle between cosmic duty *(dharma)* and the negative forces *(adharma)* opposing the natural order of the universe *(rta)*.

The core of the narrative begins with Vicitravirya, a lunar dynastic king who has two sons, Pandu and Dhritarashtra. As the oldest son, Dhritarashtra should have inherited the throne, but because he was born without sight, he is considered to be inauspicious. Therefore, Pandu ascends to the throne after his father's death and raises five sons, known collectively as the Pandavas, the sons of Pandu. When Pandu dies, Dhritarashtra assumes the throne and sends the five Pandavas to grow up with his own sons, the one hundred Kauravas. When they come of age, Duryodhana, the eldest Kaurava, claims the throne for himself and exiles the Pandavas and their co-wife Draupadi. Soon thereafter Dhritarashtra abdicates and Duryodhana becomes king, but the Pandavas challenge the Kaurava claim to the throne. In order to avoid bloodshed, Dhritarashtra divides the kingdom into two. Duryodhana rules the northern half of the kingdom, and the eldest Pandava, Yudhishthira, rules the south.

Duryodhana eventually visits the Pandava capital at Indraprasta (modern-day Delhi), where Yudhishthira insults him by laughing after he accidentally plunges into a lake. The insulted Duryodhana challenges Yudhishthira to a game of dice in order to regain his honor. The stakes are high: the entire divided kingdom to the winner. Yudhishthira ultimately loses everything, including his wife Draupadi, who is publicly humiliated in a major scene known as the disrobing of Draupadi. In it, the Kauravas attempt to unravel her sari, but the cloth is miraculously unending due to the grace of the deity Krishna. A second game is then played. This time the loser must go into exile for 13 years. Again, the Pandavas lose, and they are forced into exile.

In the fourteenth year, the Pandavas announce that they wish to have their kingdom back. Duryodhana refuses, setting the dramatic stage for the climactic battle, one that lasts 18 days. The battle takes place on the plains of Kurukshetra, where all the Kauravas are slaughtered during the carnage. Although victorious in battle, Yudhishthira is saddened by the loss of his Kaurava relatives. Grief stricken, he hands over sovereignty to a junior relative and sets off with his brothers and Draupadi in the direction of the Himalayas to enter the deity Indra's heaven. All die along the way, except Yudhishthira, who is now accompanied by a devoted dog. Indra meets him along the way and invites him to enter his heaven. Yudhishthira responds to the god by saying he will only enter if his faithful canine companion can enter along with him, at which point the dog reveals his true form as *dharma* personified. The embodied *dharma* thus guides the hero into heaven, where he sees Duryodhana. Yudhishthira is perplexed to find someone who has caused so much suffering and grief enjoying the benefits of heaven, but he quickly learns that Duryodhana was rewarded for acting in accord with his own *dharma* as a warrior.

This is the basic narrative, but true to Indic story literature form, there are many twists and turns that give birth to other narrative cycles. In fact, there is a saying in the text stating that if it is not found in the *Mahabharata,* it does not exist. Moriz Winternitz suggestively asserts that the text is not just the heroic poem of the Bharatas. It is, at the same time, "a repertory of the whole of the old bard poetry" (1972, 1: 318). The exhaustiveness of the text is what provides the raw material for so many performance genres throughout India, regardless of region or linguistic barriers. The same can be said of the *Ramayana,* the second major Sanskrit epic.

Rama kicking a demon, a page from the *Shangri Ramayana.* © Brooklyn Museum of Art / Corbis.

Ramayana

If the *Mahabharata* is the premier Hindu text on *dharma,* or duty, then the *Ramayana,* the story of King Rama, is the premier text of devotion *(bhakti).* Yet each contains elements of the other, for all the characters of both epics must act with devotion in order to fulfill their *dharma.* The *Ramayana's* composer is Valmiki. Scholars have noted that even though the text was in circulation by the time the *Mahabharata* achieved its final form, it is probably of somewhat later vintage. As with the *Mahabharata,* there are northern and southern recensions, as well as a variety of medieval vernacular renderings (cf. Bose 2004; Richman 1991; Smith 1988).

The story goes as follows: King Janaka of Videha decides to hold a contest to find a suitable husband for his daughter Sita. The test is to see who can string and bend a divine bow to shoot an arrow. Many fail, but King Dasharatha of Ayodhya's son Rama accomplishes the task and is betrothed to Sita. Dasharatha's second wife, Kaikeyi, tricks him into sending Rama into exile so that he will not inherit his father's kingdom. Rama refuses to disobey his father and goes into forest exile with his brother Lakshmana and Sita.

After numerous adventures in the Dandaka forest, a major event occurs. While the brothers are away hunting one day, Sita is abducted by a ten-headed demon named Ravana, who is the king of Lanka. Rama and Lakshmana must now assemble an army to win her back. They receive support from Sugriva, king of the monkeys, who puts together an army, among which is the super simian Hanuman, who becomes the ultimate devotee *(bhakta)* of Rama and Sita. Hanuman is in actuality the son of Vayu, the wind. He uses his superior powers to build a bridge between peninsular India and the island of Lanka, which allows Rama's army to cross for the battle against Ravana and his demon army. After Ravana is killed and his army defeated, Rama victoriously returns with Sita and Lakshmana to reclaim what is rightfully his, the kingdom of Ayodhya.

Upon return, however, the citizens of Ayodhya begin to question Sita's fidelity, suspecting that she may have been touched by the demon-king while in captivity. Sita is then forced to undergo the ordeal by fire, from which she emerges unscathed and chaste. This is proof enough for Rama, but the citizens demand her banishment. He sends her to the hermitage of Valmiki, where she gives birth to twins. Many years later, Rama hears of the birth of his sons and desires to reunite with his wife and children. Sita, on the other hand, refuses to return to Ayodhya, so she calls on the earth to consume her. In the end, she returns to the place from which she came (her name literally means "furrow"), and Rama, along with his subjects, enters into the body of the deity Vishnu, of whom Rama is an incarnation (*avatāra*).

Like the *Mahabharata,* the text is clearly structured around the dichotomous issue of good versus evil. Both are about doing one's *dharma* and doing so out of devotion. Both texts have their heroes and anti-heroes, as well as a whole host of demons; yet each fulfils his or her own *dharma,* which in the end leads to harmony. The Puranas, on the other hand, are less transparent in that they present a variety of ambiguous and competing views.

Puranas

This class of texts is a combination of myth and history, best referred to in the hyphenated form myth-history, for the line between the two genres in them is blurry at best. The main objective of these texts, composed roughly between 400 and 1000 C.E., is to extol the virtues and greatness of one deity over another. There are 18 main Purana texts *(mahāpurāṇas),* 18 minor ones *(upapurāṇas),* and 18 others claiming either *mahā* or *upa* status. Sectarian Purana texts bring the number to nearly one hundred. The combined total equals more than 2,000,000 verses, which exceeds anything of its kind in the world.

Most European Orientalists saw them as debased and obscene, and nineteenth-century Indian reformers rejected them also as promoting superstition. This notwithstanding, they were and remain the most popular texts in vernacular languages because they are encyclopedic in nature. The texts also serve as a commentary on earlier religious and moral literature, for there are verses that support the view that the Puranas help in understanding the Vedas, the earliest literature of the Hindus. They have mass popular appeal, bringing the stories of people's favorite gods down to the folk level. The Puranas are thus collections of stories that keep Vedic teachings and legends current among the masses. In other words, they were Vedas for those excluded from Vedic tradition (i.e., women and outcasts). Puranas are sometimes even collectively referred to as a fifth Veda (e.g., Vyasa says this in the *Mahabharata*); hence, the term *purāṇaveda* is used to describe them. The Puranas break with the Vedic sacrificial tradition, however, and promote sectarian positions in favor of two deities, Vishnu and Shiva.

Of the eighteen *mahāpurāṇas,* two are dedicated to Brahma the creator; one to Surya the sun; one to Agni, god of fire; ten to Shiva the destroyer; and four to Vishnu the preserver. There is clearly competition between the various deities portrayed in the texts because the purpose is to proclaim one deity greater than all the others. In reality, however, they are less sectarian and more tolerant in nature. There are repeated passages, for example, in which the claim is made that Vishnu is Shiva, and vice versa, thereby equating them. The five signs *(pañcalakṣaṇam)* structurally define the genre by listing what features are ideally supposed to frame the text. They are cosmogony; secondary creation/chronology; the genealogy of the gods; reigns *(manvantaras)* of the fourteen semidivine Manus, who rule successive cycles of time; and the history of the solar and lunar races.[7] Although these mandatory features do not figure prominently in the oral dissemination of *purāṇa* literature today, this vast corpus of literature is continuously circulated on the popular level through a variety of media (cf. Doniger 1993).

FOLKLORE IN CONTEMPORARY LITERATURE AND CULTURE

Folklore in South Asia pervades every domain of life, at every waking moment. Sometimes it even enters into dreams, as when legends circulate about a deity or saint entering a sleeping person's mind and commanding him or her to carry out a task, which is the well-known theme of the *svapnādeś* (dream command) genre. Folklore is not only casually spoken and professionally performed. It also appears in a variety of nonverbal media, such as political graffiti before an election. The slogan *rām ke nām* (in the name of Ram), for example, was plastered on walls or embroidered on banners all over north India in the years following 1990. The slogan was coined to bolster the aspiring politician L. K. Advani's campaign to build a Hindu temple to the deity Rama in the very spot where a Muslim mosque stood in the town of Ayodhya. Regular rumors of human sacrifice and organ theft appear in newspapers throughout the subcontinent, while song lyrics appear in cinema advertisement posters. Cinema song tunes then filter down into the folk stream of music to influence the compositions and performances of folk musicians (cf. Marcus 1993).

Wall art depicting mythological themes is also a common sight throughout India. It allows people to recall a particularly poignant mythic event through visual means. One that is a favorite in many parts of Hindu India is the image of the super simian Hanuman transporting a mountaintop from the Himalayas to Lanka to save Rama's brother Lakshmana, who needs herbal medicine that grows only on the peak. Rather than wasting time hunting for the correct herbs and endangering Lakshmana's life, Hanuman uproots the mountain and speedily carries it back out of devotion to Rama and his family. This episode from the *Ramayana* is much beloved, and its depiction in popular art suggests yet another medium through which the Rama story is disseminated. Slogans and poetry also grace the interiors and exteriors of painted Pakistani transport trucks, while the exteriors of cycle rickshaws in Bangladesh visually relate hagiographic stories of national martyrs who died during the nation's war for independence from Pakistan. We even find religious lore and *mantras* tattooed onto the bodies of devotees, as is the case in the Ramnami community of Madhya Pradesh.

Folklore, in other words, is multisensory. It embraces us with smells, such as when a particular spice conjures up a story heard while cooking a meal or when the scent of moist earth compels us to recall a specific genre of songs sung to welcome the monsoon. Not only is it multisensory; it is also multimediated, as we have already seen in earlier chapters. An item of

Hanuman transporting a mountaintop. © ArkReligion. com / Alamy.

folklore can just as easily move from oral to written form as it can from written to oral. Or it can be electronically mediated via radio, television, video, or cinema. In a celebrated case, a local and somewhat obscure Hindu goddess named Santoshi Ma achieved widespread popularity after a successful film was made about her and the benefits that can be accrued by worshipping her (cf. Das 1981). And then there are local legends about miracles attributed to such historical figures as Mahatma Gandhi (cf. Amin 1988) and Mother Theresa that elevate them to semidivine status. Legends and ballads also circulate about more notorious figures, such as the fabled bandit queen Phoolan Devi, who defied local police for years before she negotiated a truce with local authorities (cf. Phoolan Devi, Cuny, and Rambali 2003). She was then idolized in her own movie and went on to become a prominent politician until she was gunned down in New Delhi.

The latter examples suggest that folklore is not just something of the past, bogged down in a stagnant form of tradition. Instead, folklore is constantly being created and re-recreated to reflect modern times and current events. A good illustration of this point comes to us from Afghanistan. During the Russo-Afghan war of the late 1970s and early 1980s, Afghani refugees in Pakistan and freedom fighters started to compose anti-Marxist *jihād* (holy

Phoolan Devi, Indian "Bandit Queen" and parliamentarian, seen here during surrender with the members of the gang. © Baldev / Sygma / Corbis.

war) poetry to extol the virtues of martyrdom and also to inspire the rebels' struggles and glorify their successes in battle (cf. Edwards 1993). The profound impact that that war had on the Afghan psyche is not only reflected in the verses written by military bards.

Another fascinating phenomenon that became widespread during this period of turmoil was the so-called war rug, in which themes and the instruments of war were incorporated by Afghani rug weavers into their patterns of ornamentation. It was quite common to see helicopters, hand grenades, and Kalashnikov rifles interwoven with floral motifs and abstract patterns in rugs produced during the 1980s and 1990s. These rugs, by the way, became curious objects of collection, and some are now housed in museums in Europe and North America. They were even being peddled in flea markets, as I personally witnessed in New Mexico, during the early 1990s. Once again, we see how the things produced locally for circulation are eventually drawn into an international arena through the process of globalization, often for economic and/or ideological reasons.

We have seen that folklore has multiple existences. The textual examples culled from Sanskrit story literature, some of which were provided in chapter three, exist in various forms today, just as stories from Arabic and Persian literature circulate orally and in vernacular print in Afghanistan, Pakistan, and Bangladesh. Throughout the millennia-long journey from Veda to video, there has been a constant crisscrossing of folklore that pervades all the human senses and gradually becomes embedded in a variety of genres and media. Folklore is by nature intertextual. One Hindu saying, quoted earlier, states that if it is not found in the *Mahabharata,* it does not exist. Here the proverb comments on the epic, but within the epic itself we find numerous proverbs, as well as virtually every other genre one can possibly imagine. Of course, I have also been stressing that because folklore is multidirectional, it is virtually impossible to determine if an item moved from print to speech or the other way around. But what we can know for certain is that written folklore and oral folklore exist side by side. We have vernacular *Ramayanas* intended to be read as literature (cf. Smith 1988), and we also have vernacular *Ramayanas* that are intended to be recited ritually out loud (cf. Lutgendorf 1991).

Another example of the interaction of textual and oral comes from the Muslim sectors of South Asia. *Mushā'iras* are gatherings that serve as venues for the recitation of Urdu poetry (cf. Sequeira 1981). Sometimes they are formal in the sense that the patterns of recitation are scripted and follow the rules of *ādāb* (etiquette), but other times they are spontaneous occasions for verbal dueling, where the intensity of the listeners' cries of *vāh vāh* determines who the more talented poet is. Verbal dueling traditions are quite common in

An Afghan war rug. Graham Gower Collection.

South Asia. The *kavi gān* of West Bengal usually pits two singers against one another in competition. Normally their patron chooses a theme (e.g., the virtues and vices of women) on which each must extemporaneously compose verse in a back-and-forth manner. As in the Urdu poetry session, the audience's cries determine the more eloquent singer. In this sense, it roughly parallels the *mushā'ira,* which, although much more formal, also demonstrates the progression of a poet's thought over the course of an evening. In both instances of verbal dueling, there is a clear interaction between oral/verbal and written media, since Urdu poets and Bengali singers alike draw freely on allusions, themes, images, and motifs included in their respective classical traditions.

Four Points for Final Reflection

Throughout this volume, I have made a number of interrelated points that can be summarized as follows:

1. Folklore is lived and contextual.
2. It resides along a continuum ranging from oral to written.
3. It belongs to everyone and to no one.
4. Easy divisions for taxonomic purposes are difficult to substantiate.

Let me take each one of these issues and elaborate by using examples from contemporary South Asia.

Folklore Is Lived and Contextual

As we saw in chapters one and two, folklore is not just a jumble of texts to be read by the interested reader, for it lives in performance. Even the Vedas, the oldest Indic texts, are to be recited and heard. This tradition of aural culture in South Asia has continued down to the present day, and to understand a particular performance tradition, we need to study its meaning as it emerges in specific socially interactive situations. Take, for instance, the bazaar of storytellers in Peshawar, the capital of Pakistan's Northwest Frontier Province, which is situated on the northeastern border of Afghanistan. Although the bazaar currently includes all the modern accoutrements of contemporary life, storytelling still flourishes here (cf. Heston and Nasir 1988, 7–21). What is incredibly interesting about the bazaar of storytelling is that it is not lined with a number of bards vying for an audience's attention, as one might suspect. Rather, the medium of dissemination has changed. Although professional storytellers still inhabit the area, they now record their *badala*s (songs) on cassettes in tiny studios located behind the bazaar. These well-known stories, sung in verse form in a variety of Pashto dialects, are mass produced and sold to people in both recorded and printed versions.

The printed versions are available as inexpensive, brightly colored chapbooks (cf. Heston and Hanaway 1996) that are readily available in the bazaar alongside the recorded cassettes. What makes the stories appealing to the local population is their real-life quality. Heston and Nasir (1988, 11–15) have summarized some of the common points that pervade the *badala*s. They note that dominant narrative themes mirror Pashtun society at large. Extended-family living, with the senior male dominating decision making, is a prominent theme, as is restricted social interaction between the sexes. Women, for

Qissa Khwani storyteller's bazaar, Peshawar, Pakistan. © Robert Harding Picture Library Ltd / Alamy.

all intents and purposes, become the property of the husband's family after marriage, and they can only return to their natal home with permission from the male spouse's family. Men generally tend to congregate together in *hujras*, male guesthouses, while women attend to domestic chores.

The stories are also filled with conflict and violence, which reflects the Pashtun tribal code of honor. Quite often, the *tarbur* (paternal cousin), the father's brother's son, is defined as an enemy as well as a cousin, since he frequently appears as the antagonist in the narratives. Ethnographies of the region (e.g., Lindholm 1982) suggest that a large percentage of murders in Pashtun society are committed by close cousins or commissioned by them, often for economic reasons related to land inheritance. Murders may also be due to matters of shame and honor, what we might call revenge *(badal)* killings. Honor is a central concern in the Pashtun code of ethics, controlling as it does male and female behavior. Courage and bravery are therefore essential qualities for men, as is chastity for women. Any deviation of the strict moral code demands quick retaliation both in life and story,

Traditionally, the *badalas* were sung by village youths to each other in their local *ḥujra.* On festive occasions, such as weddings, professional performers would be hired to sing the same songs. On such occasions of large gatherings, the performance might have moved outdoors into adjacent fields to accommodate more people than could easily fit into the guesthouse. This would then allow women to listen to the performance from the rooftops of village houses. Heston and Nasir (1988, 14–15) further point out that nowadays the cassette versions are finding their way into village guesthouses, which sometimes leads to an invitation for well-known singers to perform at public functions. During such performances, the singer might be recorded, and the cassette would then be duplicated for purposes of sale and dissemination in Peshawar's bazaar of storytellers. The most popular stories then become topics for Pashto films that are later distributed as videos, adding yet another medium of transmission. Moreover, if a particular celluloid version is successful, it might be remade in other regional languages spoken in Pakistan or might be converted into a television production in Urdu, the national language of the nation. Peter Manuel (1993) has provided related data for India showing that new media for the dissemination of expressive culture are not an isolated phenomenon in South Asia. What all this suggests is that folklore is vibrant and alive. It does not simply disappear with the onslaught of modernity but adapts and changes to create ever more variety and complexity. This is why it is absolutely imperative to situate aspects of folklore in the concrete circumstances of everyday life.

It Resides along a Continuum Ranging from Oral to Written

The example used above provides a nice segue into our second theme. As I suggested numerous times in the previous pages, folklore can exist as a written text or as part of a performance context. Yet even a written text has its own context. A written text can be read individually in the solitude of one's home, it can be read out loud to an audience, it can be memorized and recited, or it can serve as a script for a staged performance. In the *vratkathā* tradition practiced in many parts of Hindu India, which I mentioned in the previous chapter, a devotional story is quite often read out loud ritually as abstract patterns are drawn on the floor (cf. Pearson 1996). The stories are readily available in chapbook form in local marketplaces. These ritual occasions, astrologically marked by regional calendars and almanacs, are opportunities for making vows and performing fasts on particular days mostly for specific goddesses, such as for the aforementioned Santoshi Ma. A senior woman in the group usually reads out the story *(kathā)* that justifies the *vrat* (vow) to the younger girls in attendance while the designs are being drawn. Through this tradition, younger girls are socialized by their female elders and taught the appropriate behavior expected of a woman. We notice in this example how a written text once again serves the purposes of orality. The story is not just to be read, for it must be performed, heard, and visualized simultaneously to achieve its proper effect on the destiny of those who perform the rite (cf. Wadley 1983).

Another regional tradition that combines the verbal and the visual and blurs the line between oral and literate comes from the Bengali linguistic region. In the previous chapter, I also mentioned briefly an artisan caste of West Bengal and Bangladesh known as *paṭuyā*. *Paṭuyās* have earned their livelihood since at least the thirteenth century by painting narrative scrolls *(paṭs)* and composing corresponding songs. The songs are then performed for audiences while the corresponding scrolls are unraveled. Traditionally, these painter bards wandered the Bengali countryside to perform for small village audiences. For these itinerant performances, the bards would receive a modest fee in kind. Increasingly, however, with the loss of local patronage, they are expanding their circuit as they enter into the region's cash economy. It is quite common today to see them wandering door to door in urban contexts, visiting tourist hotels, or traveling to folk festivals around the country to market their scrolls. A fortunate few are even traveling abroad now to capitalize on international interest in their work, which has been achieved through the intervention of culture brokers whose job it is to create a global market for the sale of the scrolls. As a result, a significant transformation has occurred. Nowadays, *paṭuyās* are selling their scrolls, rather than their songs, for in the past the scrolls served mostly as props for the sung performances (cf. Hauser 2002).

It has long been assumed that the *paṭuyās* passed on their material orally from generation to generation. While this might be true to a certain extent, a number of them with whom I have worked are able to read and write. Literacy has allowed them to expand their repertoires, while also providing them a mnemonic device for memorizing their compositions. Most literate *paṭuyās* keep songbooks in which they compose their own songs or write down the songs of other singers. The themes of their compositions cover a vast range. One can see and hear myths about gods and goddesses; legends about local Muslim, Hindu, and Christian saints; or accounts of recent current events having to do with elections, natural disasters, disease, or communal violence. The themes are often inspired not only by village gossip and discussion but also by newspapers, radios, televisions, and videos.

One remarkable example that I witnessed took place in December of 2001, only a few months after the Twin Towers were destroyed in New York City. Shortly after arriving in the village of Naya, in Medinipur district, West Bengal, where a community of *paṭuyā̃s* resides, I began seeing posters and hearing loudspeaker advertisements for an upcoming *jātrā*, a genre of popular Bengali theater (cf. Banerjee 1989; Farber 1984). The specific *jātrā* being incessantly advertised would be performed in a fallow rice paddy outside the village in the near future. Such occurrences are quite frequent in rural Bengal, where itinerant theater groups based in Kolkata (formerly Calcutta) travel to perform these lengthy plays (some lasting all night) to earn their income. What was unusual about the performance in question, however, was the title and theme. The title of the forthcoming play, highly anticipated by the local population, was *Amerika Jvalcche* (America Is Burning). The advertisements boasted a spectacular recounting of the events surrounding 9/11!

On the evening of the performance, I accompanied a number of my *paṭuyā* friends to the performance out of curiosity and to break the monotony of daily life in the village. The loudspeaker advertisements had been sent around on a flatbed rickshaw to all villages within a 50-mile radius, and the effort paid off with an energetic crowd of roughly 10,000 people, each paying about 50 cents for admission. The performance was indeed spectacular, with three stages and culminating in pyrotechnics, which held the audience in rapture for more than five hours. What made this foreign news so immediate to rural Bengali sensibilities was the way that the scriptwriter added Bengali flavor to the now-historical events. In other words, the events of 9/11 became serialized into a formulaic *jātrā* script that included both tragedy and humor while at the same time personalizing them by adding a native son as a central character to the story. In so doing, the performance was successful in making this faraway occurrence relevant to the local audience's immediate experiences.

Within one week of the staged performance, a number of scroll painters began drawing the outlines of a World Trade Center scroll, and some of the more talented among them also began composing songs about 9/11 that followed the framed action of the scrolls. By the beginning of 2005, virtually every *paṭuyā* in Naya was producing scrolls about 9/11, following the cue of an innovative few who took the initiative to incorporate the event into their repertoires. In this example, we see first a fictionalizing and localizing of someone else's history in written form, followed by a public performance, which was later reworked on the canvasses and notebooks of bards who would then orally perform the same narrative after adding their own sensibilities to the tragedy.

The *paṭuẏā* example suggests that there can be no tidy division between oral and written, or between folk, popular, and classical, as was suggested earlier and will be discussed again below. Folklore in South Asia has many social lives. It does not just live in an oral-aural world, but it moves back and forth through a number of media. The example above suggests a creation that was originally written but now exists as part of a vibrant and ever-changing oral tradition. Although the *jātrā* troupe that performed on that night in December 2001 has retired *America Is Burning,* they have moved on to other newsworthy events, such as the recent London subway bombings, the story of which is being performed in rural Bengal even as I write this section in August of 2005. Now it will only be a matter of time before the *paṭuẏā*s incorporate the London news item into their repertoires, just as they did the 2004 tsunami. The events of 9/11 may no longer exist in the urban *jātrā* form, but they are now firmly implanted in the scroll painting and singing tradition of rural Bengal. Even further, they also exist on display in the private homes of Swedish art students who purchased copies during a study trip to West Bengal in the spring of 2005 and in the collections of museums in Salem, Massachusetts; Syracuse, New York; and Santa Fe, New Mexico. When new international audiences see and hear the Bengali version of 9/11, the events will have yet another afterlife, one that is transnational and hybrid in character. Here we see yet another one of the ironies of global culture emerging as I write. A global event inspires a local expressive tradition that travels thousands of miles within the span of four years to become embedded in the lives and experiences of a completely new audience.

Similar examples of oral-written interaction could be multiplied many times over. Written epics, such as the *Mahabharata* and *Ramayana,* constantly take on new forms and acquire distinctly regional retellings, be it in the context of the Tamil *terukkūttu* or the Kannada *yakṣagāna* theater traditions of south India, or the *chau* dances of Orissa and West Bengal in the east. In Pakistan, too, we notice how the beloved Punjabi romance of Hir and Ranjha, one version of which was provided in chapter three, has multiple lives in oral, written, and celluloid media. Yet although all this border crossing and fluidity is symptomatic of modern life, it does raise dilemmas, both theoretical and practical, some of which I raised at the end of the previous chapter. Let us return to the discussion of ownership in the next section.

The opening frame of Manu Chitrakar's scroll painting titled *Oil Trade Center,* which was inspired by a popular Bengali theater production called *America Is Burning* that was performed in December 2001. By permission of the Museum of International Folk Art. Santa Fe, New Mexico. Department of Cultural Affairs. Photo by Paul Smutko.

It Belongs to Everyone and to No One

The *paṭuyā* example elaborated above raises a number of questions suitable for my third point. What gives a Bengali artist the right to appropriate an experience so deeply American as the September 11 bombings for personal gain and profit? Is it not crass commercialism to mass-produce an alien story, albeit in fictional form, for mass consumption? One could argue these questions from either an etic or an emic perspective. The etic perspective (which would be emic from an American point of view) might argue that it is hurtful to American sensibility, especially to those who lost loved ones in the conflagration. On the other hand, the emic perspective (which would be etic from the American point of view) would contend that the tragedy was universal. Because violence of other sorts and natural calamities in South Asia routinely take the lives of many more than died on 9/11, it is a narrative that rings true to everyone. It is thus not so different from Hollywood's production of *City of Joy,* a film based on a novel that fictionally relates the difficulties of growing up in a poverty-stricken ghetto of Kolkata.

Cultural flow inevitably leads to appropriation, reproduction, deviation, transformation, and change. In this sense, the production of folklore is a global process that belongs to no one. As I mentioned in the introduction and in chapter four, an earlier generation of folklorists understood the production and dissemination of folklore in a superorganic way, that is, as having a life of its own devoid of human agency. Put another way, human beings were seen only as receptacles for the dissemination of folkloric texts. Folktales, from this perspective, would only pass through individual storytellers without leaving any significant human imprint on the narrative. That is why the goal of so many early studies of folklore focused on seeking out an original source. Yet we have also seen in chapter two that certain communities in South Asia regard specific performance traditions or stories as their own, and only they have a right to them. This is even true of rural deities, who have multiple existences and forms specific to the village in which they reside (cf. Korom 1997). And there are hundreds of deceased charismatic Sufi saints known as Zinda Pir, the living saint, who are enshrined throughout the subcontinent. Yet each has his or her own distinct hagiography, as we saw in the story of Jhulelal recounted in chapter three.

The oral history of South Asia has taught us that such claims have led to conflict at times, and I have recorded legends of so-called deity thefts and kidnappings, during which one village steals another village's sacred image and installs it in their own village or holds it ransom until its demands are met by the violated village. Due to the authority of tradition, claims to ownership are taken seriously on the local level yet are difficult to enforce in any legal sense. Indeed, it is extremely difficult to copyright culture, especially if one considers the power relationships involved in doing so. When village courts cannot resolve such feuds, the deity in question often intervenes through a dream command to settle the dispute.

How then do we justify the liberal borrowing of folkloric items from one culture for use in another, or even within the same culture? Let us use the *paṭuyā* example once again to pursue this question. In the aftermath of the *America Is Burning* production, there was some debate in Naya as to who originally had the idea to transform the play into a scroll and song. No fewer than three *paṭuyā*s in the village claimed ownership, but none of them could prove it definitively. Given that the artists are highly competitive due

Image by the artist Robu on a rickshaw mud flap from Rajshahi, Bangladesh showing the film star Bobita as Nagini, who can transform herself into a cobra. Robu's painting is inspired by the film *Nag-Nagini,* which in turn was inspired by folklore. By permission of the Museum of International Folk Art, Santa Fe, New Mexico. Department of Cultural Affairs. Photo by Paul Smutko.

to decreasing patronage, even while professing caste comradeship, it is not surprising that each would want to lay a claim to the hypothetical original. But we must also remember the scriptwriter who first penned the story. Is it not his? Yes and no. One could argue that his *version* is his, but not the narrative itself. Similarly, each of the *paṭuyā* claimants could boast *his* version as *his* own. The latter point became clear to me on a crisp autumn afternoon in 2004 when one of the claimants asked me if I wanted to record a song he had composed about Satya Pir, a Muslim saint worshipped in eastern India and Bangladesh. My initial response was "Nah, I already recorded it from so-and-so." His immediate rebuttal was *āmār gān anya rakam* (my song is different), meaning the theme might be the same but the versions are different. What he was trying to tell me was that each owns his personal rendering of the song. Folk wisdom of this sort reconfirms what contemporary folklore studies teaches us about the nature of folklore production, namely, that it is

Dukhushyam Chitrakar, senior scroll painter and singer of Naya village in India, singing in front of the sacred grove of a local Muslim saint entombed there. This female saint is worshipped by both Muslims and Hindus. By permission of the Museum of International Folk Art, Santa Fe, New Mexico. Department of Cultural Affairs. Photo by Paul Smutko.

emergent and is created in specific performance contexts, as I suggested in the introduction. Therefore, no two texts produced in performance are the same, since the audience's interaction with the performer is responsible for mutually producing a specific text.

Easy Divisions for Taxonomic Purposes Are Difficult to Substantiate

The last major theme that has arisen in the course of this book is the issue of taxonomy. Taxonomy encourages us to categorize and label things

This dancer poses as Shiva shooting an arrow at the golden deer, part of a story from the classic *Ramayana* epic, 1988. Corbis.

into tidy, definable units for the purposes of academic investigation. It is an attempt to make order out of chaos. But because culture is messier than the natural order of the physical universe, generalizations are often difficult to make. The lengthy quote by Ben-Amos cited in chapter two questions universality, encouraging us to think in culturally relativist terms. I used extensive examples at the end of that chapter to make the point that a rose is not always a rose. In a region as linguistically and culturally diverse as South Asia, we must always begin with the specific indigenous point of view before attempting any sort of cross-cultural, comparative analysis to arrive at a universal conclusion. It is therefore best to understand items of folklore as existing on a continuum or sliding scale that is multidimensional and multilinear in nature.

Folklore simply cannot be reduced to a number of binary categories or either-or frameworks such as Redfield's great and little traditions, discussed in the introductory chapter. Moreover, we have already seen that indigenous categories like *mārga* and *deśī* or *śruti* and *smṛti* are more fluid than our notions of classical and folk or events heard or remembered. Yet at the same time, I have suggested that similarities and parallels do in fact exist as family resemblances. After all, a braid of hair is only a braid when individual strands of hair are intentionally intertwined and bound together to create a distinct entity known as the braid. When we undo the hair, the braid ceases to exist, but the strands remain, only to anticipate a future braiding. We have even seen in chapter two that the very concept of folklore as understood in the Western world is problematic in South Asia. Our best bet in sorting out all of South Asia's rich folkloric diversity is to continue doing ethnographic fieldwork in concrete places, while paying closer attention to the larger issues confronting folklore in the modern world that I surveyed in chapter four.

NOTES

1. It is not possible to discuss all the relevant texts at length here, but see Keith (1928, x–xii, 242–95, 352–72).

2. This was the subtitle given to the first English translation of the text in 1880.

3. See Cowell (1990, xxii). A few more recent scholars, especially Collins (1990), take issue with much of the historical evidence and suggest that the so-called Pali canon was much more fluid than fixed throughout its development. This notwithstanding, there can be no denial that *Jataka* tales do indeed appear in these scriptures.

4. This number is somewhat arbitrary and imposed upon the narratives by foreign editors and translators, as pointed out early on by Rhys Davids, who states that the number is "merely a round number reached by an entirely artificial arrangement,

and gives no clue to the actual number of stories. It is probable that our present collection contains altogether . . . between two and three thousand independent tales, fables, and riddles" (1977, lxxxi).

5. On the historical accuracy of this traditional assertion, see Rhy Davids (1977, lxii–xvi). Buddhaghosa was a fifth-century Indian Buddhist monk who was one of the earliest and greatest commentators on Theravada scripture. He composed a massive treatise on Buddhism titled the *Visuddhimagga* (the Purity Path). His work is considered authoritative. On the dating of Buddhaghosa's life, see Winternitz (1972, 2: 609–11).

6. "Vampire" is the largely agreed upon translation of the term, but it is not quite accurate, since it refers specifically to a class of ghouls that inhabit corpses.

7. The best work to consult on the Purana literature is Rocher (1986). Another indispensable source for wading through this massive corpus is Mani (1964).

Glossary

ādivāsī. The official term used in India for people of tribal origin, this literally means "primal nester."

ahiṃsā. This term is associated primarily with Mahatma Gandhi to refer to his method of nonviolent resistance to colonial rule but has origins in Indian antiquity. The concept came into prominence after the Emperor Ashoka converted to Buddhism circa 262 B.C.E.

Benfey, Theodor (1809–81). This German Indologist was well known for his translation of the *Panchatantra* and for his theories concerning the Indic origin of story literature.

bhaṅgṛā. This genre of Punjabi folk music has achieved a new form in the South Asian diaspora by combining elements of Western popular music with well-known Punjabi rhythms.

bhāoŷāiŷā. This genre of folk song, which is sung in the local dialect in the northern regions of the Bengali-speaking part of the subcontinent and in Assam, evokes the landscapes and toponyms of northern Bengal.

Bloomfield, Maurice (1855–1928). A noted Sanskrit scholar, he taught at Johns Hopkins University. He taught a number of students who would go on to teach at major American universities, urging them to study Sanskrit story literature and the prominent motifs therein.

Brown, William N. (1892–1975). One of Bloomfield's students, he went on to become a professor of Sanskrit at the University of Pennsylvania, where he taught from 1926 to 1966. Brown is well known not only for his philological work but also for his studies of Sanskrit story literature, about which he published numerous articles.

creolization. This is a linguistic term that refers to the mixing of languages in contact zones where two or more cultures come together. Gradually, it came to be used for mixed culture as well. Originally used in the context of the Caribbean, it is now used to refer to mixed cultures throughout the world. It can be thought of as a synonym of "hybridity."

darśan. This term is used widely throughout India to refer to "auspicious sight." To get *darśan* means to view a sacred object, be it a place, a building, or a person. Often this task requires performing a pilgrimage.

deśī. Roughly translated, it means "native." However, as a technical term, it refers to an item of literary culture that is less classical and more regional or vernacular in character.

dharma. It is the philosophical concept of duty in Hinduism, referring to the spiritual dispositions and appropriate behavior of each *varṇa.*

diaspora. This Greek neologism originally referred to the global dispersion of the Jewish people out of the "promised land." It gradually came to refer to any group of displaced people. The word went through a series of stages before it achieved its contemporary range of meanings. By the 1960s and 1970s, sociological uses began to emerge as academic interest was generated around the study of forced expatriation and the African slave trade. Today it is used in a variety of ways and is the subject of heated debates in academic circles.

emic. The linguist Kenneth Pike coined this term from the word "phonemic." In cultural anthropology it is used to refer to an insider's point of view of his or her own culture. It is the complementary opposite of etic.

etic. Also coined by Pike, this term comes from the word "phonetic" and refers to an outsider's point of view of someone else's culture.

ġazal. This genre of semiclassical sung poetry has achieved widespread popular appeal in South Asia. As a poetic form, it originated in Arabic literature but reached its creative height in Persian before entering the stream of Urdu poetic forms. Today it is difficult to classify the genre as classical, since it is a mainstay of Indian and Pakistani cinema. It has also entered the folk slipstream in the form of *qawwālī,* an ecstatic form of song sung at the shrines of Sufi saints but now also popular on the world music scene.

gāthā. This term is used for individual verses of the Buddhist *Jataka* fables. In Nepali, however, it refers to the ballad genre.

globalization. This refers to the political and economic processes involved in creating a world economy and order that forces various nations to interact, often unequally.

ḥujra. This is an Arabic word that means "room." In the Pashto language spoken in Afghanistan and Pakistan, it refers specifically to a male guesthouse, where it is incumbent upon the host to be hospitable to his guests.

hybridity. This botanical and biological term is used to refer to the process of grafting two species together to create a hardier new variety. Postmodern theorists use the term primarily to refer to new forms of culture and identity that result from cultural encounter and change. Theoretically, the term is similar to "creolization."

jan(a). Literally, it means "people," but it is used in some South Asian languages, especially in south India, as an equivalent to the English term "folk."

jātrā. This popular form of Bengali theatre, which incorporates current affairs, gained prominence in the nineteenth century, and it continues to be performed by itinerant theater troupes for large rural audiences.

jātaka. It is a class of Buddhist texts written in Pali concerning the former lives of the historical Buddha.

jihād. The word comes from the Arabic root for "exertion," be it mental or physical. It commonly implies holy war in Islam but also refers to a genre of resistance poetry that emerged in Afghanistan and Pakistan during the Russo-Afghan war.

kahānī. The word literally means "story" in many Indo-Aryan languages. However, in terms of indigenous classificatory schemes, it often implies a story that is fictitious in nature.

karma. Literally meaning "action" or "deed," in South Asian religious thought, it refers to the law of cause and effect shared by Hindus, Buddhists, Jains, and Sikhs. One's *karma* from previous lives determines one's status in the present birth. The goal is to extinguish it in order to end the cycle of rebirth and achieve spiritual liberation.

kathā. In Sanskrit the term refers to the genre of story literature, but in many north Indian vernaculars it implies a story that is true.

khicuṛi. This is a tasty dish that is simple but filling. It consists of rice and lentils cooked with turmeric and other spices. It is often made with leftovers from the previous day. Because it is, in the culinary sense, a dish of mixed substances, it also commonly refers to items of culture that are mixed in north India, Nepal, Bangladesh, and Pakistan.

Lang, Andrew (1844–1912). He is the folklorist who disproved the solar theories of Max Müller. He is also known for his theories of religious evolution, which postulate that monotheism preceded other religious forms, since many so-called primitive cultures harbored the concept of a high god. This kind of original monotheism then degenerated into animism, according to Lang.

lok(a). This term means "people" in the languages derived from Sanskrit. As a technical term, it came to be used as an equivalent of the English word "folk," as the academic field for the study of folklore emerged in north India during the British colonial period.

lok sāhitya. It literally means "folk literature," but some early South Asian folklorists used it to mean "folklore."

lok saṅgīt. This is a generic north Indian term meaning "folk song." However, there is a myriad of subgenres that can be classified under this rubric. The variety of folk-song subgenres in South Asia is truly vast and would need to be classified according to time, topic, occupation, and place.

Mahabharata. This is the larger of the two great Sanskrit epics of India. It follows the adventures of the five Pandava brothers and culminates in a great war against the Kauravas. It is also found in a variety of vernacular renderings throughout the subcontinent and exists in theatrical performance as well.

mārga. The term literally means "path," but in technical contexts refers to classical tradition, as opposed to its complementary term *deśī.*

māyā. Hindus, Buddhists, Jains, and Sikhs use this word to refer to the illusory nature of the earthly realm that deceives us into thinking that the mundane world is the true and ultimate reality. Illusion is what keeps us anchored in this realm and hinders us from liberating ourselves from the bondage of *karma.*

melā. The term is cognate with words meaning "to meet." In north Indian languages it refers to huge fairs and festivals that often take place during religious rituals. These fairs generally feature a number of performers, who perform a variety of entertainments ranging from storytelling and singing to fire eating and acrobatics. It is similar in many ways to a Western circus or carnival. Today it is also quite common throughout the subcontinent to use the term for organized folk festivals.

Memorate. A first-person experience narrative about an encounter with a supernatural force.

Müller, Max (1823–1900). Müller was a German Indologist who taught Sanskrit at Oxford University. He was the first to use the term "scientific" with regard to religion. For Müller, the science of religion should be based on the science of language, and it should be a discipline separate from theology. According to Müller, the earliest myths—that is, those in the Vedas—were anthropomorphic expressions, which he called "mythopoetic." He believed that later generations then forgot their meanings, and these mistaken meanings based in language error were then passed down from generation to generation, a process he referred to as the "disease of language." For him, all myths originated in the sun; hence, his solar mythology thesis.

mushā'ira. This term refers to a formalized gathering during which Urdu poetry is recited, quite often in a competitive manner. It is popular throughout Pakistan and India.

nirvāṇa. It is the Buddhist term for extinction in the sense of extinguishing a flame. The ultimate goal of Buddhists is to extinguish the flame that causes us to suffer this earthly existence. Hence, to extinguish suffering one must extinguish earthly existence itself, which means eliminating all of one's personal *kārmik* residue.

nītiśāstra. This term refers to a class of Sanskrit texts that deal with morals and ethics, such as the animal fables included in the *Panchatantra.*

Panchatantra. These five books consist of animal fables written in Sanskrit that illustrate the importance of proper behavior. Many of the stories included in it are still part of the oral tradition today.

parī. Recognized as supernatural entities throughout much of the Islamic world, they most often appear in Muslim folktales as seductive supernatural women who are the objects of romantic quests by male heroes. *Parī*s were also known in pre-Islamic times, and they are mentioned in the Avestan texts of Zoroastrianism, where they are called *paraikā.*

paṭuyā. This term refers to an occupational group of artists who paint narrative scrolls and compose songs about those same scrolls. They are most common in Bengal but are found elsewhere in the region bearing different titles. Collectively, they are also referred to as *citrakār*s (picture makers). Although the etymology is uncertain, their name is derived from *paṭ,* which refers to the actual scrolls they paint.

pūjā. The word used to refer to religious rituals performed for a god or goddess. Sometimes elaborate and other times simple, they almost always involve symbolic and substantial transactions between humans and deities. It is also of uncertain etymology, but some scholars believe that it might be related to a root that means "to smear," since such rituals often involve the application of pastes to images as well as on participants' foreheads.

purāṇa. It literally means "old" but also refers to a class of mythological texts most often dedicated to a particular deity. The Hindu Puranas are written in Sanskrit, but medieval texts for local deities later emerged in regional vernaculars as well. There are even caste *purāṇa*s that are nurtured and maintained by professional bards and genealogists.

puruṣa. The term literally means "man." In the Vedas, however, it refers to the cosmic man who is sacrificed and divided up to create the four kinds of human beings.

qiṣṣa. In Arabic, Persian, and Urdu this word means "story." In medieval Persia it referred to oral narratives about heroes and romance. However, in contemporary South Asia it refers to a popular form of chapbook literature that draws on the various storytelling traditions in the Arabic, Persian, and Sanskrit written traditions.

Ramayana. The shorter of the two great Sanskrit epics involves the adventures of the deity Rama, his wife Sita, and his brother Lakshmana while they are living in exile. Like the *Mahabharata,* it exists in a variety of regional forms, and stories from it reappear in devotional songs, heroic ballads, and theater forms.

Rig Veda. The oldest written corpus of verses from ancient India comprises one-fourth of the Vedas, considered to be revelation by Hindus. It is thought that at least portions of it existed orally for many centuries before it was written down.

ṛta. The Vedic concept of cosmic order, which was maintained through a complicated system of elaborate *yajña*s (sacrifices), some of which were communal and public, while others were domestic and private. In either case, they were reciprocal in nature, much like *pūjā*s are today.

saṃsāra. In Hindu religion and philosophy, this term refers to the slippery stream of existence through which we all pass during each successive birth due to ignorance, illusion, and *karma.* In common north Indian parlance, it can also refer to family life.

smṛti. The term refers to "that which is remembered." It is used in Hinduism to refer to all religious texts that do not belong to the Vedas. Sometimes it is erroneously translated as "secondary revelation" in English.

śruti. It is "that which is heard." It is used only for the Vedas, which Hindus believe were divinely revealed to a group of sages who were the ancestors of priestly lineages that now guard specific branches of Vedic texts and learning.

suā nāc. This is a tribal parrot dance that is performed in the Chhattisgarh province located in central India.

svadeśī. This is another term associated with Mahatma Gandhi, and it refers to the concept of self-sufficiency. Gandhi believed that each village could essentially exist autonomously, if given the opportunity. To this end, he advocated that all Indians should spin cotton daily as an alternative to buying British cloth made from Indian cotton processed in British factories. Hence, the spinning wheel became a central symbol of Indian independence.

svapnādeś. This genre is known mostly from dreams, during which a deity enters a person's mind and makes a demand. Quite often the deity complains that he or she is not being worshipped enough. The deity may threaten to bring on calamity if worship does not intensify. The sleeping individual is then instructed to bring this message to others, and the burden of responsibility for ensuring the successful worship of the deity in question falls on the shoulders of that individual.

Tagore, Rabindranath (1861–1941). Tagore is the Bengali Nobel Laureate who was deeply involved in the folklore revival movement in the nineteenth century. A romantic at heart, Tagore saw in folklore the possibility to unify a culture fragmented by colonialism. Central to the unification process was the need to bring together the urban intellectual elite and the mass of rural peasants, who all shared one thing, namely Bengali lore.

terukkūttu. This is an important form of theatrical mythic reenactment popular in northeastern Tamil Nadu. Central to this performance tradition are the stories from the *Mahabharata* that focus on Draupadi, the co-wife of the Pandava brothers in the epic.

transnationalism. Transnationalism refers to the processes of cultural flows across national borders that result in more and more complicated forms of culture. It is a concept that radically transformed anthropology by freeing it from understanding culture as something bound to a specific locality. Transnationalism allows us to view the "big picture," but it also runs the danger of being too theoretical and hypothetical in nature. One of the reasons for this is because it is difficult and expensive to conduct fieldwork in more than one place at a time. Nonetheless, transnational anthropologists have been calling for multisided fieldwork, which would allow us to follow the trajectory of a single aspect of culture across national borders.

varṇa. *Varṇa* means "hue" or "color." It refers specifically to spiritual class, to the four groups of humans that result from the division of the cosmic man's body in Rig Veda 10.90. It is often erroneously translated as "caste" in English, but I prefer "spiritual class," since caste has more to do with occupational specialization. Each *varṇa* contains a variety of occupational castes.

vetāla. *Vetāla* is the term used for the vampire character in the text known as the *Vetalapanchavimshatika.* Although not an exact translation, vampire is the closest folkloric concept in English to describe it.

vil pāṭṭu. It is a genre of bow song sung in temple festivals organized throughout the southern districts of Tamil Nadu and parts of southern Kerala. The Tamil bow song belongs to a larger tradition, including the Malayalam *teyyam* and the Tulu *bhūta kōla,* in which deified dead heroes are praised in song to bring about possession.

vrat. *Vrat* refers to a fast and vow undertaken by an individual for a specific deity in order to be granted some sort of boon, such as lifelong prosperity, health, etc. Usually, the *vrat* is accompanied by a variety of ritual acts, including storytelling and floor drawings.

yakṣagāna. This dramatic form comes from the combination of *yakṣa,* the dwarf servant of Kubera, the Hindu god of wealth, and *gāna,* a distinct kind of vocal music prevalent in Andhra Pradesh and Karnataka. The genre combines elaborate masks and ornate costumes with dance and song to enact stories from the Sanskrit epics and Puranas.

Bibliography

REFERENCE WORKS

Arnold, Alison, ed. 2000. *The Garland Encyclopedia of Music.* Vol. 5, *South Asia: The Indian Subcontinent.* New York: Garland Publishing.

Bhattacharya, Sushil Kumar. 1989. *Folk Heritage of India.* Varanasi, India: Bibliographical Society of India.

Bødker, Laurits. 1957. *Indian Animal Tales: A Preliminary Survey.* Helsinki, Finland: Suomalainen Tiedeakatemia.

Handoo, Jawaharlal. 1977. *A Bibliography of Indian Folk Literature.* Mysore, India: Central Institute of Indian Languages.

Jain, Sushil Kumar. 1967. *Folklore of India and Pakistan: A Complete Catalogue of Publications in English Language.* Regina, Canada: University of Saskatchewan Campus Library.

Jason, Heda. 1988. *Types of Indic Oral Tales: Supplement.* Helsinki, Finland: Suomalainen Tiedeakatemia.

Jatoi, Iqbal Ali. 1980. *Bibliography of Folk Literature.* Islamabad, Pakistan: National Institute of Folk Heritage.

Khan, Shamsuzzaman, and M. Chowdhury, eds. 1987. *Bibliography of Folklore of Bangladesh.* Dhaka, Bangladesh: Bangla Academy.

Kirkland, Edward C. 1966. *A Bibliography of South Asian Folklore.* Bloomington: Indiana University Press.

Korom, Frank J. 1988. *Pakistani Folk Culture: A Select Annotated Bibliography.* Islamabad, Pakistan: Lok Virsa Research Institute.

Kumar, Sushil, and N. Kumar, eds. 2003. *Encyclopedia of Folklore and Folktales of South Asia.* New Delhi: Anmol.

Mani, Vetam. 1975. *Purāṇic Encyclopaedia.* Delhi: Motilal Banarsidass.

Mills, Margaret A., Peter Claus, and Sarah Diamond, eds. 2003. *South Asian Folklore: An Encyclopedia.* New York: Routledge.

Roberts, Warren E. 1961. "A Tale Type Index for India and Pakistan." In *Internationale Kongress der Volkserzählungsforscher in Kiel und Kopenhagen: Vorträge und Referate*, ed. K. Ranke, 338–40. Berlin: DeGruyter.

Sengupta, Sankar. 1967. *A Bibliography of Indian Folklore and Related Subjects.* Calcutta: Indian Publications.

———. 1967. *A Survey of Folklore Study in Bengal: West Bengal and East Pakistan.* Calcutta: Indian Publications.

Thompson, Stith, and Tony Balys. 1958. *Oral Tales of India.* Bloomington: Indiana University Press.

Thompson, Stith, and Warren Roberts. 1960. *Tale-Types of India, Pakistan, Ceylon.* Helsinki, Finland: Suomalainen Tiedeakatemia.

COLLECTIONS, ANTHOLOGIES, AND TRANSLATIONS

Acworth, Harry Arbuthnot. 1894. *Ballads of the Marathas, Rendered into English Verse from the Marathi Originals.* London: Longmans, Green and Co.

Amore, Roy C., and Larry Shinn, eds. 1981. *Lustful Maidens and Ascetic Kings: Buddhist and Hindu Stories of Life.* New York: Oxford University Press.

Anderson, James D. 1895. *A Collection of Kachári Folk-Tales and Rhymes.* Shillong, India: Assam Secretariat Printing Press.

Beck, Brenda E. F., P. J. Claus, P. Goswami, and J. Handoo, eds. 1987. *Folktales of India.* Chicago: University of Chicago Press.

Benfey, Theodor. 1859. *Pantschatantra. Fünf Bücher indischer Fabeln, Märchen und Erzählungen.* 2 vols. Leipzig, Germany: F. A. Brockhaus.

Bodding, P. O. 1940. *Santal Riddles.* Oslo, Norway: A. W. Brøggers Boktryykkeri.

Bompas, Cecil H. 1909. *Folk Lore of the Santal Parganas.* New Delhi: Ajay Book Service, 1981.

Brown, William N., and N. Mayeda. 1974. *Tawi Tales: Folk Tales from Jammu.* New Haven, CT: American Oriental Society.

Buitenen, J.A.B. van. 1959. *Tales of Ancient India.* Chicago: University of Chicago Press.

Burton, Sir Richard. 1893. *Vikram and the Vampire or Tales of Hindu Devilry.* New York: Dover Publications, 1969.

Cornelius, Judson K. *Campus Humor.* Hyderabad, India: Manikyam Mansion, 1997.

Cowell, Edward B., ed. 1895. *The Jātaka or the Stories of the Buddha's Former Births.* 6 vols. Varanasi, India: Motilal Banarsidass, 1990.

Cunningham, Alexander, ed. 1871–87. *The Archaeological Survey.* 23 vols. Simla, India: Government of India Publications.

Darmesteter, James. 1888–90. *Chants populaires des afghans.* Paris: Imprimirie Nationale.

Day, Lal Behari. 1883. *Folk-Tales of Bengal.* London: Macmillan.

Dimmit, Cornelia, and J.A.B. van Buitenen, eds. 1978. *Classical Hindu Mythology: A Reader in the Sanskrit Purāṇas.* Philadelphia: Temple University Press.

Emeneau, Murray B. 1944. *Kota Texts.* Berkeley: University of California Press.

Frere, Mary. 1868. *Old Deccan Days; or, Hindoo Fairy Legends Current in Southern India.* London: Murray.

Gordon, E. M. 1908. *Indian Folk Tales, Being Side-Lights on Village Life in Bilaspore, Central Provinces.* London: Stock.

Gover, Charles E. 1871. *The Folk Songs of Southern India.* Madras, India: Higginbotham and Co.

Gray, John. 1961. *Indian Folk Tales and Legends.* Oxford: Oxford University Press.

Grierson, George. 1903–28. *The Linguistic Survey of India.* 11 vols. Calcutta: Government of India Publications.

Griffith, Ralph T. H., trans. 1963. *The Hymns of the Rgveda.* Delhi: Motilal Banarsidass.

Hertel, Johannes. 1915. *The Panchatantra: A Collection of Ancient Hindu Tales.* Cambridge, MA: Harvard University Press.

Heston, Wilma, and M. Nasir. 1988. *The Bazaar of Storytellers.* Islamabad, Pakistan: Lok Virsa Publishing House.

Khan, Shamsuzzaman. 1985. *Folk Tales of Bangladesh.* Dhaka, Bangladesh: Bangla Academy.

———. 1986. *Folk Poems from Bangladesh.* Dhaka, Bangladesh: Bangla Academy.

Kingscote, Georgiana W., and Natesa Sastri. 1890. *Tales of the Sun; or, Folklore of Southern India.* London: Allen.

Knowles, James. H. 1893. *Kashmiri Folk Tales.* Islamabad, Pakistan: National Institute of Folk Heritage, 1981.

Lorimer, D. L. R. 1934. *Folk Tales from Hunza.* Islamabad, Pakistan: Lok Virsa Publishing House, 1987.

Manwaring, Alfred. 1899. *Marathi Proverbs: Collected and Translated.* Oxford: Clarendon Press.

McNair, F. F. A. and T. L. Barlow. 1908. *Oral Tradition from the Indus. Comprised in Tales.* Brighton, England: Gosden.

Naithani, Sadhana, ed. 2000. *Folktales from Northern India.* Santa Barbara, CA: ABC-CLIO Press.

Olivelle, Patrick, trans. 1997. *Panchatantra.* New York: Oxford University Press.

Parker, Henry. 1910–14. *Village Folk Tales of Ceylon.* 3 vols. London: Luzac.

Penzer, Norman, ed. 1924. *The Ocean of Story, Being C. H. Tawney's Translation of Somadeva's Kathā Sarit Sāgara.* 10 vols. Delhi: Motilal Banarsidass, 1968.

Ramanujan, A. K., ed. 1991. *Folktales from India: A Selection of Oral Tales from Twenty-two Languages.* New York: Pantheon.

———. 1997. *A Flowering Tree: And Other Oral Tales from India.* Berkeley: University of California Press.

Rhys Davids, Thomas W. 1880. *Buddhist Birth Stories.* New York: Arno Press, 1970.

Ryder, Arthur., trans. 1925. *The Panchatantra: Complete and Unabridged.* Bombay: Jaico Publishing House, 1949.

———. 1932. *Twenty-two Goblins.* New York: E. P. Dutton.

Schiefner, Anton von. 1926. *Tibetan Tales: Derived from Indian Sources.* London: Routledge.

Sen, Dineshchandra. 1932. *The Ballads of Bengal.* 4 vols. Delhi: Mittal Publications, 1988.

Siddique, Ashraf, and M. Lerch. 1998. *Pakistani Folk Tales.* New York: Hippocrene.

Steele, Flora A. 1894. *Tales of the Punjab.* London: Macmillan.

Swynnerton, Charles. 1892. *Folk Tales from the Upper Indus.* Islamabad, Pakistan: Lok Virsa Publishing House, 1987.

Temple, Richard Carnac, trans. 1884. *The Legends of the Panjab.* 2 vols. Islamabad, Pakistan: Institute of Folk Heritage, 1981.

Tod, James. 1920. *Annals and Antiquities of Rajasthan.* 3 vols. London: Milford.

Usborne, Charles F., trans. 1966. *The Adventures of Hir and Ranjha.* Karachi, Pakistan: Lion Art Press.

Wilkins, Charles. 1886. *Fables and Proverbs from the Sanskrit, Being the Hitopadesha.* Gainesville, FL: Scholars' Facsimiles and Reprints, 1968.

GENERAL BIBLIOGRAPHY

Abrahams, Roger D. 1993. "Phantoms of Romantic Nationalism in Folkloristics." *Journal of American Folklore* 106 (419): 3–37.

Adams, R. 1961. "The Tales of Greed and Punishment: A Study of an Indian Oral Tale." *Journal of the Asiatic Royal Society* 15: 22–36.

Aijmer, Göran, ed. 1995. *Syncretism and the Commerce of Symbols.* Göteborg, Sweden: Institute for Advanced Studies in Social Anthropology.

Aiyappan, A. 1976. "Deified Men and Humanized Gods: Some Folk Bases of Hindu Theology." In *The Realm of the Extra-Human: Agents and Audiences,* ed. A. Bhatari, 139–48. The Hague: Mouton Publishers.

Amin, Shahid. 1988. "Gandhi as Mahatma: Gorakhpur District, Eastern UP, 1921–2." In *Selected Subaltern Studies,* ed. R. Guha and G. Spivak, 288–348. Oxford: Oxford University Press.

Anderson, Benedict. 1991. *Imagined Communities: Reflections on the Origins and Spread of Nationalism.* London: Verso.

Angelo, Michael. 1997. *The Sikh Diaspora: Tradition and Change in an Immigrant Community.* New York: Garland Publishing.

Anzulovic, Branomir. 1999. *Heavenly Serbia: From Myth to Genocide.* New York: New York University Press.

Ao, Temsula. n.d. *The Ao-Naga Oral Tradition.* Baroda, India: Bhasha Publications.

Apache Indian. 1992. *No Reservations.* New York: Island Records. Compact disc.

Appadurai, Arjun. 1996. *Modernity at Large: Cultural Dimensions of Globalization.* Minneapolis: University of Minnesota Press.

Appadurai, Arjue, F.J. Korom, M. A. Mills, eds. 1991. *Gender, Genre, and Power in South Asian Expressive Traditions.* Philadelphia: University of Pennsylvania Press.

Archer, William G. 1985. *Songs for the Bride: Wedding Rites of Rural India.* New York: Columbia University Press.

Armstrong, John. 1995. "Mobilized and Proletarian Diasporas." *American Political Science Review* 70 (2): 393–408.

Arya, Satya P. 1984. "Proverbs in Northern India." In *Indian and Japanese Folklore: An Introductory Assessment,* ed. R. Mathur and M. Manabe, 425–69. Tokyo: KUFS Publications.

Asani, Ali. 1988. "Sufi Poetry in the Folk Tradition of Indo-Pakistan." *R & L* 20 (1): 81–94.

Bakhtin, Mikhail. 1981. *The Dialogic Imagination.* Austin: University of Texas Press.

———. 1986. *Speech Genres and Other Late Essays.* Austin: University of Texas Press.

Banerjee, Sumanta. 1989. *The Parlour and the Streets: Elite and Popular Culture in Nineteenth Century Calcutta.* Calcutta: Seagull Press.

Banerji, S. C., and C. Chakraborty. 1991. *Folklore in Ancient and Medieval India.* Calcutta: Punthi Pustak.

Baron, Robert and N. Spitzer, eds. 1992. *Public Folklore.* Washington, DC: Smithsonian Institution Press.

Basch, Linda, Nina Glick Schiller, and Cristina Szanton Blan, eds. 1994. *Nations Unbound: Transnational Projects, Postcolonial Predicaments, and Deterritorialized Nation-States.* Langhorne, PA: Gordon and Breach.

Basu, Ranu. 1975. "Some Aspects of the Composition of the Elite in Bengal. 1850–1872." In *Studies on Bengal. 1975,* ed. W. M. Gunderson, 107–24. East Lansing: Michigan State University Press.

Bauman, Richard. 1975. "Verbal Art as Performance." *American Anthropologist* 77 (2): 290–311.

Baumann, Gerd. 1990. "The Re-invention of *Bhangra.* Social Change and Aesthetic Shifts in a Punjabi Music in Britain." *The World of Music* 32 (2): 81–97.

Beck, Brenda E. F. 1972. "Body Imagery in the Tamil Proverbs of South India." *Western Folklore* 38 (1): 21–41.

———. 1978. "The Hero in a Contemporary Local Tamil Epic." *Journal of Indian Folkloristics* 1 (1): 26–39.

———. 1982a. "Indian Minstrels as Sociologists: Political Strategies Depicted in a Local Epic." *Contributions to Indian Sociology* 16 (1): 35–57.

———. 1982b. *The Three Twins: The Telling of a South Indian Folk Epic.* Bloomington: Indiana University Press.

———. 1986. "Social Dyads in Indic Folktales." In *Another Harmony: New Essays on the Folklore of India,* ed. S. H. Blackburn and A. K. Ramanujan, 76–104. Berkeley: University of California Press.

Bédier, Joseph. 1925. *Les fabliaux: Études de littérature populaire et d'histoire du moyen age.* Paris: E. Champion.

Ben-Amos, Dan. 1972. "Toward a Definition of Folklore in Context." In *Toward New Perspectives in Folklore,* ed. A. Paredes and R. Bauman, 2–15. Austin: University of Texas Press.

————. 1976. "Analytical Categories and Ethnic Genres." In *Folklore Genres,* ed. D. Ben-Amos, 215–42. Austin: University of Texas Press.

Beyer, Peter. 1998. "The Religious System of Global Society: A Sociological Look at Contemporary Religion and Religions." *Numen* 45 (1): 1–29.

Bhabha, Homi, ed. 1990. *Nation and Narration.* London: Routledge.

————. 1994. *The Location of Culture.* London: Routledge.

Bhachu, Parminder. 1985. *Twice Migrants: East African Sikh Settlers in Britain.* London: Tavistock Publications.

Bhagwat, Durga. 1943. "The Riddles of Death." *Man in India* 23: 342–46.

————. 1965. *The Riddle in Indian Life, Lore and Literature.* Bombay: Popular Prakashan.

————. 1984. "The Riddle Form in India." In *Indian and Japanese Folklore: An Introductory Assessment,* ed. R. Mathur and M. Manabe, 517–39. Tokyo: KUFS Publication.

Bharati, Agehananda. 1970. "The Hindu Renaissance and Its Apologetic Patterns." *Journal of Asian Studies* 29 (2): 267–87.

Bharucha, Rustom. 2000. *The Politics of Cultural Practice: Thinking through Theatre in an Age of Globalization.* Hanover, CT: Wesleyan University Press.

Bhattarai, Harihar. 1985. "Folklore Studies in Nepal." *Himalayan Culture* 3 (1): 10–14.

Bhatti, F. M. n.d. "An Aspect of Punjabi Folklore: Heer and Ranjha." London: Inner London Education Authority, Resource Centre for Asian Studies.

Bilimoria, Purushottama. 1995. *The Hindus and Sikhs in Australia.* Canberra: Australian Government Publishing Service.

Blackburn, Stuart H. 1978. "The Folk Hero and Class Interests in Tamil Heroic Ballads." *Asian Folklore Studies* 37: 131–49.

————. 1985. "Death and Deification: Folk Cults in Hinduism." *History of Religions* 24 (3): 255–74.

————. 1987. "Epic Transmission and Adaptation: A Folk Ramayana in South India." In *The Heroic Process: Form, Function, and Fantasy in Folk Epic,* ed. B. Almqvist, S. Catháin, and P. Ó Héalaí, 569–90. Dublin: Glendale Press.

————. 1988. *Singing of Birth and Death: Texts in Performance.* Philadelphia: University of Pennsylvania Press.

————. 1996a. "The Brahmin and the Mongoose: The Narrative Context of a Well-Travelled Tale." *Bulletin of the School of Oriental and African Studies* 59 (3): 494–507.

————. 1996b. *Inside the Drama-House: Rama Stories and Shadow Puppets in South India.* Berkeley: University of California Press.

————. 2001. *Moral Fictions: Tamil Folktales from Oral Tradition.* Helsinki, Finland: Suomalainen Tiedeakatemia.

————. 2003. *Print, Folklore, and Nationalism in Colonial South India.* Delhi: Permanent Black.

Blackburn, Stuart H., P. J. Claus, J. B. Flueckiger, and S. S. Wadley, eds. 1989. *Oral Epics in India.* Berkeley: University of California Press.

Blackburn, Stuart H., and A. K. Ramanujan, eds. 1986a. *Another Harmony: New Essays on the Folklore of India.* Berkeley: University of California Press.

———. 1986b. "Introduction." In *Another Harmony: New Essays on the Folklore of India,* ed. S. H. Blackburn and A. K. Ramanujan, 1–37. Berkeley: University of California Press.

Bloomfield, Maurice. 1916. "On Recurring Psychic Motifs in Hindu Fiction, and the Laugh and Cry Motif." *Journal of the American Oriental Society* 36: 54–89.

———. 1917. "On the Art of Entering Another's Body: A Hindu Fiction Motif." *Proceedings of the American Philosophical Society* 56: 1–43.

———. 1919. "The Fable of the Crow and the Palm-Tree: A Psychic Motif in Hindu Fiction." *American Journal of Philology* 40: 1–36.

———. 1920a. "The Dohada or Craving of Pregnant Women: A Motif of Hindu Fiction." *Journal of the American Oriental Society* 40: 1–24.

———. 1920b. "On Overhearing as a Motif of Hindu Fiction." *American Journal of Philology* 41: 309–35.

Bonazzoli, Giorgio. 1983. "Composition, Transmission and Recitation of the Purana-s." *Purana* 25: 254–80.

Booth, Gregory D. 1995. "Traditional Content and Narrative Structure in the Hindi Commercial Cinema." *Asian Folklore Studies* 54 (2): 169–90.

———. 2000. "Religion, Gossip, Narrative Conventions and the Construction of Meaning in Hindi Film Songs." *Popular Music* 19 (2): 125–45.

Bose, Mandakranta, ed. 2004. *The Rāmāyaṇa Revisited.* Oxford: Oxford University Press.

Bose, N. S. 1969. *The Indian Awakening and Bengal.* Calcutta: Firma K. L. Mukhopadhyay.

Braziel, Jane E., and A. Mannur, eds. 2003. *Theorizing Diaspora: A Reader.* Malden, MA: Blackwell Publishing.

Bregenhøj, Carsten. 1987. *Rg Veda as the Key to Folklore: An Imagery Experiment.* Copenhagen: Nyt Nordisk Forlag A. Busck.

Brenneis, Don, and Ram Padarath. 1975. "'About Those Scoundrels I'll Let Everyone Know': Challenge Singing in a Fiji Indian Community." *Journal of American Folklore* 88 (349): 283–91.

Brown, Michael. 2003. *Who Owns Native Culture?* Cambridge, MA: Harvard University Press.

Brown, William N. 1919a. "The Pañcatantra in Modern Indian Folklore." *Journal of the American Oriental Society* 39: 1–54.

———. 1919b. "The Wandering Skull. New Light on Tantrakhyana." *American Journal of Philology* 40: 423–30.

———. 1920. "Escaping One's Fate: A Hindu Paradox and Its Use as a Psychic Motif in Hindu Fiction." In *Studies in Honor of Maurice Bloomfield,* ed. W. N. Brown, 89–104. New Haven, CT: Yale University Press.

———. 1921. "Vyāghramārī, or the Lady Tiger-Killer: A Study of the Motif of Bluff in Hindu Fiction." *American Journal of Philology* 42: 122–51.

———. 1922a. "The Silence Wager Stories: Their Origin and Their Diffusion." *American Journal of Philology* 49: 289–317.

———. 1922b. "The Tar Baby Story at Home." *Scientific Monthly* 15: 227–33.

———. 1927. "Change of Sex as a Hindu Story Motif." *Journal of the American Oriental Society* 47: 3–24.

———. 1933. *The Swastika: A Study of the Nazi Claims of Its Aryan Origin.* New York: Emerson Books.

———. 1937. "The Stickfast Motif in the Tar-Baby Story." In *Twenty-fifth Anniversary Studies, Philadelphia Anthropological Society,* ed. D. S. Davidson, 1–12. Philadelphia: Philadelphia Anthropological Society.

Brukman, Jan. 1975. "'Tongue Play': Constitutive and Interpretive Properties of Sexual Joking Encounters among the Koya of South India." In *Sociocultural Dimensions of Language Use,* ed. M. Sanches and B. Blount, 235–68. New York: Academic Press.

Buitenen, Hans van. 1958. "The Indian Hero as Vidyadhara." *Journal of American Folklore* 71 (281): 305–11.

Burlingame, Eugene W. 1917. "The Act of Truth (*Saccakiriya*): A Hindu Spell and Its Employment as Psychic Motif in Hindu Fiction." *Journal of the Royal Asiatic Society,* n.s., 429–67.

Caplan, Lionel. 1985. "The Popular Culture of Evil in Urban India." In *The Anthropology of Evil,* ed. D. Parkin, 110–27. New York: Basil Blackwell.

Chatterji, Roma. 1985. "Folklore and the Formation of Popular Consciousness in a Village in the Purulia District of West Bengal." PhD diss., Delhi School of Economics, University of Delhi.

Clarke, Colin, C. Peach, and S. Vertovec, eds. 1990. *South Asians Overseas: Migration and Ethnicity.* Cambridge: Cambridge University Press.

Claus, Peter J. 1978a. "Heroes and Heroines in the Conceptual Framework of Tulu Culture." *Journal of Indian Folkloristics* 1 (2): 28–42.

———. 1978b. "Oral Traditions, Royal Cults and Material for the Consideration of the Caste System in South India." *Journal of Indian Folkloristics* 1 (1): 1–25.

———. 1981. "Indian Folk Epics." In *Indian Folklore I,* ed. D. P. Pattanayak and P. J. Claus, 6–21. Mysore, India: Central Institute of Indian Languages.

———. 1985. "The New Folklore: Review and Comment." In *Studies of South India: An Anthology of Recent Research and Scholarship,* ed. R. Frykenberg and P. Kolenda, 195–216. New Delhi: American Institute of Indian Studies.

———. 1995. "Designing Regional Folklife Documentation Centres." In *Computerizing Cultures,* ed. B. Saraswati, 122–35. New Delhi: New Age Publishers.

———. 1998. "Folklore." In *India's Worlds and U.S. Scholars, 1947–1997,* ed. J. W. Elder, E. C. Dimock, Jr., and A. T. Embree, 211–36. New Delhi: Manohar.

Claus, Peter J., J. Handoo, and D. P. Pattanayak, eds. 1987. *Indian Folklore II.* Mysore, India: Central Institute of Indian Languages.

Claus, Peter J., and Frank J. Korom. 1991. *Folkloristics and Indian Folklore.* Udupi, India: Regional Resources Centre for the Folk Performing Arts.

Clifford, James. 1994. "Diasporas." *Cultural Anthropology* 9 (3): 302–38.

Coburn, Thomas. 1980. "The Study of the Purāṇas and the Study of Religion." *Religious Studies* 16 (3): 341–52.

———. 1984. "Scripture in India: Towards a Typology of the Word in Hindu Life." *Journal of the American Academy of Religion* 52: 435–59.

Cocchiara, Giusseppe. 1981. *The History of Folklore in Europe.* Philadelphia: Institute for the Study of Human Issues.

Cohen, Robin. 1997. *Global Diasporas: An Introduction.* London: UCL Press.

Collingwood, R. G. 1993. *An Essay on Philosophical Method.* Oxford: Clarendon Press.

Collins, Steven. 1990. "On the Very Idea of the Pali Canon." *Journal of the Pali Text Society* 15: 89–125.

Coomaraswamy, Anand K. 1937. "The Nature of 'Folklore' and 'Popular Art.'" *The Indian Arts and Letters* 11 (2): 76–84.

Cosquin, Emmanuel. 1922. *Études folkloriques, recherches sur les migrations des contes populaires et leur point de départ.* Paris: É. Champion.

Coward, Harold, J. R. Hinnels, and R. B. Brady, eds. 2000. *The South Asian Religious Diaspora in Britain, Canada and the United States.* Albany: State University of New York Press.

Crooke, William. 1896. *The Popular Religion and Folklore of Northern India.* 2 vols. New Delhi: Munshiram Manoharlal, 1978.

Dalton, Edward Taite. 1872. *A Descriptive Ethnology of Bengal.* Calcutta: Office of the Superintendent of Government Printing.

Das, Veena. 1981. "The Mythological Film and Its Framework of Meaning: An Analysis of Jai Santoshi Ma." *India International Quarterly* 8 (1): 43–55.

Dave, Trimbaklal N. 1951. "Institutions of Bards in Western India." *Eastern Anthropologist* 4: 166–71.

De, Sushil Kumar. 1962. *Bengali Literature in the Nineteenth Century.* Calcutta: University of Calcutta Press.

de Caro, Frank A. 1970. "A Hindu Religious Anecdote." *Journal of Popular Culture* 4: 240–43.

———. 1988. "Differential Uses of Narrative." *Fabula* 29 (1–2): 143–49.

de Caro, Frank, and Rosan A. Jordan. 1984. "The Wrong *Topi:* Personal Narratives, Ritual, and the Sun Helmet as a Symbol." *Western Folklore* 43 (4): 233–48.

Detienne, Marcel. 1981. *L' invention de la mythologie.* Paris: Gallimand.

Deva, Indra. 1972. "Folklore Studies." In *A Survey of Research in Sociology and Anthropology,* ed. Indian Council of Social Science Research, 197–239. Vol. 3. Bombay: Popular Prakashan.

———. 1984. "Folk Beliefs in Northern India." In *Indian and Japanese Folklore: An Introductory Assessment,* ed. R. Mathur and M. Manabe, 351–77. Tokyo: KUFS Publication.

———. 1989. *Folk Culture and Peasant Society in India.* Jaipur, India: Rawat Publications.

Devi, Phoolan, M.-T. Cuny, and P. Rambali. 2003. *The Bandit Queen of India: An Indian Woman's Amazing Journey from Peasant to International Legend.* Guilford, CT: Lyons Press.

Dimock, Edward. 1959. "Tagore: Greatest of the Bauls." *Journal of Asian Studies* 19: 33–52.

Doctor, Raymond. 1986. "Gujerati Proverbs: An Analytical Study." *Lore and Language* 4 (1): 1–30.

———. 1986. "Predictive Sayings in Gujerati." *Folklore* 97 (1): 41–55.

Doctor, Roma. 1985. "Sindhi Folklore: An Introductory Survey." *Folklore* 96 (2): 223–33.

———. 1986. "The Logic of Riddles Re-examined: An Apologue to Maranda." *Lore and Language* 5 (2): 13–33.

Doniger, Wendy. 1987. *Tales of Sex and Violence: Folklore, Sacrifice, and Danger in the Jaiminiya Brahmana.* Delhi: Motilal Banarsidass.

———. 1993. *Purāṇa Perennis: Reciprocity and Transformation in Hindu and Jaina Texts.* Albany: State University of New York Press.

Dorson, Richard. 1955. "The Eclipse of Solar Mythology." *Journal of American Folklore* 68: 393–416.

———. 1968. *The British Folklorists: A History.* London: Routledge and Kegan Paul.

Dube, Saurabh. 1998. *Untouchable Pasts: Religion, Identity, and Power among a Central Indian Community, 1780–1950.* Albany: State University of New York Press.

Dumézil, Georges. 1968. *Mythe et épopee.* Paris: Gallimard.

Dundes, Alan. 1977. "Who Are the Folk?" In *Frontiers of Folklore,* ed. W. R. Bascom, 17–35. Boulder, CO: Westview Press.

———. 1990. "The American Concept of Folklore." In *Essays in Folklore Theory and Method,* 3–27. Madras, India: Cre-A.

Dundes, Alan, and Ved Prakash Vatuk. 1990. "Some Characteristic Meters of Hindi Riddle Prosody." In *Essays in Folklore Theory and Method,* 61–132. Madras, India: Cre-A.

Dunham, Mary. 1997. *Jarigan: Muslim Epic Songs of Bangladesh.* Dhaka, Bangladesh: University of Dhaka Press.

Dutt, Gurusaday. 1936. "The Living Traditions of the Folk Arts in Bengal." *The Indian Art and Letters* 10: 22–34.

Eaton, Richard. 1974. "Sufi Folk Literature and the Expansion of Islam." *History of Religions* 14 (2): 117–27.

Edgerton, Franklin. 1924. *The Panchatantra Reconstructed.* 2 vols. New Haven, CT: American Oriental Society.

Edwards, David B. 1993. "Words in the Balance: The Poetics of Political Dissent in Afghanistan." In *Russia's Muslim Frontiers: New Directions in Cross-Cultural Analysis,* ed. D. F. Eickelman, 114–29. Bloomington: Indiana University Press.

———. 1994. "Afghanistan, Ethnography, and the New World Order." *Cultural Anthropology* 9 (3): 345–60.

Embree, Ainslee. 1976. "Bengal as the Image of India in the Late 18th and Early 19th Centuries: Notes Towards the Definition of an Imperial Experience." In *Bengal*

Studies in Literature, Society and History, ed. M. Davis, 131–40. East Lansing: Michigan State University Press.

Emeneau, Murray B. 1940. "A Classical Indian Folk-Tale as a Reported Modern Event: The Brahman and the Mongoose." *Proceedings of the American Philosophical Society* 83:503–13.

———. 1943. "Studies in Folktales of India II: The Old Woman and Her Pig." *Journal of American Folklore* 56: 272–88.

———. 1958. "Oral Poets of South India—The Todas." *Journal of American Folklore* 71 (281): 312–24.

———. 1964. "India as a Linguistic Region." In *Language in Culture and Society: A Reader in Linguistics and Anthropology*, ed. D. Hymes, 642–53. New York: Harper and Row.

Erdman, Joan L., ed. 1992. *Arts Patronage in India: Methods, Motives and Markets*. New Delhi: Manohar.

Eriksen, Thomas Hylland. 1991. "The Cultural Contexts of Ethnic Differences." *Man* 26:1, 127–44.

Farber, Carole M. 1984. "Performing Social and Cultural Change: The Jatra of West Bengal, India." *South Asian Anthropologist* 5 (2): 121–35.

Ferro-Luzzi, Garbiella E. 1986. "Language, Thought, and Tamil Verbal Humor." *Current Anthropology* 27 (3): 265–72.

Flick, Hugh M. 1983. "The Transmission of Folk Wisdom in Ancient India." *The Harvard Advocate* 117 (3): 54–57.

Flueckiger, Joyce B. 1988. "He Should Have Worn a Sari: A 'Failed' Performance of a Central Indian Oral Epic." *Tisch Drama Review* 32 (1): 159–69.

———. 1996. *Gender and Genre in the Folklore of Middle India*. Ithaca, NY: Cornell University Press.

Flueckiger, Joyce B., and L. Sears, eds. *Boundaries of the Text: Epic Performances in South and Southeast Asia*. Ann Arbor, MI: Center for South and Southeast Asian Studies.

Frasca, Richard A. 1990. *The Theater of the* Mahābhārata: Terrukkūttu *Performances in South India*. Honolulu: University of Hawaii Press.

Furedy, C. 1972. "A Neglected Minority: Muslims in the Calcutta Municipality. 1876–1900." In *West Bengal and Bangladesh. Perspectives from 1972*, ed. B. Thomas and S. Lavan, 125–46. East Lansing: Michigan State University Press.

Fürer-Haimendorf, Christoph von. 1961. "Historical Value of Indian Bardic Literature." In *Historians of India, Pakistan and Ceylon*, ed. C. H. Phillips, 87–93. London: University of London. School of Oriental and African Studies.

Gangulee, N. 1947. *Indians in the Empire Overseas*. London: New India Publishing House.

Geertz, Clifford. 1983. "Blurred Genres: The Refiguration of Social Thought." In *Local Knowledge: Further Essays in Interpretive Anthropology*, 19–35. New York: Basic Books.

George, K. M., ed. 1984. *Comparative Indian Literature*. Vol. 1. Madras, India: Macmillan India.

Georges, Robert, and A. Dundes. 1963. "Toward a Structural Definition of the Riddle." *Journal of American Folklore* 76: 111–18.

Ginzberg, Carlo. 1983. *The Night Battles: Witchcraft and Agrarian Cults in the Sixteenth and Seventeenth Centuries.* Baltimore: Johns Hopkins University Press.

Gluckman, Max. 1954. *Rituals of Rebellion.* Manchester: Manchester University Press.

Gold, Ann G. 1992. *A Carnival of Parting.* Berkeley: University of California Press.

Gomme, George Lawrence. 1887. *A Hand-Book of Folk-Lore.* London: Folk-Lore Society Publications.

Gossen, Gary H. 1974. "Chamula Genres of Verbal Behavior." *Journal of American Folklore* 84: 145–67.

Gowda, D. Javare. 1984. "Folk Beliefs in Southern India." In *Indian and Japanese Folklore: An Introductory Assessment*, ed. R. Mathur and M. Manabe, 378–402. Tokyo: KUFS Publication.

Grintser, Pavel A. 1963. *Drevneindijskaya Proza* [Old Indic prose]. Moscow: Akademia Nauk SSR.

———. 1974. *Drevneindijkij Epos: Genesis i Tipologija* [Old Indic epic: Genesis and typology]. Moscow: Akademia Nauk SSR.

Gumperz, John, and D. Hymes, eds. 1964. *The Ethnography of Communication.* Washington, DC: American Anthropological Association.

Gupta, Akhil. 1998. *Postcolonial Developments: Agriculture in the Making of Modern India.* Durham, NC: Duke University Press.

Gupta, Atul Chandra. 1958. *Studies in the Bengali Renaissance.* Calcutta: National Council for Education.

Hacker, Paul. 1959. *Prahlāda: Werden und Wandlungen einer Idealgestalt: Beiträge zur Geshichte des Hinduismus.* 2 vols. Mainz, Germany: Akademie der Wissenschaften und der Literatur.

Halbfass, Wilhelm. 1988. *India and Europe: An Essay in Understanding.* Albany: State University of New York Press.

Halliday, W. R. 1923. "Notes upon Indo-European Folk-Tales and the Problem of Their Diffusion." *Folk Lore* 34: 117–40.

Hanchett, Suzanne. 1978. "Recent Trends in the Study of Folk Hinduism and India's Folklore." *Journal of Indian Folkloristics* 1 (1): 40–54.

Handoo, Jawaharlal. 1987. "South Indian Folklore Studies." *Journal of Folklore Research* 24 (2): 135–56.

Handoo, Jawaharlal, ed. 1998. *Folklore in Modern India.* Mysore, India: Central Institute of Indian Languages.

Handoo, Lalita. 1980. "The Syntagmatic Structure of Kashmiri Folktales." *Journal of Indian Folkloristics* 3 (5–6): 121–29.

Hannerz, Ulf. 1987. "The World in Creolisation." *Africa* 57 (4): 546–59.

———. 1989. "Notes on the Global Ecumene." *Public Culture* 1 (2): 66–75.

Hansen, Kathryn. 1992. *Grounds for Play: The Nautanki Theatre of North India.* Berkeley: University of California Press.

Haque, Abu S. M. 1967. "Folklore in the Nationalist Thought and Literary Expression of Rabindranath Tagore." PhD diss., Indiana University.

———. 1975. "The Use of Folklore in Nationalist Movements and Liberation Struggles: A Case Study of Bangladesh." *Journal of the Folklore Institute* 12 (2–3): 211–40.

Hariyappa, H. L. 1953. *Ṛgvedic Legends through the Ages.* Poona, India: S. M. Katre.

Harlan, Lindsey. 1992. *Religion and Rajput Women: The Ethic of Protection in Contemporary Narratives.* Berkeley: University of California Press.

———. 2003. *The Goddess' Henchmen: Gender in Indian Hero Worship.* Oxford: Oxford University Press.

Hartnack, Christiane. 1990. "Vishnu on Freud's Desk: Psychoanalysis in Colonial India." *Social Research* 57 (4): 921–49

Hauser, Beatrix. 2002. "From Oral Tradition to 'Folk Art': Reevaluating Bengali Scroll Paintings." *Asian Folklore Studies* 61 (1): 105–22.

Heelas, Paul, ed. 1998. *Religion, Modernity and Postmodernity.* Oxford: Blackwell Publishers.

Heginbotham, Stanley. 1975. *Cultures in Conflict: The Four Faces of Indian Bureaucracy.* New York: Columbia University Press.

Helweg, Arthur W., and Usha M. Helweg. 1990. *An Immigrant Success Story: East Indians in America.* Philadelphia: University of Pennsylvania Press.

Henry, Edward O. 1977. "Music in the Thinking of North Indian Villagers." *Asian Music* 9 (1): 1–12.

———. 1976. "The Variety of Music in a North Indian Village." *Ethnomusicology* 20 (1): 49–66.

Hertel, Johannes. 1914. *Das Panchatantra. Seine Geschichte und seine Verbreitung.* Leipzig, Germany: B. G. Teubner.

———. 1915. *The Panchatantra. A Collection of Hindu Tales. In Its Oldest Recension, the Kashmirian, Entitled Tantrakhyayika.* Cambridge, MA: Harvard University Press.

Heston, Wilma, and W. Hannaway, eds. 1996. *Studies in Pakistani Culture.* Islamabad, Pakistan: Lok Virsa Publishing House.

Hiltebeitel, Alf. 1992. "Colonial Lenses on the South Indian Draupadī Cult." In *Ritual, State and History,* ed. D.H.A. Kolff and M. S. Oort, 507–31. Leiden, Holland: E. J. Brill.

———. 1999. *Rethinking India's Oral and Classical Epics.* Chicago: University of Chicago Press.

———. 2001. *Rethinking the Mahābhārata: A Reader's Guide to the Education of the Dharma King.* Chicago: University of Chicago Press.

Hinnells, John R., ed. 1998. *A New Handbook of Living Religions.* New York: Penguin Putnam.

Hobsbawm, Eric. 1983. "Introduction: Inventing Traditions." In *The Invention of Tradition,* ed. E. Hobsbawm and T. Ranger, 1–14. Cambridge: Cambridge University Press.

Honko, Lauri. 1968. "Genre Analysis in Folkloristics and Comparative Religion." *Temenos* 3: 48–66.

————. 1995. "Training Folklore Scholars in Bangladesh." *Studies* (Dhaka) October: 13–18.

————. 1998a. *The Siri Epic as Performed by Gopala Naika.* 2 vols. Helsinki, Finland: Suomalainen Tiedeakatemia.

————. 1998b. *Textualizing the Siri Epic.* Helsinki, Finland: Suomalainen Tiedeakatemia.

Huda, Mohammad N. 1995. "The Egg Phenomenon of Creative Process and Personlore." *Studies* (Dhaka). October: 19–32.

Hymes, Dell, ed. 1999. *Reinventing Anthropology.* Ann Arbor: University of Michigan Press.

Indian Lion. 1994. *Under Cover.* Middlesex, UK: Multitone Records. Compact disc.

Islam, Makbul. 2001. "Rethinking Tusu: Diffusion and Transformation." *Folklore Research Journal* 7: 35–69.

Islam, Mazharul. 1970. *A History of Folktale Collections in India and Pakistan.* Dhaka, Bangladesh: Bangla Academy.

————. 1974. *Phoklor Pariciti Ebang Lok Sāhityer Paṭhan-Pāṭhan* [An introduction to folklore and the studying and teaching of folk literature]. Dhaka, Bangladesh: Bāṅgla Akademī.

————. 1985. *Folklore: The Pulse of the People.* New Delhi: Concept Publishing Company.

Jain, Jagdishchandra. 1981. *Prakrit Narrative Literature: Origin and Growth.* New Delhi: Munshiram Manoharlal.

————. 1986. "Folktales in Prakrit Literature." In *Sanskrit and World Culture,* ed. W. Morgenroth, 673–80. Berlin: Akademie-Verlag.

Jameson, Fredric. 1991. *Postmodernism, or, The Cultural Logic of Late Capitalism.* Durham, NC: Duke University Press.

Jason, Heda. 1983. "India on the Map of 'Hard Science' Folkloristics." *Folklore* 94 (2): 105–7.

Jayawardena, Chandra. 1968. "Migration and Social Change: A Survey of Indian Communities Overseas" *The Geographical Review* 58 (3): 437–49.

Jhala, Jayasinhji. 1995. "Aesthetic Choice and Innovation in Western India: Views from the Street." *Journal of Popular Culture* 29 (1): 71–92.

Jong, J. W. de. 1975. "Recent Russian Publications on the Indian Epic." *Adyar Library Bulletin* 39: 1–42.

Jordon, Rosan A., and Frank de Caro. 1996. *British Voices from South Asia.* Baton Rouge, LA: Louisiana State University Libraries, Special Collections.

Junghare, Indira. 1983. "Songs of the Mahars: An Untouchable Caste of Maharashtra, India." *Ethnomusicology* 27 (2): 271–98.

Karan, P. P. 1984. "Landscape, Religion and Folk Art in Mithila: An Indian Cultural Region." *Journal of Cultural Geography* 5: 85–102.

Karim, Anwarul. 1988. *The Myths of Bangladesh.* Kushtia, Bangladesh: Folklore Research Institute.

Kaur, Raminder. 2003. *Performative Politics and the Cultures of Hinduism.* Delhi: Permanent Black.

Kearney, Michael. 1995. "The Local and the Global: The Anthropology of Globalization and Transnationalism." *Annual Review of Anthropology* 24: 547–65.

Keith, Arthur B. 1928. *A History of Sanskrit Literature.* Oxford: Oxford University Press.

Kelly, John. 1991. *A Politics of Virtue: Hinduism, Sexuality, and Countercultural Discourse in Fiji.* Chicago: University of Chicago Press.

Keyes, Charles F., and E. V. Daniel, eds. 1983. *Karma: An Anthropological Inquiry.* Berkeley: University of California.

Khan, Shamsuzzaman, ed. 1987. *The Folklore of Bangladesh.* Dhaka, Bangladesh: Bangla Academy.

———. 1995. "Folklore Fieldwork, Problems and Prospects: Perspective Bangladesh." *Studies.* October: 1–18.

Kilambi, Jyotsna. 1985. "Toward an Understanding of the *Muggu*: Threshold Drawings in Hyderabad." *RES* 10: 71–102.

Kirshenblatt-Gimblett, Barbara. 1996. "The Electronic Vernacular." In *Connected: Engagements with Media,* ed. George E. Marcus, 1–45. Chicago: University of Chicago Press.

Kirtley, Bacil F. 1963. "The Ear-Sleepers: Some Permutations of a Traveler's Tale." *Journal of American Folklore* 76: 119–130.

Klass, Morton. 1988. *East Indians in Trinidad: A Study in Cultural Persistence.* Prospect Heights, IL: Waveland Press.

Köhler, Rheinhold. 1898–1990. *Kleinere Schriften.* Vol. 1. Weimar, Germany: E. Felber.

Kondapi, C. 1951. *Indians Overseas 1838–1949.* Bombay: Oxford University Press.

Kopf, David. 1969. *British Orientalism and the Bengali Renaissance: The Dynamics of Indian Modernization. 1773–1835.* Berkeley: University of California Press.

Korom, Frank J. 1982a. Field Notes, Varanasi, Uttar Pradesh, India.

———. 1982b. Field Notes, Cooch Behar, West Bengal, India.

———. 1985. Field Notes, Islamabad, Pakistan.

———. 1988. "Why Folklore?" *Inaugural Address for the International Workshops in Folkloristics.* Udupi, India: Regional Resource Centre for the Folk Performing Arts.

———. 1989a. "Inventing Traditions: Folklore and Nationalism as Historical Process in Bengal." In *Folklore and Historical Process,* ed. D. Rihtman-Auguštin and M. Povrzanović, 57–84. Zagreb, Croatia: Institute of Folklore Research.

———. 1989b. "Review of *Oral Epics in India.*" *Karnataka Folklore Newsletter* 1 (4): 15–19.

———. 1990. Field Notes, Goalpara Village, Birbhum District, West Bengal, India.

———. 1992. "Review of *Types of Indic Oral Tales: Supplement.*" *Journal of American Folklore* 106 (420): 233–34.

———. 1994. "Memory, Innovation, and Emergent Ethnicity: The Creolization of an Indo-Trinidadian Performance." *Diaspora* 3 (2): 135–55.

———. 1995. "The South Asian Diaspora: A Review Essay." *Middle East & South Asia Folklore Bulletin* 12 (1): 2–4.

———. 1997. "Oral Exegesis: Local Interpretations of a Bengali Folk Deity." *Western Folklore* 56 (2): 155–73.

———. 1999. "Reconciling the Local and the Global: The Ritual Space of Shi'i Islam in Trinidad." *Journal of Ritual Studies* 12 (1): 21–36.

———. 2000. "South Asian Religions and Diaspora Studies." *Religious Studies Review* 26 (1): 21–28.

———. 2003. *Hosay Trinidad: Muḥarram Performances in an Indo-Caribbean Diaspora*. Philadelphia: University of Pennsylvania Press.

———. 2004. "Uncharted Waters of Folklore Theory." *Lokoshruti* 3 (1): 45–56.

Kothari, Sunil. 1984. "The Technique of Seraikella Chhau Dance." *Folk India* 1: 20–26.

Kripalini, Krishna. 1980. *Rabindranath Tagore: A Biography.* Calcutta: Visvabharati.

Krishnamurti, B. 1991. "Shift of Authority in Written and Oral Texts." Paper presented at "Authoritative Words: Strategies of Communication in South and Southeast Asia," Madison, WI, 9–11 May.

Krishnaswamy, Revathi. 1998. "Mythologies of Migrancy: Postcolonialism, Postmodernism and the Politics of (Dis)location." *ARIEL* 26 (1): 125–46.

Kuckertz, Josef. 1975–76. "Origin and Construction of the Melodies in Baul Songs of Bengal." *Yearbook of the International Folk Music Council* 7: 85–91.

Künig D. and G. Bandini. 1980. "Some Examples of the Life-Token Motif in Indian Literature." *South Asian Digest of Regional Writing* 9: 30–41.

Kurin, Richard. 1983. "The Structure of Blessedness at a Muslim Shrine in Pakistan." *Middle Eastern Studies* 19 (3): 312–25.

Lal, Vinay. 1999. "The Politics of History on the Internet: Cyber-Diasporic Hinduism and North American Hindu Diaspora." *Diaspora* 8 (2): 137–72.

Landau, Marcus. 1884. *Die Quellen des Dacameron*. Stuttgart, Germany: J. Scheibe.

Lapointe, Elwyn C. 1978. "The Epic of Guga: A North Indian Oral Tradition." In *American Studies in the Anthropology of India,* ed. S. Vatuk, 281–308. New Delhi: Manohar.

Laufer, Berthold. 1898. "Fünf indische Fabeln aus dem Mongolischen." *Zeitschrift der Deutschen Morgenländischen Gesellschaft* 52: 283–88.

Lawrence, Bruce. 1976. *Shahrastani on the Indian Religions*. The Hague: Mouton Publishers.

Layard, John. 1937. "Labyrinth Ritual in South India: Threshold and Tatto Designs." *Folk-Lore* 48 (2): 116–82.

Leavitt, J. 1981. "Himalayan Versions of 'The Three Golden Sons': The Effect of Context on Narrative Content." *Journal of Indian Folkloristics* 4 (7–8): 1–17.

Lebra-Chapman, Joyce. 1986. *The Rani of Jhansi: A Study in Female Heroism in India.* Honolulu: University of Hawaii Press.

Limón, Jose, and M. J. Young. 1986. "Frontiers, Settlements, and Development in Folklore Studies, 1972–1985." *Annual Review in Anthropology* 15: 437–60.

Lincoln, Bruce. 1999. *Theorizing Myth: Myth, Narrative, and Scholarship.* Chicago: University of Chicago Press.

Lindholm, Charles. 1982. *Generosity and Jealousy: The Swat Pakhtun of Northern Pakistan*. New York: Columbia University Press.

Loiseleur-Deslonchamps, Auguste. 1838. *Essai sur les fables indiennes et sur leur introduction en Europe*. Paris: Techener.

Lourdu, S. D. 1984. "Proverbs in Southern India." In *Indian and Japanese Folklore*, ed. R. Mathur and M. Manabe, 470–94. Tokyo: KUFS Publication.

Lüders, Heinrich. 1904. "Die Jātakas und die Epik." *Zeitschrift der Deutschen Morgenländischen Gesellschaft* 58: 687–714.

Lutgendorf, Philip. 1989. "The View from the Ghats: Traditional Exegesis of a Hindu Epic." *Journal of Asian Studies* 48 (2): 272–88.

———. 1990a. "The Power of Sacred Story: *Ramayana* Recitation in Contemporary North India." *Journal of Ritual Studies* 4 (2): 115–48.

———. 1990b. "Ramayana: The Video." *Tisch Drama Review* 34 (2): 127–76.

———. 1991. *The Life of a Text: Performing the* Rāmcaritmānas *of Tulsidas*. Berkeley: University of California Press.

Lüthi, Damaris. 1993. "Krishna and Catir Nāccu: Feature Film as a Political Medium." *Visual Anthropology* 5: 271–84.

Macaulay, T. B. 1835. *Speeches*. New York: AMS Press.

Macdonnel, Arthur A. 1900. *A History of Sanskrit Literature*. New York: Haskell House Publishers, 1960.

Majumdar, Ramesh C. 1960. *Glimpses of Bengal in the Nineteenth Century*. Calcutta: Firma K. L. Mukhopadhyay.

Malik, Aditya. 2005. *Nectar Gaze and Poison Breath: An Analysis and Translation of the Rajasthani Oral Narrative of Devnārāyaṇ;*. New York: Oxford University Press.

Malik, Madhu, 1986. "Of Princes and Paupers: The Maintenance of Social Roles through Folktales." *India International Center Quarterly* 13 (2): 165–80.

Malinowski, Bronislaw. 1948. "Myth in Primitive Psychology." In *Magic, Science and Religion And Other Essays*, ed. Bronislaw Malinowski, 93–148. Prospect Heights, IL: Waveland Press, 1992.

Maloney, Clarence. 1974. *Peoples of South Asia*. New York: Holt, Rinehart and Winston.

Manuel, Peter. 1988. "A Historical Survey of the Urdu Gazal-Song in India." *Asian Music* 20 (1): 93–113.

———. 1993. *Cassette Culture: Popular Music and Technology in North India*. Chicago: University of Chicago Press.

———. 1994. "Syncretism and Adaptation in Rasiya, A Braj Folksong Genre." *Journal of Vaiṣṇava Studies* 3 (1): 33–60.

Marcus, Scott. 1993. "Recycling Indian Film Songs: Popular Music as a Source of Melodies for North Indian Folk Musicians." *Asian Music* 24 (1): 101–10.

Marriott, McKim. 1958. "Networks and Centres of Integration in Indian Civilization." *Journal of Social Research* 1: 1–9.

———. 1961. "Changing Channels of Cultural Transmission in Indian Civilization." *Journal of Social Research* 4: 13–25.

Marshall, Peter J., ed. 1970. *The British Discovery of Hinduism in the Eighteenth Century.* Cambridge: Cambridge University Press.

Masani, Zareer. 1987. *Indian Tales of the Raj.* Berkeley: University of California Press.

Maskiell, Michelle, and Adrienne Mayor. 2001a. "Killer Khilats, Part 1: Legends of Poisoned 'Robes of Honour' in India." *Folklore* 112 (1): 23–45.

———. 2001b. "Killer Khilats, Part 2: Imperial Collecting of Poison Dress Legends in India." *Folklore* 112 (2): 163–82.

Mathur, R., and M. Manabe, eds. 1984. *Indian and Japanese Folklore: An Introductory Assessment.* Tokyo: KUFS Publication.

McCormack, W. C. 1979. *Language and Society: Anthropological Issues.* New York: Mouton Publishers.

McDowell, Christopher. 1997. *A Tamil Asylum Diaspora.* Providence, RI: Berghahn Books.

Mehrotra, Suman and Satyendra. 1984. "History of North Indian Folk Literature." In *Indian and Japanese Folklore: An Introductory Assessment,* ed. R. Mathur and M. Manabe, 39–56. Tokyo: KUFS Publication.

Mills, Margaret A. 1991. *Rhetorics and Politics in Afghan Traditional Storytelling.* Philadelphia: University of Pennsylvania Press.

Minkowski, Christopher Z. 1989. "Janamejaya's Sattra and Ritual Structure." *Journal of the American Oriental Society* 109 (3): 401–20.

Mode, Heinz. 1961. "Types and Motifs of the Folk Tales of Bengal." *Folklore* (Calcutta) 2 (4): 201–5.

Morris, Brian. 1987. *Anthropological Studies of Religion.* New York: Cambridge University Press.

Mukherjee, Sima. 1962. "Folk Sentiments and Folk Background in *Bratachari* Songs." *Folklore* (Calcutta) 3 (12): 569–72.

Mukhopadhyay, Durgadas. 1989. *Culture, Performance, Communication.* Delhi: B. R. Publications.

Mulla, Majan. 1997. "Professionelle Märchenerzähler im südindischen Karnataka." *Fabula: Zeitschrift für Erzählforschung* 38 (1–2): 101–11.

Müller, Max. 1889. *Natural Religion.* London: Longmans.

Myers, Helen. 1998. *Music of Hindu Trinidad: Songs from the India Diaspora.* Chicago: University of Chicago Press.

Naithani, Sadhana. 1996. "Political Ideology and Modernization of Folklore." *Jahrbuch für Volksliedforschung* 41: 71–75.

———. 1997. "The Colonizer Folklorist." *Journal of Folklore Research* 34: 1–14.

———. 2001a. "An Axis Jump: British Colonialism in the Oral Folk Narratives of Nineteenth-Century India." *Folklore* 112 (2): 183–88.

———. 2001b. "Prefaced Space: Tales of the Colonial British Collectors of Indian Folktales." In *Imagined States,* ed. L. Del Guidice and G. Porter, 64–79. Logan: Utah State University Press.,

Nambiar, A. K. 1987. "Theyyam—Ritual and Performance." *Ruchi* 1 (6): 61–74.

Nandy, Ashis. 1990. "The Discreet Charms of Indian Terrorism." *Journal of Commonwealth and Comparative Politics* 28 (1): 25–43.

Narayan, Kirin. 1986. "Birds on a Branch: Girlfriends and Wedding Songs in Kangra." *Ethos* 14: 47–75.

———. 1989. *Storytellers, Saints, and Scoundrels: Folk Narrative in Hindu Religious Teaching.* Philadelphia: University of Pennsylvania Press.

———. 1993. "Banana Republics and V. I. Degrees: Rethinking Indian Folklore in the Postcolonial World." *Asian Folklore Studies* 52: 177–204.

———. 1995a. "Shared Stories." In *Bridges to Humanity: Narratives on Anthropology and Friendship,* ed. B. Grindal and F. Salamone, 86–98. Prospect Heights, IL: Waveland Press.

———. 1995b. "The Practice of Oral Literary Criticism: Women's Songs in Kangra, India." *Journal of American Folklore* 108 (429): 243–64.

———. 1995c. "Taking Oral Literary Criticism Seriously: Reflections on a Kangra Women's Song." In *Folklore Interpreted: Essays in Honor of Alan Dundes,* ed. R. Bendix and R. L. Zumwalt, 237–64. New York: Garland Publishing.

———. 1996. "Songs Lodged in Some Hearts: Displacements of Women's Knowledge in Kangra." In *Displacement, Diaspora, and Geographies of Identity,* ed. S. Levie and T. Swedenburg, 181–213. Durham, NC: Duke University Press.

———. 1997. *Mondays on the Dark Night of the Moon: Himalayan Foothill Folktales.* New York: Oxford University Press.

Nasir, Mumtaz. 1987. "*Baiṭhak:* Exorcism in Peshawar (Pakistan)." *Asian Folklore Studies* 46 (2):159–78.

Nicholas, Ralph. 1982. "The Bengali Calendar and the Hindu Religious Year in Bengal." In *The Study of Bengal: New Contributions to the Humanities and Social Sciences,* ed. P. Bertocci, 17–29. East Lansing: Michigan State University Press.

Nida, Eugene. 1960. *Message and Mission: The Communication of the Christian Faith.* New York: Harper.

Norton, R. 1920. "The Life-Index, a Hindu Fiction Motif." In *Studies in Honor of Maurice Bloomfield,* ed. W. N. Brown, 211–24. New Haven, CT: American Oriental Society.

Oberoi, Harjot. 1992. "Popular Saints, Goddesses, and Village Sacred Sites: Rereading Sikh Experience in the Nineteenth Century." *History of Religions* 31 (4) 363–84.

Obeyesekere, Gananath. 1963. "The Great Tradition and the Little in the Perspective of Sinhalese Buddhism." *Journal of Asian Studies* 22 (2): 323–42.

O'Gorman, Edmundo. 1970. *The Invention of America.* Bloomington: Indiana University Press.

Opler, Morris and Shaligram Shukla. 1968. "Palanquin Symbolism: The Special Vocabulary of the Palanquin-Bearing Castes of North Central India." *Journal of American Folklore* 81 (321): 216–34.

Pande, Trilochan. 1963. "The Concept of Folklore in India and Pakistan." *Schweizerisches Archiv für Volkskunde* 59: 25–30.

Panditaradhya, M.N.V. 1975. *On Riddles: A Definition and Analysis.* Mysore, India: Prabodha Publications.

Parkes, Peter. 1987. "Livestock Symbolism and Pastoral Ideology among the Kafirs of the Hindu Kush." *Man,* n.s., 22: 637–60.

Peabody, Norbert. 1997. "Inchoate in Kota? Contesting Authority through a South Indian Passion Play." *American Ethnologist* 24 (3): 559–84.

Pearson, Anne M. 1996. *"Because it Gives Me Peace of Mind": Ritual Fasts in the Religious Lives of Hindu Women.* Albany: State University of New York Press.

Pierce, David C. 1969. "The Middle Way of the Jātaka Tales." *Journal of American Folklore* 82 (325): 245–54.

Pinney, Christopher. 1992. "The Iconology of Hindu Oleographs: Linear and Mythic Narrative in Popular Indian Art." *RES* 22: 33–61.

Poddar, Arabinda. 1970. *Renaissance in Bengal: Quests and Confrontations. 1800–1860.* Simla, India: Indian Institute for Advanced Studies.

———. 1977. *Renaissance in Bengal: Search for Identity.* Simla, India: Indian Institute for Advanced Studies.

Pollock, Sheldon. 1997. "The 'Revelation' of 'Tradition:' Śruti, Smṛti, and the Sanskrit Discourse of Power." In *Lex et Litterae: Studies in Honour of Professor Oscar Botto,* ed. S. Lienhard and I. Piovano, 395–417. Allessandria, Italy: Edizioni dell'Orso.

Pritchett, Frances. 1986. *Marvelous Encounters: Folk Romance in Hindi and Urdu Literature.* Riverdale, MD: Riverdale Co.

Qureshi, Mahmud S. 1971. *Étude sur l'évolution intellectuelle chez les musulmans du Bengale. 1857–1947.* Paris: Mouton and Co.

Qureshi, Regula. 1995. *Sufi Music in India and Pakistan: Sound, Context, and Meaning in Qawwali.* Chicago: University of Chicago Press.

Raghavan, V. 1958. "Methods of Popular Religious Instruction in South India." *Journal of American Folklore* 71 (281): 336–44.

Raheja, Gloria G., and A. G. Gold. 1994. *Listen to the Heron's Words: Reimagining Gender and Kinship in North India.* Berkeley: University of California Press.

Rai, Amit. 1995. "India On-Line: Electronic Bulletin Boards and the Construction of a Diasporic Hindu Identity." *Diaspora* 4 (1): 31–57.

Ramanujan, A. K. 1987. "Foreword." In *Folktales of India,* ed. B. E. F. Beck, P. J. Claus, P. Goswami, and J. Handoo, xi–xxi. Chicago: University of Chicago Press.

———. 1989. "Where Mirrors are Windows: Toward an Anthology of Reflections." *History of Religions* 28 (3): 187–216.

———. 1990. "Who Needs Folklore? The Relevance of Oral Traditions to South Asian Studies." South Asia Occasional Paper 1, University of Hawaii.

Rama Raju, B. 1984. "South Indian Folksongs." In *Indian and Japanese Folklore: An Introductory Assessment,* ed. R. Mathur and M. Manabe, 100–57. Tokyo: KUFS Publication.

Rao, V. Narayana. 1981. "Proverbs and Riddles." In *Indian Folklore I,* ed. D. P. Pattanayak and P. J. Claus, 22–31. Mysore, India: Central Institute of Indian Languages.

Read, D.H.M., and S. C. ,Roy. 1921. "Folklore and the Folklore Society." *Man in India* 1: 40–47.

Redfield, Robert. 1960. *The Little Community and Peasant Society and Culture.* Chicago: University of Chicago Press.

Richman, Paula. 1991. *Many Rāmāyaṇas: The Diversity of a Narrative Tradition in South Asia.* Berkeley: University of California Press.

Richter, Julius. 1908. *A History of Missions in India.* Edinburgh: Oliphant, Anderson and Ferrier.

Risley, Herbert H. 1892. *The Tribes and Castes of Bengal.* 2 vols. Calcutta: Bengal Secretariat Press.

Robertson, Roland. 1995. "Glocalization: Time-Space and Homogeneity-Heterogeneity." In *Global Modernities*, ed. M. Featherstone, S. Lash, and R. Robertson, 27–44. London: Sage Publications.

Rocher, Ludo. 1986. *The Puranas.* Wiesbaden, Germany: Otto Harrassowitz.

Rodrigues, Lucio 1954. "Konkani Folk Songs of Goa." *Journal of the University of Bombay* 22 (4): 65–88.

Roghair, Gene H. 1982. *The Epic of Palnadu: A Study and Translation of Palnati Virula Katha.* New York: Clarendon Press.

Roy, Manisha. 1972. *Bengali Women.* Chicago: University of Chicago Press.

Roy, Sarat Chandra. 1932. "The Study of Folk-Lore and Tradition in India." *Journal of the Bihar and Orissa Research Society* 18: 353–81.

Rudolph, S. H., and Lloyd I. Rudolph. 1967. *Gandhi: The Traditional Roots of Charisma.* Chicago: University of Chicago Press.

Rudolph, Susanne, and James Piscatori, eds. 1997. *Transnational Religion: Fading States.* Boulder, CO: Westview Press.

Safran, William. 1991. "Diasporas in Modern Societies: Myths of Homeland and Return." *Diaspora* 1 (1): 83–99.

Sakhi, Satnam, and Khavo Makhan Makhi. 2003. *Virtual Bera Paar.* "Story of Jhulelal." http://mysite.verizon.net/satnamsakhi/jhulelal/story.html

Sakthivel, S. 1984. "History of South Indian Folk Literature." In *Indian and Japanese Folklore: An Introductory Assessment*, ed. R. Mathur and M. Manabe, 57–84. Tokyo: KUFS Publication.

Sankaran, S. G. 1984. "Folktales of Southern India." In *Indian and Japanese Folklore: An Introductory Assessment*, ed. R. Mathur and M. Manabe, 273–314, Tokyo: KUFS Publication.

Sax, William S. 1990. "The Ramnagar Ramlila: Text, Performance, Pilgrimage." *History of Religions* 30 (2): 129–53.

———. 2002. *Dancing the Self: Personhood and Performance in the Pāṇḍav Līlā of Garwhal.* New York: Oxford University Press.

Schlanger, Judith. 1970. "Metaphor and Invention." *Diogenes* 69: 12–27.

Scott, James. 1985. *Weapons of the Weak: Everyday Forms of Peasant Resistance.* New Haven, CT: Yale University Press.

———. 1990. *Domination and the Arts of Resistance: Hidden Transcripts.* New Haven, CT: Yale University Press.

Sen, Dinesh Chandra. 1911. *The History of Bengali Language and Literature.* Calcutta: University of Calcutta Press.

———. 1920. *The Folk-Literature of Bengal.* Calcutta: University of Calcutta Press.

Sen, Nabaneeta. 1966. "Comparative Studies in Oral Epic Poetry and the *Vālmīki Rāmāyaṇa:* A Report on the *Bālākāṇḍa.*" *Journal of the American Oriental Society* 86 (4): 397–409.

Sen, Soumen. 2004. *Khasi Jaintia Folklore: Context, Discourse, and History.* Chennai, India: National Folklore Support Centre.

Sen, Suchismita R. 1991. "A Comparative Study of a Folktale: The Bengali Tale of Itu." PhD diss., Penn State University.

———. 1995. "The Tale of Itu: Structure of a Ritual Tale in Context." *Asian Folklore Studies* 54 (1): 69–117.

———. 1996. "Tagore's *Lokasahitya:* The Oral Tradition in Bengali Children's Rhymes." *Asian Folklore Studies* 55 (1) 1–47.

Sengupta, Sankar. 1963. "Rabindranath Tagore's Role in Bengal's Folklore Movement." *Folklore* (Calcutta) 4: 137–52.

———. 1965. *Folklorists of Bengal.* Calcutta: Indian Publications.

———. 1984. "North Indian Folk Music: Its Wealth, Wisdom and Social Significance." In *Indian and Japanese Folklore: An Introductory Assessment,* ed. R. Mathur and M. Manabe, 158–223. Tokyo: KUFS Publication.

Sequeira, Isaac. 1981. "The Mystique of Mushaira." *Journal of Popular Culture* 15 (1): 1–8.

Shah, A. M., and R. G. Shroff. 1958. "The Vahivanca Barots of Gujarat: A Caste of Genealogists and Mythographers." *Journal of American Folklore* 71 (281): 246–76.

Sharma, R. K. 1986. "Oral Tradition as Reflected in the Great Epics." In *Sanskrit and World Culture,* ed. W. Morgenroth, 643–47. Berlin: Akademie-Verlag.

Siddique, Ashraf Hossain. 1979–80. "Bengali Folklore Collections and Studies During the British Period (1800–1947): A Critical Survey." *Bangla Academy Journal* 7 (3): 1–207.

Siiger, Halfdan, et al. 1991. "Small Functional Items and Regeneration of Society. Dough Figurines from the Kalash People of Chitral, Northern Pakistan." *Folk* 33: 37–66.

Silvestre de Sacy, Antoine. 1816. *Calila et Dimna, ou fables de Bidpai en arabe.* Paris: Imprimerie Royale.

Singer, Milton. 1961. "Text and Context in the Study of Contemporary Hinduism." *Adyar Library Bulletin* 25: 274–303.

———. 1972. *When a Great Tradition Modernizes: An Anthropological Approach to Indian Civilization.* New York: Praeger Publishers.

Singhal, Damodar P. 1972. *Pakistan.* Englewood Cliffs, NJ: Prentice-Hall.

Sinha, Mrinalini. 1992. *Colonial Masculinity: The 'Manly Englishman' and the 'Effeminate Bengali' in the Late Nineteenth Century.* Manchester: Manchester University Press.

Sinha, Surajit. 1958. "Tribal Cultures in Peninsular India as a Dimension of Little Tradition in the Study of Indian Civilization: A Preliminary Study." *Journal of American Folklore* 71 (281): 504–18.

Sircar, Sanjay. 1997. "An Annotated *Chhara-Punthi:* Nursery Rhymes from Bengal." *Asian Folklore Studies* 51 (1): 79–108.

Slymovics, Susan. 1990. *Wedding Song: Henna Art among Pakistani Women in New York City.* New York: Queens Council on the Arts.

Smith, John D. 1987. "Formulaic Language in the Epics of India." In *The Heroic Process: Form, Function, and Fantasy in Folk Epic,* ed. B. Almqvist, S. Catháin, and P. Ó Héalaí, 591–611. Dublin: Glendale Press.

———. 1990. "Worlds Apart: Orality, Literacy, and the Rajasthani Folk-*Mahabharata.*" *Oral Tradition* 5 (1): 3–19.

———. 1991. *The Epic of Pabuji: A Study, Transcription and Translation.* Cambridge: Cambridge University Press.

Smith, Jonathan Z. 1982. "In Comparison a Magic Dwells." In *Imagining Religion: From Babylon to Jonestown,* ed. Jonathan Z. Smith, 19–35. Chicago: University of Chicago Press.

Smith, William L. 1981. "Kīrttibās and the Pandits: The Revision of the Bengali Rāmāyaṇa." *Studia Orientalia* 50: 229–40.

———. 1988. *Rāmāyaṇa Traditions in Eastern India.* Stockholm: University of Stockholm Press.

Sokolov, Y. M. 1950. *Russian Folklore.* New York: Macmillan.

Spear, Percival, ed. 1958. *The Oxford History of India.* New Delhi: Oxford University Press.

Spitzer, Nicholas, and R. Baron, eds. 1992. *Public Folklore.* Washington, DC: Smithsonian Institution Press.

Srivastava, N. P. 1984. "Folktales of Northern India." In *Indian and Japanese Folklore: An Introductory Assessment,* ed. R. Mathur and M. Manabe, 330–50. Tokyo: KUFS Publication.

Srivastava, Shah L. 1974. *Folk Culture and Oral Tradition: A Comparative Study of Regions in Rajasthan and Eastern U.P.* New Delhi: Abhinav Publications.

Staal, J. Frits. 1974. "The Origin and Development of Linguistics in India." In *Studies in the History of Linguistics: Traditions and Paradigms,* ed. D. Hymes, 63–74. Bloomington: Indiana University Press.

Steerman-Imre, Gabriella. 1977. *Untersuchungen des Königswahlmotivs in der indischen Märchenliteratur: Pañcadivyādhivāsa.* Wiesbaden, Germany: Franz Steiner Verlag.

Stewart, Charles, and R. Shaw, eds. 1994. *Syncretism/Anti-Syncretism: The Politics of Religious Synthesis.* London: Routledge.

Stutley, Margaret. 1980. *Ancient Indian Magic and Folklore.* London: Routledge and Keegan Paul.

Swiderski, Richard M. 1988. "Oral Text: A South Indian Instance." *Oral Tradition* 3 (1–2): 122–37.

Tagore, Rabindranath. 1917. *Nationalism.* New York: Macmillan.

————. 1945. *My Boyhood Days*. Calcutta: Visvabharati.

————. 1956–58. *Ravindra Racanāvalī* [Collected works]. 26 vols. Calcutta: Visvabharati.

Tewari, Laxmi G. 1989. "An Elementary Reading of the Alhakhand." *South Asia Research* 9 (1): 3–20.

Thapar, Romila. 1989. "Epic and History: Tradition, Dissent and Politics in India." *Past and Present* 125: 3–26.

Thiel-Horstmann, Monika. 1978. *Sadani-Lieder: Studien zu einer nordindischen Volksliteratur.* Wiesbaden, Germany: Otto Harrasowitz.

Thompson, E. P. 1966. *The Making of the English Working Class.* New York: Vintage.

Thompson, Stith 1946. *The Folktale.* New York: Holt, Rinehart and Winston.

Tölölyan, Khachig. 1996. "Rethinking *Diaspora*(s): Stateless Power in the Transnational Moment." *Diaspora* 5 (1): 3–36.

Töttössy, C. 1969. "Character and Genre of the Stories of the Sukasaptati." *Indian Antiquity* 17 (1969): 433–41.

Toulmin, Steven. 1972. *Human Understanding.* Vol. 1. Princeton, NJ: Princeton University Press.

Toynbee, Arnold. 1962. *A Study of History.* Vol. 5. New York: Oxford University Press.

Trawick, Margaret 1988. "Ambiguity in the Oral Exegesis of a Sacred Text: *Tirukkōvaiyār."* *Cultural Anthropology* 3 (3): 316–51.

Troger, Rolf. 1966. *A Comparative Study of a Bengali Folktale: An Analysis of the Bengal Folktale Type: The Pursuit of Blowing Cotton—AT 480.* Calcutta: Indian Publications.

Tyler, Stephen. 1973. *India: An Anthropological Perspective.* Pacific Palisades, CA: Goodyear Publishing.

Uččida, Norihiko. 1979. *Oral Literature of the Saurashtrans.* Calcutta: Simant Publications.

Upadhyaya, Hari S. 1965. "A Survey of Hindi Folklore." *Southern Folklore Quarterly* 29 (3): 239–250.

Upadhyaya, K. D. 1954 "A General Survey of Folklore Activities in India." *Midwest Folklore* 4 (4): 201–12.

————. 1959. "A General Survey of Indian Folk-Tales." *Indian Folk-Lore* 2 (4): 292–297; 325–29.

————. 1965. "The Classification and Chief-Characteristics of Indian (Hindi) Folk Tales." *Fabula* 7: 225–29.

————. 1967. "Society as Depicted in Indian Folk-Narratives." *Fabula* 9 (1–3): 155–61.

Upadhyāya, V. n.d. *Śrī Kāśī Pañcakrośī Dev-Yātrā* [The Sacred Kashi Five Krosh Deity Pilgrimage].Varanasi, India: Śrī Bhṛguprakāśan.

Vatsyayan, Kapila. 1984. "The Chhau Dance of Mayurbhanj." *Folk India* 1: 1–12.

Vatuk, Ved P. 1965. "Craving for a Child in the Folksongs of East Indians in British Guiana." *Journal of the Folklore Institute* 2 (1): 55–77.

———. 1969. "Amir Khusro and Indian Riddle Traditions." *Journal of American Folklore* 82: 142–54.

———. 1979. *Studies in Indian Folk Traditions.* Delhi: Manohar.

Veer, Peter van der, ed. 1995. *Nation and Migration: The Politics of Space in the South Asian Diaspora.* Philadelphia: University of Pennsylvania Press.

Veer, Peter van der, and Steven Vertovec. 1991. "Brahmanism Abroad: On Caribbean Hinduism as an Ethnic Religion." *Ethnology* 30 (2): 149–66.

Venu, G. 1981. "Tolpava Koothu: The Traditional Shadow Puppet Play of Kerala." *National Centre for the Performing Arts Quarterly Journal* 10 (4): 25–36.

Venugopal, Saraswati. 1982. "Some Perceptions of Deity and Their Change as Reflected in Folk Songs of Tamilnadu." In *Images of Man: Religion and Historical Process in South Asia,* ed. F. W. Clothey, 196–216. Madras, India: New Era Publications.

Veselovskiĭ, Aleksandr N. 1883. *Zamietki po literaturie i narodnoi slovesnost* [Notes on literature and oral folklore]. Moscow: n.p.

Vidyarthi, Lalita P., ed. 1973. *Essays in Indian Folklore.* Calcutta: Indian Publications.

Wadley, Susan S. 1978. "Texts in Contexts: Oral Traditions and the Study of Religion in Karimpur." In *American Studies in the Anthropology of India,* ed. S. Vatuk, 309–41. New Delhi: Manohar.

———. 1983. "Vrats: Transformers of Destiny." In *Karma: An Anthropological Inquiry,* ed. V. Daniel and C. Keyes, 147–62. Berkeley: University of California Press.

———. 2004. *Raja Nal and the Goddess: The North Indian Epic Dhola in Performance.* Bloomington: Indiana University Press.

Wagner, Roy. 1975. *The Invention of Culture.* Chicago: University of Chicago Press.

Wallace, Anthony F. C. 1956. "Revitalization Movements." *American Anthropologist* 58: 264–81.

Wankhade, Manohar 1965. "Some Aspects of Maratha Society as Reflected in Maratha Ballads." *Southern Folklore Quarterly* 29 (3): 251–58.

Werbner, Pnina, and Tariq Modood, eds. 1997. *Debating Cultural Hybridity: Multi-Cultural Identities and the Politics of Racism.* London: Zed Books.

Wilkins, William J. 1882. *Hindu Mythology.* Calcutta: Rupa and Company, 1978.

Winternitz, Moriz. 1908–20. *Geschichte der indischen Literatur.* 3 vols. Leipzig, Germany: Amelang.

———. 1933. *A History of Indian Literature.* 2 vols. New Delhi: Munshiram Manoharlal, 1972.

Wittgenstein, Ludwig. 1976. *Philosophical Investigations.* Oxford: Basil Blackwell.

Witzel, Michael. 1987. "On the Origin of the Literary Device of the 'Frame Story' in Old Indian Literature." In *Hinduismus und Buddhismus: Festschrift Ulrich Schneider,* ed. H. Falk, 380–414. Freiburg, Germany: Hedwig Falk.

Young, Robert. 1995. *Colonial Desire: Hybridity in Theory, Culture and Race.* London: Routledge.

Zachariae, Theodor. 1914. "Rätsel der Königin von Saba in Indien." *Zeitschrift für Volkskunde* 24: 421–24.

Zbavitel, Dušan. 1961. "Rabindranath and the Folk-Literature of Bengal." *Folklore* (Calcutta) 2: 9–14.

———. 1983. *Bengali Folk-Ballads from Mymensingh and the Problem of Their Authenticity.* Calcutta: University of Calcutta Press.

Zimmer, Heinrich. 1971. *The King and the Corpse: Tales of the Soul's Conquest of Evil.* Princeton, NJ: Princeton University Press.

Zograph, G.A. 1982. *Languages of South Asia: A Guide.* London: Routledge and Kegan Paul.

Web Resources

GENERAL

southasia.net: This powerful search engine for the region is arranged categorically.

wwwcrl.uchicago.edu/dsal: This digital South Asian library is the result of a collaborative effort to make South Asian resources available online. The site includes reference sources, images, maps, statistics, bibliographies, and much more.

www.umlib.um.edu.my: Billed as the "Yahoo! of South Asian resources," this site provides links to many others.

www.une.edu.au/~arts/SouthAsiaNet/san.htm: The homepage of South Asia Net, an international group of scholars interested in the region. The site is based in Australia and links to a number of journals that publish articles on the region.

lcweb2.loc.gov/frd/cs/cshome.html: Part of the Library of Congress's Web site, this section provides LOC publications on country profiles, each of which covers historical chronologies, geographic and demographic information, cultural and religious diversity, international relations, etc. Each volume also includes an extensive bibliography for further research.

wwwcrl.uchicago.edu/info/samp.htm: The site of the South Asia Microform Project contains a catalog of holdings, a list of member institutions, and more.

www.columbia.edu/cu/libraries/indiv/area/sarai: Home of SARAI, South Asia Resource Access on the Internet, this is one of the best sites for obtaining quick and easy access to information on the region.

www.lib.washington.edu/libinfo/libunits/suzzallo/s-asia: Based at the University of Washington, this site links to bibliographies on South Asian topics.

library.berkeley.edu/SSEAL/SouthAsia/diaspora.html: This is the site of the University of California's South Asian diaspora project, which documents the global dispersal of people from the region in both the past and the present. The site includes an archive, bibliographies, and other electronic resources.

www.asiasource.org/links: This source provides links to a variety of sites that explore the cultures of Asia. There are many links that connect you to the cultures and literatures of South Asia.

www.aasianst.org/asiawww.htm: This invaluable site is a guide to Asian studies resources on the web. From here, you can go directly to the South Asian resources section and explore sites generally by country.

imp.lss.wisc.edu/~gbuhnema: This site features an archive of resources for Indologists, including texts, language resources, dictionaries, art, journals, etc.

www.meadev.gov.in: Homepage of the government of India

www.censusindia.net: The home of the Census of India provides state-by-state information on population, demography, etc. Extensive maps are also included.

jan.ucc.nau.edu/~vdk/india/indianew.html: Links to other sites concerning India. The links are listed by category.

www.northeastvigil.com: This not-for-profit journal is dedicated to following events in the northeastern region of India, the least understood part of the country. It contains updated news, op-ed pieces, and feature articles on the seven northeastern provinces.

www.clas.ufl.edu/users/gthursby/pak: This Pakistani virtual library is run by a professor from the University of Florida. The wide range of subjects that it covers is nearly comprehensive.

www.bangla.net/bd_news: This site offers daily news, governmental statistics, newsgroups, and more from the Academy of Media and Information Technology in Bangladesh.

www.dhaka-bangladesh.com: This is a composite news site run by Bangladeshis living in the United States. The articles are culled from a variety of sources and are updated daily. The site covers not only current affairs but also the arts and culture.

http://bicn.com: The site for the *Bangladesh International Community News* provides information of interest to visitors and expatriates alike.

www.macalester.edu/~guneratne/index.html: This is the homepage for the Nepal Studies Association. It covers a wide range of issues pertaining to the Himalayas and also provides information on teaching and research resources.

TOPIC SPECIFIC SITES

www.pitt.edu/~dash/folktexts.html#I: This site is maintained by an academic folklorist and provides access to a variety of electronic texts from South Asia. The site also provides links to other sites pertaining to folk and fairy tales, myths, legends, etc.

www.indianfolklore.org: This is the official Web site of the National Folklore Support Centre in Chennai, India. The NFSC is a fairly recent organization established to further research on and understanding of the role that folklore plays in Indian life. The center also publishes a quarterly newsletter entitled *Indian Folklife* as well as the *Indian Folklore Research Journal,* another quarterly publication.

www.seattleartmuseum.org/exhibit/interactives/intimateWorlds/enter.asp: This Web site accompanies the museum's exhibition on the Hindu deity Krishna. It narrates his entire life story in words and images.

www.webpak.net/~ricksha/index.htm: This excellent interactive site explores the social and aesthetic role of painted rickshaws in Bangladesh, many of which draw on Bengali folklore for their content.

www.uiowa.edu/~incinema: This is the Web site of a professor who teaches a course on Indian cinema. It provides overviews, comments, and history of a number of popular films produced in Mumbai (formerly Bombay). The site also contains a variety of visuals to accompany the texts.

www.ciil.org/culture/folklore.html: The Central Institute of Indian Languages in Mysore, India runs this well-documented site. A number of valuable folklore resources, such as bibliographies, research centers, etc., can be accessed from here.

www.indianmythology.com: Part of the homepage of *Encyclopedia Mythica*, this site is dedicated to Hindu mythology and offers a variety of features, ranging from access to myths online to visual images of Hindu deities.

www.asiatica.org/publications/ejvs: This e-journal for Vedic studies, edited by Michael Witzel, includes articles, book reviews, and more.

www.south-asian-initiative.org/epw: This is the homepage of *Economic and Political Weekly*, a social science journal with full-length articles and reviews covering political science, economics, sociology, and anthropology. The site contains the full texts of the most recently published issue and abstracts of previously published articles.

world.std.com/~metta/lib/index/html: This is a Theravada Buddhist text archive. Translations of texts from the Pali canon can be downloaded here.

www.accesstoinsight.org/lib/bps/leaves/bl135.html;
www.accesstoinsight.org/lib/bps/leaves/bl138.html;
www.accesstoinsight.org/lib/bps/leaves/bl142.html: These three addresses provide a number of tales from the *Jatakas* retold by Ken and Visakha Kawasaki.

is.rice.edu/~riddle/play/sasialit: This site is designed specifically for South Asian literature both at home and in the diaspora.

www.amarchitrakatha.com: This is the homepage of Amar Chitra Katha, the well-known publisher of Indian comic books. Here you can find a variety of folklore texts in comic-book form.

www.hindunet.org/scriptures: A variety of Hindu scriptures can be found here, including the epics and mythical Puranas.

bombay.oriental.cam.ac.uk/john/mahabharata/statement.html: The entire *Mahabharata* is available here as an electronic text for subscribed users. The site also provides a link to John D. Smith's homepage, where one can access the Pabuji oral epic from Rajasthan.

www.maxwell.syr.edu/maxpages/special/ramayana: This site provides a useful introduction to the *Ramayana* epic in its myriad written and oral forms. Short and long synopses are also included.

panchatantra.org/#third: The tales from the *Panchatantra* along with illustrations are available at this site.

banglapedia.search.com.bd/HT/B_0134.HTM: Here you will find an overview of the founding and history of work being done at Dhaka's Bangla Academy, the premier research institute in Bangladesh for folklore research. The site provides a link to a discussion of Bengali folktales and other genres of folk literature covered in the *Banglapedia,* an encyclopedia of Bangladeshi culture.

www.heritage.gov.pk: This is the official site for Pakistan's National Fund for Cultural Heritage, which provides links to a variety of informative sites, including Lok Virsa, Pakistan's Institute for Folk Heritage.

www.mythinglinks.org/home.html: The homepage of Myth*ing Links provides a variety of resources to explore the folklore, mythology, and sacred art of the various countries of South Asia. It also provides annotated descriptions of other related sites on Afghanistan, Pakistan, Nepal, India, etc.

www.lankalibrary.com/myths.html: This site is a section of the virtual library of Sri Lanka. It provides a link to a section on Sri Lankan myths and other folkloric materials.

ignca.nic.in: This is the homepage for the Indira Gandhi National Centre for the Arts. The site is multifaceted, dealing with all aspects of Indian culture. Links to other sites are also provided.

www.sscnet.ucla.edu/southasia: This is the homepage for Manas, a Web site run by a professor of history at the University of California, Los Angeles. It provides much useful background information on the Indian subcontinent and also includes a valuable section on the diaspora.

Index

About the Author

FRANK J. KOROM is Associate Professor of Religion and Anthropology at Boston University. He has published several books, and his work has appeared in such journals as *Asian Folklore Studies, Western Folklore,* and *Journal of South Asian Literature.*